A Vagrant \

Florence Warden

Alpha Editions

This edition published in 2024

ISBN : 9789362094490

Design and Setting By
Alpha Editions
www.alphaedis.com
Email - info@alphaedis.com

Contents

CHAPTER I.

The country town of Beckham was astir. It was a cloudy, changeful May afternoon, and the white-capped country lasses who were alighting from all sorts of strange vehicles at the churchyard gate had to hold up their clean cotton frocks with what untutored grace they might, as they trod the worn, wet flagstones that led up to the church door. Three or four hundred lads and lasses of Beckham and the neighborhood were collecting at the sound of the church-bells for the bishop to lay his hands on their empty heads and confirm them in the faith in which they were baptized.

The big bare building filled quickly, the vicar on Sunday never gathered such a congregation. The candidates filled the two middle aisles, the girls occupying the whole of one and the front benches of the other, the boys the rest. The latter looked shame-faced, the former self-conscious but content.

Long before the bishop's appearance the church was full in every part, for it was a pretty sight even to those who had no personal interest in any of the candidates.

When from time to time the sun burst through the swift-flying clouds and shone through the long windows full upon the young faces crowned with the demure little white caps, women whispered to each other softly that it looked like heaven. There were thoughts not unworthy of this simile in some of the young minds, especially in those of the girls; others, while trying to fix their thoughts—as they had been told to do—upon the Catechism, could not help wishing they could renounce the pomps and vanities in white cashmere with pretty frills of lace at throat and wrists, like Miss Mainwaring of Garstone Vicarage, who looked so like a picture of some fair-haired saint, as she sat with her starry blue eyes fixed steadily on the communion table in front of her, that it was impossible to guess that she was thinking more of her new ivory-bound church-service than of the ceremony she was about to go through. She and the girl by her side attracted more attention than any others. There were a few of their class present, but of types as commonplace and faces as vacuous as those of the village-girls.

Betty Mainwaring was sixteen. Her fresh young face was sweet and silly, charming by the look of modest purity which passed so easily under the tulle cap and veil for the expression of pious devotion; but in truth Betty's very innocence, and the fact that she had passed her whole life in an atmosphere of the simplest, strictest religion, had made it impossible for her to concentrate much earnest thought upon this important step in the Christian life. She had read through the devotional works prescribed for her as attentively as she could, and had accepted all the formulas and dogmas of the

Church with the unshrinking faith of the most complete ignorance of their meaning. She had been taught that confirmation is one of the most serious events of life, and she believed it and let the fact rest, while her innocent thoughts wandered to a consideration of the backs of the row of girls in front of her, and to the reflection how strange it seemed to be confirmed with one's own governess.

For the girl beside her, with the passionate dark eyes and set, serious face, only eighteen herself, and already carrying on her young shoulders the responsibility of directing the minds of girls of her own age, was Miss Lane, who taught "advanced" English, French, German, Italian, music, and singing to the two grown-up Misses Mainwaring, and the earlier stages of the same to their two younger sisters and their seven-year-old brother. To her life was a serious hard-working affair enough, and her tardy confirmation an event of quite desperate importance, involving much doubt and anxious self-examining. She had even thought of asking the vicar, her pupils' father, for a private interview, of laying bare the bewildered state of her mind, and of asking him whether he thought her fit for confirmation. The papers on the subject which he had given her to read had proved but dry bones to the eager, earnest girl; but she had a strong conviction that confession would procure little more. The Reverend John Mainwaring's religion was not of the hysterical, but of the independent sort; and the girl felt that all he could do would be to throw her back on prayer and her own conscience for an answer to her doubts. What was certain was that he would unhesitatingly have pronounced the conscientious little worker, striving hard to live up to an ideal standard of excellence in her dull profession, as fitter for confirmation than almost any member of his flock.

So she sat by her pupil's side, with downcast eyes and mind fixed on the service she was about to hear, curiously conscious at the same time—being keenly alive to outward things and not without a young girl's vanity—of the interest her pretty, modest appearance was exciting.

But, just before the entrance of the bishop, three persons came in to whom all eyes turned at once, and there was almost a murmur of admiration even in the hush of the sacred building at sight of the girl who, at the foot of the middle aisle, stopped for her mother and brother to take off the long white mantle which was wrapped round her, and then followed the Reverend John Mainwaring up the aisle to the seat he had kept for her in the pew with his own daughter and the governess, Annie Lane.

Lilian Braithwaite came of a handsome race. Tall, with a well-molded figure, gray eyes, brown hair, and complexion rich enough in its tints to promise something more lovely still when a season or two in town should have toned down its coloring, she gave promise of beauty distinguished enough to hold its own amongst the fairest women she might meet. The plain white cashmere which looked so simple on Betty Mainwaring had quite a different effect upon her handsome figure, and the tulle headdress, half cap, half veil, which she wore in common with the other candidates of her own class, had as much of the veil and as little of the cap about it as possible. Already, at seventeen, she walked through the crowd of admiring faces with a bearing which showed more of the dignity of an acknowledged beauty than of the modesty of a young girl. She smiled at the young governess good-humoredly enough, however, and would even have entered into a whispered conversation, with scornfully critical remarks upon the rest of the candidates, if Miss Lane had not received her overtures shyly and with all the primness of her profession. Miss Braithwaite, who was not easily repulsed, gave a little amused shrug of the shoulders, and said, in a loud whisper:

"Are you afraid the vicar is looking at you?"

And then she met his rather uneasy glance in her own direction with a bland smile.

It had been rather a difficult matter for him to bring himself to believe that Miss Braithwaite was in all respects fit for confirmation; but, as no scruple had ever entered her own head, and as, moreover, she was technically prepared for the rite, being able to repeat the Lord's Prayer, the Ten Commandments, and the Catechism with perfect fluency, he had no choice but to bring her to the bishop with the rest of the candidates.

When the service was over, and she rejoined her mother and brother, a young man with a rather handsome face, but deformed and resting on crutches, came up to her and stood silently by while her brother wrapped her again in the long, white mantle she had come in.

"You here, Stephen! How did you come? The doctor said you were not to go out until your cough was better," said Miss Braithwaite, in a voice scarcely as low as it ought to have been.

"I wanted to see you—all in white like a bride, making all the other girls look ugly and clumsy," whispered the cripple, with his face flushing; "so I got Thompson to get the pony-carriage ready, and followed you as fast as I could."

Stephen Lawler's contempt for the appearance of the rest of the candidates was not shared by his cousin, Harry Braithwaite, who turned to watch one of the girls admiringly, and whispered:

"I say, Lilian, how awfully fetching little 'Miss Prim' looks in that get-up!" "Little Miss Prim" was Annie Lane, the governess.

"Yes, she is a pretty girl," answered his sister, who was handsome enough to be able to afford to acknowledge beauty in others.

Meanwhile the crowd was surging toward the door, and Harry Braithwaite kept his mother and sister as near the Vicarage party as he could. At the church door they discovered that a heavy shower of rain was coming down, and Mrs. Mainwaring was lamenting piteously that her husband, who had come on the box of the brougham beside the coachman, would lose his voice entirely if he were to return in the same way through the rain. Harry Braithwaite whispered a few words into his mother's ear, and, raising his hat, stepped forward and placed a seat in their own carriage at the disposal of the vicar's wife, in his mother's name.

"If Miss Lane will come with us, there will be lots of room in the brougham for you and your two daughters and the vicar too," said he.

And before Mrs. Mainwaring could say more than "Oh, thank you, but," he had severed Miss Lane from her pupils and was escorting her under an umbrella to the big Braithwaite barouche.

Mrs. Mainwaring looked uneasy; her two daughters, Joan and Betty, looked displeased.

"I am sure papa will not approve of that arrangement, mamma," said Joan, the eldest of the family, who had come to see her sister confirmed.

"Well, what could I do, Joan? He meant to be good-natured; and it would not do for the wife of the vicar of the parish to show any prejudice. Of course I should not have allowed you or Betty to go, but with Miss Lane it is different; she can take care of herself."

"I should think so!" said Joan, sharply.

And then the vicar came up, and his wife hurried him into the brougham, saying there was plenty of room; and it was not until they were on the point of stating that she confessed, in answer to his inquiries, that Miss Lane was going home in the Braithwaites' carriage.

"That was Master Harry's doing, I suppose?" said the vicar, with a very grave face.

"It was all done so quickly, it was impossible for me to stop him," said his wife, deprecatingly. "You know you would not have minded if it had been anybody else's carriage; and, if they are rather a wild set, we cannot reform them by holding aloof from them. And it is not as if I had let one of the girls go," said she, hurriedly, lowering her voice.

"But you have let 'one of the girls' go. Miss Lane is only a few months older than Joan," he answered, more gravely than ever.

And she, being a wise woman, dropped the conversation, to take it up again when they two should be alone together.

This little incident and the discussion it had caused disturbed the peace of all the occupants of the carriage. The vicar was annoyed that a member of his household should be thrown into such very uncongenial and perhaps dangerous society on the very day of her confirmation. His wife was uneasy on account of his annoyance. Joan and Betty were somewhat agitated, too; but they gave no vent to their feelings except in a little soft-toned wrangle about the amount of space each was authorized to take on the rather small front seat of the brougham. When the Braithwaite carriage passed them they became suddenly silent, both gazing eagerly out until it had passed out of sight. They had time to see the portly Lady Braithwaite and her handsome daughter leaning back comfortably on one seat, while Miss Lane and Harry Braithwaite sat opposite; he was talking to her, and did not notice the brougham.

When the Vicarage was reached, a group of children rushed to the hall door to criticise their elder sister in her white gown, and the missing governess.

"Hasn't Miss Lane come back yet?" asked Mrs. Mainwaring, rather anxiously. "Their carriage passed us a long time ago," she added, when the children had shaken their heads in surprise.

"She will stay at the Grange to tea, of course, mamma," said Joan, acidly.

And again Mrs. Mainwaring, with a glance at her husband, dropped the subject.

The Grange was a sort of an ogre's castle to the simple lady, and not quite without reason. There is in most quiet country neighborhoods a house with this sort of reputation, where there lives a wicked man who does not come regularly to church, and who goes to bed and gets up again at unorthodox hours, and whose guests do the same and worse things besides; where there is a tribe of servants who find it difficult to obtain places in the neighborhood on leaving; and where, above all, there is a family of healthy, high-spirited, ill-disciplined children, rough girls and rougher boys, who grow up with a bad name, which becomes steadily worse as the wild lads grow into manhood, and the girls, without any one's saying that there is any "harm in them," acquire the stigma of being "fast." The Grange was more worthy of its bad reputation than most homes of the same type. Sir George Braithwaite, the present owner, had in his youth on several occasions narrowly escaped appearing in the London police courts; he had sobered down somewhat on coming into the baronetcy; but in four wild sons, whose doings were the scandal of the neighborhood, he saw the follies of his own youth repeated and developed.

When, two years before, the Reverend John Mainwaring became Vicar of Garstone, the inmates of the Grange had made advances to the new-comers, had petted the pretty Betty and invited the elder boys to fish and shoot during the holidays. But the vicar and his wife soon took alarm, and, while striving to maintain an appearance of perfect good-will, discouraged the intimacy between the younger members of the families, until the proud Braithwaites, seeing at last through the civil excuses and regrets, drew back suddenly and held themselves as far aloof as Mrs. Mainwaring could wish. The intimacy thus abruptly checked had never been renewed, and, although the members of the two families greeted each other without apparent ill-will when by chance they met, there was no cordiality on either side—the Grange laughed at the Vicarage as "slow," the Vicarage shuddered at the Grange as "fast."

The interest the latter took in the prim little Vicarage girls and their brothers had died out long since, while, on the other hand, the "wild Braithwaites" had an ever-increased secret attraction for the clergyman's family. Joan and Betty were more constrained than usual when accident brought them face to face with any of the handsome Braithwaite boys, and they both in their hearts sat in judgment upon their parents, and thought that a policy of conciliation would be a much more Christian way of treating the scapegraces. And each of these demure and somewhat stiff maidens began, as she left the schoolroom, to think she saw signs of redeeming grace in one of the Grange lads, and to feel that she would like to have a hand in his reform.

So that, when Miss Lane—who, however prim and staid her manner might be, was undeniably a very pretty girl—was carried off before their eyes by one of their wicked neighbors, and taken to the interesting Grange, feelings which their simple-minded mother never dreamed of mingled with the indignation Joan expressed. Betty was silent, but inclined to be tearful.

The Mainwarings were a somewhat stolid race, and meals at which no stranger was present were very solemn feasts indeed. On this occasion tea-time was passed in dead silence—even Marian and Bertram, the two youngest, scarcely dared kick each other under the table. When they all rose, a tear was rolling down Betty's fair cheek. Her mother caressed her anxiously, fearing that the excitement of the solemn vows she had made that day had proved too much for her. Betty gave way.

"Oh, how that Miss Lane must be enjoying herself at the Grange!" she cried bitterly.

CHAPTER II.

Meanwhile the Braithwaite carriage had reached the Grange, and, Miss Lane's timid remonstrances having been overcome, it had been arranged that she was to stay to dine there, and a boy was sent to the Vicarage with a message to that effect. Harry, who had gone to Beckham on horseback, and had sent his horse home and returned in the carriage to be near the pretty governess, was suffering from a certain sense of disappointment. Miss Lane proved even prettier on closer inspection than she had given promise at a distance of being. As he sat beside her in the carriage, he thought to himself that there was a beauty in the rich yet delicate tints of a brunette complexion which no lily fairness could vie with, and that the sweep of long, dark eyelashes over a girl's cheeks was the loveliest thing in the world. But he saw too much of those eyelashes and not enough of the eyes they shaded—only a swift, shy look as she answered any question of his, and then they fell again or turned to his sister, who chattered on fast about the ceremony they had just passed through, and the people who had been in the church.

Harry himself was less talkative than usual; he could not think of anything to say worthy the attention of this beautiful, brave girl with the soft voice and steady, brown eyes. He became impatient at last, snubbed his sister for being a magpie, and told her gruffly to "shut up," when she made an angry reply. He was glad when they reached the Grange and the ladies went up-stairs; then he strolled into the stable-yard and met his eldest brother George.

"Who was that in the carriage?"

"Only little Miss Lane, the Mainwarings' governess."

"Eh? Oh, that was why you came home with the family-party! What is she like?"

"Like? Oh, like—a governess! Stiff, prim—won't talk, or can't talk. Awful mistake for her to have such a pretty face; it's thrown away on a girl like that."

"Perhaps she'll talk by and by. I think life at the Vicarage doesn't encourage liveliness much. Where is she now?"

"Up-stairs with mamma and Lil. I say, she's my discovery; I brought her here, and I won't have you monopolizing her. I've seen you staring at her in church, and wrinkling up your ugly face with annoyance because she wouldn't look at you; but——"

"My dear boy, you shall have undisturbed possession of your prize, as far as I am concerned. I don't look for my goddesses in the Sunday-school. I admire your wisdom, though, all the same. She can do you no possible harm, and will give you some excellent advice as a reward for your attentions."

"Hope she'll give you a snub as a reward for yours!" said Harry, with a heartiness which went beyond brotherly pleasantry.

Both faces were darkening into frowns when the dinner-bell rang. When they entered the dining-room, as they did together a few minutes later, they found little Miss Lane completely engrossed by their youngest brother, a great overgrown lad of fifteen or sixteen, whose usual shyness with women had been overcome in a quarter of an hour's *tête-à-tête* with the governess in the drawing-room. He had placed her in the seat between his own and his father's; but, before he had had time to sit down, George dropped quietly into the chair he was holding.

"That's my place," said he roughly.

"Mine for to-night, dear William," answered his elder brother coolly, bending his handsome face close to that of the girl by his side. "This is a pleasure I have long wished for, Miss Lane," he said, in the tender tones of the experienced flirt.

She looked at him shyly, laughed and blushed.

"It is very unkind of you to laugh. Don't you believe me?"

"Not quite, I think."

"Somebody has been poisoning your mind against me already, I see," he said, with mock fierceness. "You would not pay any attention to what the juvenile William might say. It must have been Harry. It was Harry, was it not?"

"Which is 'Harry'?"

"Harry is the grumpy-looking one over there—the one who came back in the carriage with you. He would give the world at this moment to pitch me out of the window."

"Why?"

"Never mind why. It is his nasty temper."

"He wouldn't find it so easy, I should think."

"No. We should be always pitching each other out of the window if we were not so well matched; as it is, when any of us are excited beyond endurance, we pitch the child out."

"The child?"

"Yes—that great gawky boy who thought he was going to have all your conversation to himself by putting you between himself and my father. He hasn't come to his full strength yet. We can still do great execution upon him if we take him unawares."

The talk continued chiefly on his side until the general conversation turned upon racing, and he hastened, with an eager interest which no woman could excite in him, to join in the argument that was going forward. When he again glanced at the girl by his side, she was looking puzzled and rather prim.

"Our talk about horses and betting shocks you, I see," he laughed. "You think it very wicked."

"No, indeed, I don't. But I am not used to it. It is so new to me, at least, since I have been a governess."

"Since you have been a governess? Well, that can't be very long. And did you hear talk like ours before?"

"Not—quite like yours; but I have heard gentlemen talk about racing and theaters, and—things like that, at home, before my father died."

"Is that long ago?"

"No"—rather tremulously.

"Are you happy at the Vicarage?"

"Oh, yes, they are very kind to me!"

"So that now any conversation that is not serious surprises and distresses you?"

"Oh, no; I like it!"

"You like our profane conversation? Then why were you looking so prim just now? When I turned to you, you looked so solemn and severe, that the first words that occurred to me froze on my lips. I hadn't a word to say."

"That was because I can't talk about horses."

The little governess plucked up spirit enough to fire this shot under cover of the rising of the ladies, and George Braithwaite followed the small retreating figure with his eyes with more interest than he had yet felt in her. In the talk with his father and brothers which now went on unrestrainedly upon their favorite topics, Harry found occasion to disagree with his eldest brother upon every point. George bore this with a good-humor he seldom showed except when he wished to be irritating. The younger was already almost at boiling-point when they left the dining-room, where it had been unanimously decided that Miss Lane was very pretty, but had no spirit, no "go," and that the Vicarage had crushed all the youth out of everything about her but her face.

George and Harry left the dining-room, the former by the door, the latter by the French window; and they entered the drawing-room at the same moment. Their mother and sister were at the piano looking for a missing song, but the demure little figure in white was not in the room. George merely asked if either of them had seen his cigar-case; but Harry burst out:

"Where's Miss Lane?"

"Oh, the child has taken her off somewhere to play with him!" said Lilian. "You all seem very much excited about the governess," she added rather contemptuously.

But Harry left the room. Miss Lane was prim, certainly, and had nothing to say for herself; but she was very pretty, and, moreover, he felt bound to show George that he was not to have it all his own way, as he had seemed at dinner to think he was doing.

He searched the billiard-room, the morning-room, opened the windows, and looked out on to the lawn. At last he thought he heard the sound of laughter up-stairs, and, mounting the staircase in a few bounds, he was led by the excited cries of "the child!"—"Take care!"—"Well done!"—"Caught, by Jove!"—and by girlish laughter and the scuffling of feet toward the picture-gallery. On the inner side of the door by which he entered it hung a heavy curtain; he pulled it aside just far enough to peep through into the long half-lighted gallery.

There stood the grave, sedate, prematurely old governess of half an hour before panting with laughter and exertion in the pause after a game of shuttlecock. There was no mistaking the fact; for she still held the battledoor in one hand while she rallied William on his clumsiness.

"If you try to catch it so, you must miss it, and perhaps lose your balance, besides exhibiting yourself in an extremely ungraceful attitude;" and she threw out her arms in laughing imitation of him in the act of saving himself from a fall. "Now try again. Are you ready?"

"Yes, I should think so! You sha'n't laugh at me this time!"

The game began again. The shuttlecock was tossed from the one to the other amid cries and more laughter, both combatants being nimble, quick of eye and hand, and as much excited as if their very lives depended on the keeping up of the flimsy thing of leather and feathers. Harry's own breath came and went as fast as theirs as he watched, not the game, but the graceful, active little player in white, whose movements in the *abandon* of the game had a fascination such as no famous dancer he had ever seen had exercised upon him; and when, as, once more pausing, the shuttlecock fell to the ground, she stood panting under the soft light of a Chinese lantern, her cheeks flushed, her dark eyes sparkling, her beautiful brown hair shining as her head moved, and her lips parted with smiles, the blood mounted to his face, and he watched her, with all the passionate admiration of his twenty years in his heart and in his eyes. He dared not move; he would not for the world have broken the charm by letting her know that the game had a spectator.

A minute later the shuttlecock was flying again. Opposite to the door where Harry was standing hidden was another door; and, as, with her eyes fixed upon the toy in the air above her head, Miss Lane tripped backward against the curtain, her foot caught in its folds, she stumbled, and might have fallen, had not an arm from behind the curtain caught and saved her. It was George's. He had taken up his position just as his brother had taken his a few minutes later, at the opposite door.

Quick as thought, Miss Lane had shrunk at the touch of the unexpected hand into the shell of demure propriety she generally wore.

She showed not even surprise, only a little shame and confusion.

"Thank you. I am much obliged to you," said she, modestly, without raising her eyes, extricating herself gently from the obliging arm. "I—I caught the curtain with my foot."

"Are you sure you have not twisted your ankle?" asked George, bending down over her with great solicitude.

"Quite, thank you."

George bowed his handsome head still lower, and murmured mischievously.

"Now I see why I couldn't amuse you at dinner. It was because I can't talk about shuttlecocks!"

She colored, but made no answer, except by a mischievous smile as she raised her eyes to his face. Harry came out from behind his curtain.

"Will you come and have a game at billiards, Miss Lane? I'll teach you."

"I can play a little; but I musn't now, thank you. I must go back to the Vicarage."

"How anxious you are to get away from us!" said George.

"Oh, indeed, it is not that! I haven't been so happy for, oh, I don't know how long, as I have been here to-day!"

"Then why are you in such a hurry to get away?"

"I am not in a hurry; it is because I must go," said she, the almost child-like gayety quite gone out of her voice, which remained sweet, but low and grave; "besides, I—I ought not to have enjoyed myself so much. I had forgotten."

"Forgotten what?" said George, kindly.

"To-day—my confirmation. It was wrong, very wrong of me! Such an example for my pupil Betty, too!"

George could not help smiling.

"I don't think your bad example would do much harm to Betty, Miss Lane. I dare say she wishes she had a chance of spending her evening in the same way."

"I am afraid she does," said the governess, simply.

Then, hearing the voices of Lady Braithwaite and her daughter outside, she went out to meet them, followed by "the child," and leaving the two elder brothers face to face.

"Charming little creature! That dash of the prig leaves her a delicious spice of novelty," said George, lighting a cigar, and seeming not to notice his brother's frowns.

"I thought 'you didn't choose your goddesses out of the Sunday-school'? I thought I 'was to have undisturbed enjoyment of my discovery, as far as you were concerned'?"

"And so you might have had, if you had had the wit to forestall me. The pleasure of her society was absolutely forced upon me, for I could not leave a defenseless woman to be bored to death all through dinner by William and Sir George."

"Where are you going?" asked the other, sharply, for George had his hand upon the door.

"To the stables, if you have no objection."

"You are not going to see Miss Lane home?" shouted Harry.

"By Jove, I never thought of it! But it would be a good action to save the poor little woman from a *tête-à-tête* with such a cub."

In his delight at tormenting his fiery-tempered brother, George had gone a little too far. As he lounged against the doorway, a sudden blow had sent him reeling back into the gallery, the door was slammed, and his brother was at the other end of the corridor before he could say a word. Harry met his sister in the corridor.

"Where's Miss Lane?"

"Why? What do you want with Miss Lane?"

"Never mind. Where is she?"

But his sister was in a teasing mood. She had more than George's cruelty in her disposition, and, being a girl, she could give it freer rein. She delighted in watching the excited working of Harry's face as she evaded his questions.

"My dear boy, I am not Miss Lane's guardian-angel. You should ask 'the child' where she is."

"For Heaven's sake, don't torment me so! You met her outside the picture-gallery a few minutes ago, and took her away with you."

"Oh, so I did! But you see I've dropped her somewhere."

Harry seized her arm and shook it roughly. But the action only roused the girl's spirit from idle teasing to hot defiance.

"Do you think you can make me tell you? If you were to kill me, I wouldn't tell you unless I chose!"—and she shook herself free with a violence which sent him staggering a few paces.

He changed his tactics.

"Don't be silly, Lil. You know I didn't mean to hurt you; and, if we did come to blows, you would be just as likely to hurt me. But do tell me where Miss Lane is."

"She's gone."

"Gone! Alone?"

"No. Stephen has gone with her; and it was I who sent him," said she, defiantly.

"Oh, to annoy me, I suppose?"

"Partly, perhaps—you and George. I thought there had been quite fuss enough made about the little governess, and I thought that Stephen, being a cripple, and, therefore, not quite so rough as you, would make her a safer escort."

Without a word in answer, Harry gave her a sharp box on the ear, and swung himself into the hall over the balusters, dashed into the garden, and plunging into a shrubbery to a short cut to the road, came out scratched and breathless a few yards behind Miss Lane and Stephen.

"You had better go in, Stephen, or you'll make your cold worse. I'll see Miss Lane safely home," said he, abruptly.

A hot flush came over the cripple's face.

"You've grown very considerate for me—for once," he said, bitterly. "Did Lilian send you?"

"No; it would have been better for her if she had."

"What have you done to her?" cried Stephen, anxiously.

"I've only boxed her ears for impertinence," said Harry, haughtily.

"You brute! How dared you? I wish George had seen you."

"George was lying on his back in the picture-gallery, where I left him."

A sharp cry escaped the lips of the little governess.

"What! You have hurt your brother—perhaps killed him!"

"I haven't hurt him, Miss Lane," said Harry, with an uncomfortable blush. "I shouldn't have touched him if he hadn't wanted to prevent my seeing you home. You will let me now, won't you?" said he, with sudden gentleness.

"Thank you. Mr. Lawler has offered to take me," answered she, freezingly.

"But Mr. Lawler has a bad cold, and ought not to be out at night."

"Then I will go home alone."

Harry turned white with rage. The handsome lad was not used to snubs from women of any class, when he took the trouble to pay them any attention. Stephen's eyes gleamed maliciously.

"You won't send me back? The air won't hurt me in the least; I am out in it every night," said he, eagerly.

She could not refuse the cripple, and, bowing very coldly to Harry, she went on with Stephen toward the Vicarage.

It was always a terrible ordeal to the sensitive little Southron to shake four cold hands and smile "good-night" up into four cold faces when, the day's work over, she could run through the garden to the cottage built in one corner of it, where she lived with an old servant of the family to wait upon her. But to-night it was far more terrible than it had ever been before. One degree more of frost in the manner of papa, mamma, eldest girl, and second girl made her feel that her sin, in letting herself be carried off by those worldlings, and possibly enjoying their godless society, was grievous indeed. But they never guessed the pain they were inflicting. Nay, they meant to be rather kind about it; and Mrs. Mainwaring asked, not without veiled curiosity:

"Well, did you enjoy yourself at the Grange? I suppose they were very kind to you?"

"Oh, yes, very kind."

"You had a beautiful dinner, didn't you?" asked Betty, who was rather a *gourmand.*

"Yes, very nice," answered Miss Lane, who had indeed not been insensible to the difference between the cookery of the Grange and that of the Vicarage.

"Did they all get tipsy?" asked Bertram, aged seven, very shyly.

"Oh, no! What makes you ask that, Bertram?"

"Ben said they did," whispered he, sheepishly withdrawing—Ben was the coachman, with a dash of gardener.

"Did you think them nice?" asked Joan, inquisitorially.

"They were all very kind; but, oh, they quarrel dreadfully!"

"You wouldn't like to be governess there, I suppose?"

"Oh, no, Mrs. Mainwaring!" answered Miss Lane, fervently and sincerely.

Yet, when she was once more alone, trying faithfully to banish outward thoughts and prepare herself for her prayers, the admiration, the warm kindliness of the wrong-headed Braithwaites would rush in and contrast itself with the logical conduct of the Mainwarings, who hung about her when she was in high spirits and neglected her when she was unhappy and unwell.

"I do hope he is not hurt!" was her last thought.

CHAPTER III.

Meanwhile Stephen Lawler had returned to the Grange, happy in the favor pretty Miss Lane had accorded him at the expense of Harry, whom he hated with a hatred which, if unreasonable, was not without excuse. He joined his cousins in the billiard-room, where a hot quarrel between George and Harry was only just kept from blazing forth afresh by the presence of their father, the only power on earth which could keep in check the ungovernable passions of his unruly brood. Stephen glanced from one to the other of the two angry, flushed faces, and rolled the spot-ball along the table in an idle manner, through which the least glimpse of the conqueror showed. George laughed unpleasantly.

"Stephen looks happy."

"He's the fox who carried off the lamb while the lion and tiger were fighting about it," said Wilfred, the second son, quoting from Æsop's fables rather at random.

"Was she kind, Stephen?" asked George, mockingly.

"Very kind—much kinder than she was to you."

"That goes without saying, my dear fellow," answered George, with a cruel patronage in his tone which made the cripple wince.

"All women don't worship brutes! I wouldn't enter the lists with you for your Molly and Sukey; but ladies are different."

"Different from what? From Molly and Sukey, or from Miss Lane, the governess?"

"Ah, you can look down upon 'Miss Lane, the governess,' since she calls you a brute!"

"When did she call me a brute? It's a lie!" said George, sharply.

"It's not a lie! She said you and Harry were both brutes; and, by Jove, she was right!"

George raised his fist, but dropped it with an ostentatious self-restraint.

"You are a privileged person," said he, coolly.

Stephen sprung forward and struck him in the face; but George remained as irritatingly quiet as ever.

"But you shouldn't presume upon your advantages. You can tell lies as other gentlemen may not do, and you can strike a man without getting struck back;

but you can't expect to hold your own with a woman against me, or even Harry. It's absurd!"

"What do you mean by 'even Harry?'" asked the third brother, savagely.

"What I mean by it in this case is that, by a little careful management you might have got the *tête-à-tête* you wanted with pretty Miss Lane, but that, if I had stepped in, not all the management in the world would have availed you to get what you wanted."

"You think yourself irresistible?"

"No, I don't. But I think I know more about women than you do; and I'm not quite such a cub as to think I can impress a woman favorably by merely staring across the dinner-table at her and insulting everybody who is civil to her."

Harry grew red at this home-thrust.

"And I suppose you think you have impressed her very favorably by drawling compliments into her ear one minute and turning your back to her the next?"

"That's all his science," said Wilfred, who had been drinking more than the rest, but who had as much wit when he was tipsy as his brothers had when they were sober.

"Well, haven't we exhausted the little governess?" asked George, yawning.

"Yes; let us talk of the Duchess of Shoreditch," proposed Wilfred, mimicking him.

"Oh, y-e-s, we will!" said Harry, following his example rather clumsily. "You might have condescended to see a duchess home yourself, perhaps?"

"To the man of principle all women are duchesses," answered Wilfred, who was becoming tiresome.

"My dear Wilfred, what do you know about the man of principle?" asked his eldest brother, with a look which recalled to the sententious one various occasions on which his morality had given way rather suddenly. "All women are not duchesses; and I would rather see a governess home on a moonlit evening than a duchess, for the simple reason that I should get better paid for my trouble."

"Not by Miss Lane!" cried Harry, starting up, his face aflame.

George did not answer.

"Not by Miss Lane!" said Harry again, in a louder voice. "Answer, you— conceited liar!"

"It is of no use to continue the discussion if you only lose your temper and throw your manners to the winds——"

"Harry's manners!" chuckled Wilfred; but nobody took any notice of him.

"Say what you mean then, or by——"

"I only mean that I should have neglected my opportunities, and put a cruel slight upon a very pretty girl, if I had not got a kiss when I wished her good-night."

"She would never have spoken to you again if you had done such a thing. She would have boxed your ears——"

"She would have done nothing of the kind. Your experience being confined to barmaids, who very naturally resent your rough overtures in the free-and-easy manner you describe, you cannot tell how a woman of more refinement accepts the homage due to her charms when it is properly offered."

"I think this is blackguard talk," said Wilfred; but the time had long gone past for him to get a hearing.

"You think she would have let you kiss her willingly?" said Harry, not so loudly as before, but with his whole frame quivering with restless excitement.

"I don't wish to be boastful, but I think it most likely."

"It's a——"

Stephen shook his cousin's arm.

"Let him prove it, Harry; let him prove it."

But Harry shrunk from that. He was as thoughtless and unprincipled as the rest of them; but he was not *blasé*. He was only twenty; and some instincts of chivalry and respect for the beautiful girl whose name was being bandied about so freely made him hesitate.

"He knows better than to agree to that!" sneered George.

"Why don't you try to be beforehand with him?" suggested Stephen.

"I will, by Jove!" said Harry, stung and excited past all scruples. "We'll see if my rough overtures may not be more to her taste than your what-do-you-call-it homage. I bet Fire King to a five-pound note I'll have a kiss from her to-morrow."

"Willingly, mind?"

"Willingly."

"Done, then! But how am I to be sure you have won fairly if you come and claim it?"

"You will have my word."

There was a general laugh. There are some families, as lawless as the Braithwaites, in which truth is part of their code, and a lie held to be beneath a gentleman; but the Braithwaites, while fiercely proud of their birth, considered that it placed them above obligations, and that the title "gentleman," descended to them from their fathers, was a sort of inherited, inalienable fortune which required no effort of theirs to support or to increase.

However, Harry having refused to let the bet hold except on this condition, it was resolved to trust him, George having fully made up his mind to supplement his brother's account of the interview by the evidence of his own eyes.

The next morning, at breakfast time, when the wine was gone out of his head and his temper was cooler, Harry was a little ashamed of his bet, for to increase his compunction came the very strongest doubts as to his power to win it. However, when George asked with a sneer whether he did not wish the bet were off, his brother answered fiercely that he never made bets which he did not intend to keep. So George only shrugged his shoulders, told him he was a fool, and walked off to the stable-yard, already looking upon his brother's favorite horse, Fire King, as his own by right, although he did not expect to enter into possession without a struggle. In spite of his ostentatiously cynical speeches the night before, his own respect for the demure girl-governess stood higher than he wished to have it believed, and he thought it extremely unlikely that his younger brother, who was still at the stage of being alternately boisterous and shy with women, would even risk a meeting with Miss Lane.

But Harry, nerved by the danger of losing Fire King, had strung himself up to do great things. Fate favored him.

It was Saturday; and on that day the vicar's children always had a half holiday, and their governess was free to spend the afternoon as she liked. When it was fine she generally used her liberty to enjoy her one chance in the week of a walk by herself, and with a book—some solidly instructive book in her hand, just to justify her ramble to herself and relieve her conscience of the reproach of "wasting her time." So on this Saturday afternoon she had strolled out with a sketch-book and a small camp-stool, and, after wandering through the fields alongside the hedges, watching the young rabbits playing about their holes, gathering a few late primroses, singing to herself all the while very happily, she opened her camp-stool in the corner of a field where there was a pond half surrounded by trees, seated herself, and began to draw.

On the other side of the pond, divided from it by a stretch of uneven grass-covered ground, ran a private road, and beyond that was a thick plantation from which, unknown to her, Harry had for some time been watching the governess; and further along the road were some stables and outbuildings, in the shelter of which his brother George had been for some time watching Harry.

Miss Lane set to work with the dry enthusiasm of the conscientious amateur, and was soon too much absorbed in calculating distances and making little dots on the paper with her pencil to notice Harry, until, by making a long circuit through the plantation, across the road and along the edge of the field she was in, he came through the long grass to her side. Filled with the guilty consciousness of the enterprise he had in hand, he was half sheepish, half bold, and Miss Lane's greeting, which was a rather cold little bow and a complete ignoring of his proffered hand, did not help him to recover his self-possession.

"You are drawing, I see," he remarked, rather huskily.

"Yes," said she. Then, as there was a pause which her companion evidently did not know how to fill, she added, glancing first at her paper, and then at the pond in front of her, "It doesn't look much like it yet, does it?"

"I dare say it will look more like when it is finished."

"No, it won't," said Miss Lane, candidly; "that is the worst of it. I can't draw, though I really do try very hard."

"Then why do you give yourself all the trouble of trying?"

Harry felt that his share in the talk was not in the style he had intended, but her rather stiff simplicity of manner disconcerted him.

"It is an excuse for coming out of doors."

"An excuse? I never want one. I only want excuses for not coming home. I hate houses—they are so beastly stuffy; don't you think so?"

He felt he was getting further and further from the lover-like manner which was to overcome Miss Lane; but he could not help it. She considered a little before answering.

"I like houses too—some houses, I wonder you don't like yours. I think it is one of the nicest I have ever been in."

"Do you? Do you like it better than the Vicarage?"

"Oh, yes! The Vicarage is only a place to eat and drink and sleep in!" she said, scornfully. "As for the drawing-room, everything in it is an insult to one's eyes."

"I suppose you mean that it is not artistic," said Harry. "But it isn't the furniture that insults me; it is the people. I feel as if I were in church, or as if I had had a bucket of cold water over me when I didn't expect it, directly I get inside the house."

"Oh, don't say that! They are all very kind."

"Then you like the Vicarage people better than the Grange people?"

"I did not say that. But I know them better."

"Oh, yes; I remember! You said we were a set of brutes."

He felt that this was worse and worse; he was getting positively rude.

"I have never said anything of the kind, Mr. Braithwaite," said she, coldly.

"Didn't you tell Stephen that George and I were brutes?"

"I did say it was brutal to box your sister's ears and knock your brother down just because they contradicted you; and I think so," said Miss Lane, quietly.

"But it was about you. It was because they wouldn't tell me where you were, and wouldn't let me see you home."

"That doesn't make any difference."

This answer was a blow. Miss Lane was the first woman who had ever excited in him any but the most fleeting admiration. He looked upon women as a nuisance in the hunting-field and a positive danger at a *battue*, pretty things whose society at any sort of gathering gave one more trouble than it was worth, and who ought accordingly to feel deeply grateful for any admiration that might be cast to them. Of course this applied only to his equals; with women of a lower rank he was at his ease; and it was a current prophecy that he would be a bachelor till he was forty-five, and then marry his cook. So he looked down at Miss Lane in amazement without speaking, when she thus candidly stated that his admiration "didn't make any difference."

"Then you hate me, I see," said he, at last, deeply hurt and offended.

"Hate you? No; indeed I don't, Mr. Braithwaite!" she answered, rising.

It had only just dawned upon her that his unusually restless manner and his flushed face were the result of anything but his natural awkwardness, and she was anxious to cut the interview short, for fear any of the Mainwarings should pass—they would perhaps not even believe she had met him by accident.

"Then why do you want to run away from me? I may be a brute; but I won't hurt you."

"Oh, no; I am not afraid of that!" said she, her face breaking into the bright, child-like smile that made her so charming to him. "But it is really time for me to go in."

She held out her hand; but he did not seem to see it. He was positively shaking with nervousness, preparing for a bold stroke.

"Won't you shake hands, or have I offended you too deeply?" she asked, with simple, smiling coquetry.

Harry jerked his head suddenly down to her upturned face, and kissed her. George, who was observing this scene, watched for the girl's start, listened for the scream.

But there was neither. She remained quite still, without a sound but a short, quick sob that George was too far off to hear, and he could only see that she bent her head, without being able to catch the expression of her face. He watched a moment longer, then, with a curious look of cynical surprise, turned and sauntered back to the Grange.

But Harry was near enough to know better. He saw the color leave her cheeks and her very lips, and he knew that his impertinence had made her dumb and still with horror. Then the tears began to gather in her eyes; she stooped to feel blindly for the book she had dropped, then turned her back upon him without a word.

In a moment he was mad with remorse.

"Miss Lane!" said he huskily; but she took no notice, and began to walk away.

All his better instincts were aroused, and moved him to words less boorish than usual.

"Miss Lane," he repeated, "I would give my right hand to undo my impertinence or to make you forget it! Upon my soul, you cannot hate me for it as much as I hate myself! Won't you—won't you just look at me? Only just let me see you look again as you looked before—even if you don't speak. Good heavens, you look like stone!"

But she shook her head without looking up.

"Go away, please," was all she said, in a voice from which the bright ring had gone.

Harry was sobbing himself.

"You—you are more cruel than I," said he, unsteadily.

But he dared not stay. Those few words of dismissal were too cutting for him to try any more entreaties. He scrambled through the hedge, rather anxious that she should see he was hurting himself in his eagerness to obey her. But she never looked round. She made her way back to her cottage more quietly, without even shedding any more tears. She was too much excited for that. But, when she was once more in her little sitting-room, she gave way, threw herself on the floor by the sofa, and cried until she could scarcely see. She was so proud, so haughtily reserved to men, that this outrage to her dignity and self-respect wounded her far more deeply than it would have done an ordinary girl.

"He would not have dared if I hadn't been 'only a governess,'" she thought bitterly.

In the meantime Harry had slunk home to the Grange, where the first person he met was George.

"By Jove, Harry, I didn't think you had it in you!" was his greeting.

"What the deuce do you mean?"

"Nothing but what is complimentary on this occasion. Here are your five pounds, fairly won."

He took out his pocket-book, and handed a note leisurely to his brother, who crumpled it in his hand and tossed it into a flower-bed.

"What! Have you suddenly grown above filthy lucre? Very well, I'll take it back again;" and George was stooping over a geranium to pick it up when his brother brought his hand roughly down upon his shoulder.

"What do you mean by this tomfoolery?"

"Well, to be frank, I watched your interview, quite by accident, and saw you win your bet."

"I didn't win it," said the other, surlily.

"Not win it? Why, I saw you!"

"I—tell—you—I—didn't—win—it," said Harry, savagely. "I kissed her— like a beastly cad—and she looked as if I had killed her."

He turned round quickly and made for the house. His brother followed.

"Here, but I say, Harry——"

The other paid no attention, but disappeared into the house.

But the consequences of the act were not over. When tea-time came, and, having bathed her red and swollen eyes, Miss Lane appeared in the family circle, a deadlier chill than usual was evidently upon them. Joan looked like an ugly statue of disgust or some kindred emotion; Betty's cheeks were flushed, and her pretty vacant eyes bright with anger; Mrs. Mainwaring was cold and nervous; the Rev. Mr. Mainwaring, above all human passions, was quietly attentive to his tea and toast, as usual. The governess' heart sunk.

After tea, when she had said "Good-night" in an agony under this frigidity, Mrs. Mainwaring followed her into the hall and asked her to come into the schoolroom for a few minutes. After closing the door with ominous carefulness, the elder lady faced her victim.

"I am very sorry to have to say anything of this kind to you, Miss Lane; but I must ask whether there is any sort of engagement between you and Mr. Harry Braithwaite?"

"None, Mrs. Mainwaring," said the girl, white to the lips.

"And is it true—excuse me for asking—that he kissed you this afternoon?"

"Yes, Mrs. Mainwaring." The answer came at once, clear and cold.

The elder lady was disconcerted for a moment by this prompt reply; then she said, between tightly compressed lips:

"I did not think you would allow a gentleman you were not engaged to to take such a liberty."

Miss Lane gave a little hard laugh.

"Not a liberty, Mrs. Mainwaring; surely you make a mistake! Mr. Braithwaite did not wait to be allowed; he was good enough to give me a kiss as he would, with his easy good nature to any dependent. I only wonder you did not know me better than to think I could object."

Mrs. Mainwaring read the acute misery in the girl's face. She was sorry for her. However, as she murmured out rather incoherently, Betty was out walking and had seen the kiss given, and of course it was not a proper sight for her, and would Miss Lane kindly understand she must leave at the end of the quarter?

And Miss Lane said she would be very glad to do so. And so she would have been, if she had known where to go.

CHAPTER IV.

It was now the end of May, and Miss Lane was to leave Garstone Vicarage in the last days of June. She went through the dull round of her daily duties as carefully as ever; but the buoyancy of spirit that had formerly made her the children's favorite play-fellow out of school-hours had deserted her.

The meals, at which the bright young girl had once set the talk going, were once more the most solemn of ceremonies. The Reverend Mr. Mainwaring wished that that unlucky kiss had been ignored; he saw in fancy her inevitable successor, the usual under-bred, old-young governess, without an idea, but with a fund of chirpy small-talk, of the kind which he had suffered before the advent of Miss Lane. He knew she must be blameless in this matter; but he was not a man given to interference in domestic affairs, and, as his wife had decreed that she should go, he made a half-hearted remonstrance, forbade her being sent away before the end of the quarter, and submitted.

Joan and Betty, especially the latter, would have liked to show their resentment more openly had they dared; but it was not easy in face of their victim's well-judged conduct. She was so grave, so matter-of-fact, so painstaking with them in school-hours, put it so plainly before them that their heads could find out for themselves as much as she could tell them—which was far from being the case—that they could not but treat her with respect in the schoolroom; while out of it she scarcely spoke to them more than was absolutely necessary. But it was a dull life for her; and, shut out thus from the world around her, she found a resource in writing. This little creature was full of fiery ambitions, and one of them was to make a name some day as an author. So, when tea was over, and she could throw off the Mainwarings for the day, she hurried through the garden to her cottage, and spent the last hours of the day, half in quiet study for self-improvement, half with pen, paper, and her own fancy.

So the weeks went on toward the time of her departure; and meanwhile she saw no more of the Braithwaites, except when one or other of the brothers would ride past her and the children in their morning walks.

But George was interested enough in the pretty little governess to find out, without apparent curiosity, that she was going to leave; and he kept this discovery to himself. He did not neglect to warn Harry not to force himself into the girl's society again; but he resolved to have a farewell interview with her himself. The chance came in the third week in June, when a grand flower-show, held just outside Beckham, had brought all the scattered neighborhood together.

It was a showery day, and the festivities suffered. Showily-dressed and sometimes well-dressed women made their way over sodden grass and slippery earth from one dripping tent to another under the umbrellas of men who were only looking out for a chance of slipping away for a cigar, and did not care a straw for the roses which their companions told them were "lovely," and were roused only to a limp enthusiasm by some uninteresting patent invention in the "agricultural implement" tent.

The Mainwarings were all there. Gardening was a hobby with the elders; they knew, and called all flowers by their Latin names, and Mrs. Mainwaring's happiest hours were spent, with dress tucked up, hands hugely gloved, and face glowing with enthusiasm, bedding out geraniums, or collecting and carrying off for destruction myriads of slugs which threatened her favorite plants. Joan and Betty did not care much for flowers; but they were glad of an opportunity to wear new and particularly tasteless dull-green gowns trimmed with many little bits of fringe of a different shade, and their appearance might chance to get them an invitation to a dance or a garden-party. The children had begged to go, to get a holiday, and Miss Lane went to look after them.

So that, when George Braithwaite came on to the ground, in dutiful attendance upon his mother and sister, a rapid inspection of the tents soon convinced him that his opportunity was come. He knew better than to set to work with Harry's clumsiness. He went up to the Mainwaring children, talked to them a little while without taking any notice of the governess beyond raising his hat to her, and then drew Mrs. Mainwaring's attention to a plant which he said had a strange history, which she must ask the owner to tell her, insinuated a compliment to lean pink-eyed Joan, and talked to mother and daughters for some time in what he considered his best manner. And then he told Bertram, whose hand he held all the while, that there was "a grand gentleman" making a speech in another of the tents, and asked him if he would not like to see him, and then asked the two younger girls if they would not like to go too; and they all thought they should like to go anywhere with this nice, kind gentleman, and they all said, "Yes." Then Mr. Braithwaite was afraid he could not take them all three across without their getting wet, but said to the elder of the two small girls:

"Ask your governess to take you under one umbrella, and I will take care of these two little ones."

And the nice, kind gentleman ran off with Bertram and Marian, directing Miss Lane to follow with Ellen. But when, through the rain, they reached the long, damp tent where the people were crowding round a narrow deal-table to listen to the speech which an insignificant-looking little gentleman, standing in the mud, was delivering in a very low, monotonous voice, the little ones were disappointed; and Bertram said he did not look grand at all, in a voice much louder than the speaker's. But George still pushed him benevolently forward through the crowd, until, by civil words and strong shoulders, he had managed to get all three children quite close to the table, where they could "hear Lord Ben Nevis distinctly" as he whispered. Then he dropped unselfishly into the back row of the crowd himself, and joined the governess.

"You will get your feet wet standing in all this slush," said he.

And he found a board for her to put her feet on, and a box for her to sit on, and then stood bending down to talk to her with courteous attention which would have brought tears of envy to Joan's eyes, had she seen him.

"What a shame of them to drag you out in the rain," said he sympathetically.

"Oh, no!" she answered, smiling. "I am glad to be dragged anywhere, in any weather, as a change from the musty old school room."

"I suppose you are. I can't imagine how any girl can become a governess."

She looked up at him in pathetic surprise.

"I don't suppose any girl likes to be a governess; but there is nothing else for her if she is poor."

"Oh, yes, there is—there's the Thames!"

"But you wouldn't recommend that, surely?"

"I don't know that I wouldn't. I would try it myself, rather than endeavor to cram knowledge into the heads of little fools who will never be any the better for it."

"Oh, don't say that," she entreated. "It is just what I am tempted to think myself sometimes; but, if I gave way and really did believe I wasn't doing them any good at all, just think what a martyrdom my life would be!"

"So it is," said he, looking with his eyes a stronger meaning than his words bore.

She cast hers down and blushed. She had all a girl's thirst for admiration, and the unaccustomed attention of a handsome man threw fresh charm into her manner, brightened her eyes, and made her lovelier than she dreamed.

"If not the Thames, what is there—what profession?" she asked as his eyes answered her.

"Well, there is the stage."

"The stage!" she echoed, in horror. "You wouldn't advise that, surely!"

"You speak of it with more horror than of the Thames."

"Why, yes! I'd rather be a corpse than an actress!"

"But you wouldn't have such a lively time of it," said he, dryly.

"But, oh, to be stared at by everybody, and to paint, and be among horrid people, and for everybody else to look down upon you, and——Oh, I should not like it at all."

"Well, isn't it better to be looked at by everybody than not to be looked at, at all? But I suggested it only as an alternative to the Thames. Seriously, the Vicarage schoolroom must be a dull place."

"It is. But I am going to leave it," she answered, looking away, and her face flushing.

"Are you? I thought you would not be able to stand it long. You may do much better, and, at any rate, you have the satisfaction of knowing that you can't do worse."

"I don't know about that," said she, very gravely.

"At any rate, you will have a pleasant holiday among your friends first."

She gave a rather grim smile.

"I don't know about that, either. A semi-detached villa in the suburbs, among a family of children compared to whom the Mainwarings are angels, is not the place one would choose for a holiday."

"You have a lot of young brothers and sisters, then?"

"Oh, no, I have none! I am an orphan; so I have to spend my spare time with an aunt who doesn't particularly want me."

"That is hard lines. Then you will teach again?"

"Yes, if I can get any pupils," said she, rather sadly, thinking how much the shortness of her stay at the Vicarage would be against her chances of getting another engagement. "Not like this, though! I shall take lodgings in London and try to get daily pupils, for music, perhaps. Then I shall have more time to myself, and I can study better."

"But you know enough already; and you will be frightfully dull if you live by yourself."

"Not so dull as I am here. And, when I have got on with music and other things, I shall take another resident engagement—abroad this time. I think I should like to go to Russia or Canada."

"Have you many friends in London?"

"No. I had some once, before papa died. But one falls out of the way of one's friends somehow when one gets very poor. It isn't their fault, and it doesn't seem to be one's own; but it always happens."

"I want you to promise me something," said George, in a low voice.

She looked up inquiringly.

"I want you to promise to give me your address in London if you settle there by yourself."

Miss Lane hesitated. She was very much touched by his sympathy, very anxious not to lose it by offending him; but she did not think his request was one which she could or ought to grant. Independence had made her careful.

"I have not the least idea where I shall be, or if I shall be able to carry out my plan at all," said she, evasively.

"Where there is a will there is a way, you know; and I should think that is more the case with you than with most people."

"You are laughing at me. You think me too strong-minded."

"I will tell you what I think of you when you have answered me. Now will you promise?"

"I don't see of what use knowing my address would be to you, because as I shall be living quite alone, I can't ever see any one."

"That doesn't follow. Do you mean that you would live the life of a hermit, and condemn yourself to solitary confinement of your own free will?"

"For a time. There is no help for it."

"Yes, there is. We are going up to town, some of us, before long. I will ask my mother and Lilian to call on you. But I must know your address. And I could send you tickets for concerts and things, where you could go with your pupils, if you wouldn't let any one accompany you who would enjoy it more. Would you let me take you to a concert?" he said, bending lower.

Miss Lane looked nervously down, then entreatingly up.

"I couldn't," she said, in a low voice.

He saw the pleading reluctance in her eyes, and pressed his advantage.

"You do not know how unhappy it makes me to think of your sacrificing your bright life alone in a dingy London lodging. However nice your pupils and their friends may be to you, their affection or—or esteem—can never be so strong as that of your own disinterested friends."

He knew how to throw into these words a feeling and warmth which made the girl's cheeks flush. There was a pause.

"You do believe in my friendship, do you not?" he asked, more softly still.

"Of course I do," answered the girl, looking up with an effort. "I—I—am sure you mean to be very kind, Mr. Braithwaite."

"Then don't be too unkind to me. Promise me that you will send me your address in town."

"I cannot," said the girl; then, glancing round, she saw fixed upon her glassily the light, colorless eyes of her eldest pupil Joan.

Defiant bitterness and a dozen kindred feelings woke up within the little governess.

"I promise," said she; and she let him take her hand and press it gently in his.

He turned and saw Joan—saw the malignant look in her eyes, and knew that she had been watching them. Nothing could have pleased him better.

"Ah, Miss Mainwaring, have you too been listening to Lord Ben Nevis' speech? Not a bad speaker, though he gets rather in a tangle with his quotations sometimes."

Joan would have liked to say something satirical, but nothing occurred to her. She had even to swallow her indignation so far as to talk quite amicably to this deceitful Lovelace, and to persuade herself into thinking that, though he might amuse himself for a few odd moments with that little Miss Lane, he found a taller, slimmer, less talky woman more permanently attractive. Still he had certainly been looking at Miss Lane, as he bent over her, where she sat in a corner of the tent, in an irritatingly admiring manner.

The truth was, though he scarcely acknowledged it to himself, that he was really a little in love with Miss Lane. She was not only sweetly pretty, but "good style," the best-dressed woman there, in his opinion, not even excepting his sister. And he had no intention of losing sight of her. And why should he? She was already predisposed in his favor; she had few friends—none who could warn her that he was a dangerous acquaintance; she was going to live alone a dull life which would make her hail with gratitude any companionship as pleasant as he felt his to be to her; he would have many a dull and idle hour in town which might be pleasantly filled up by the charitable act of taking the pretty, prim little lady to a theater, or he would not even mind a picture-gallery, if she proved entertaining enough to reward him for such waste of his time. It would be pleasant for her, pleasant for him; and, as she had no friends, it could do her no harm in the eyes of the world which ignored her. He left the ground, satisfied that he had put this matter well in train.

She, meanwhile, in spite of one more degree of frost in the manner of her companions, went back to the Vicarage with them, feeling happier than she had felt for a long time. The kindly sympathy of this man, whose handsome face grew so soft when he spoke to her, and who had been her favorite among the Braithwaite brothers from the first, had taken her out of the shell of reserve she wore among the torpid natures around her. As she thought over the event of the day to her, that low-spoken conversation in the corner of the tent; recalled again each tone, each look of his; felt again in fancy the warm pressure of his hand, the question would rise in her mind, "Does he love me?" And she fell asleep, scarcely daring to hope, yet half believing that he did. At the moment when he said good-bye he had contrived to ask her on what day she was going back to London, and, almost without thinking what she was doing, she had told him. Would he be there to see her off, she wondered.

But the little fantastic dream she was indulging was not to last long. Joan was the person to destroy it. Within a few days of Miss Lane's departure she asked her mother at tea-time if she had heard that George Braithwaite was going to be married.

"Dear me, no!" said Mrs. Mainwaring. "Who told you about it, Joan?"

"I heard it at the Lawsons'. It is to some cotton-lady, it appears, with large feet and a large fortune. I wonder how they will get on together; they say he never admires any woman of his own rank. But, then, I suppose he doesn't consider a cotton-lady to be of his own rank; or perhaps he thinks more of her fortune than her face. I suppose that is necessary, with such a character for being dissipated as he has."

Mrs. Mainwaring gave a warning glance from her eldest daughter to her husband. But the vicar did not mind a little bit of mild scandal—it amused him; and the reputation of the Braithwaite boys could hardly be injured by anything Joan might say. So she went on with all she had heard, and her own comments thereon, every word inflicting a wound, as, perhaps, she meant it to do upon one of her hearers.

Annie Lane walked back to her cottage that night with heart too sore for study. So he had been only amusing himself with her, after all, as she might have known he was doing! She should have known better than to trust another Braithwaite after Harry's conduct toward her. She felt utterly humiliated and fierce with indignation against them. She had been the plaything of both, and the girlish pleasure she had felt in their admiration and attention had been dearly paid for.

She had one small revenge upon George. On Sunday, the day before her departure, he went to church and found an opportunity to whisper to her as they came out:

"I am going to see you off to-morrow. I shall be at the station."

All the girl's proud spirit flashed from her dark eyes as she raised her little head, and looking full into his face, said distinctly:

"I must beg that you will do nothing of the kind."

He was amazed, but was clever enough to suppress everything but one quick glance of annoyance and surprise. Then he merely elevated his eyebrows, raised his hat, and with a careless "As you please," went on to Joan Mainwaring.

The next day Miss Lane took a cold farewell of the family in which she had worked so hard, and was allowed to go by herself in a cab to Beckham Station. She had been able to remain calm in the face of them all; but before the two-mile drive was over, she was half-blind with tears. To be dismissed so coldly when she had tried so hard to do her duty well and to please them! To be dismissed, too, with an undeserved stain upon her character! It was too hard, too cruel, that at the outset of her life, when her very livelihood depended upon her own efforts, she should find herself clogged by this most unjust burden.

She was drying her eyes and trying to look as if she had not been crying as the cab reached the town, when a young man on horseback, who was riding in the opposite direction, passed, caught sight of her, and turning his horse's head, followed the cab into the station. She was late, and the ticket-office was already open. She had just taken her ticket, and was walking away, with her eyes upon the purse in her hand, when a voice by her side made her look up with a start. It was Harry's.

He was all mud-splashed with hard riding, his face was red and ashamed, and his voice was low and unsteady.

"Miss Lane, let me see after your luggage. Do—do let me, or—or I shall never forgive myself!"

She pointed it out to him very quietly, without a word except "Thank you."

He saw it put into the van, found a corner-seat for her in an empty second class carriage, helped her in, and stood by the door nervously twisting the heavy handle.

"When are the holidays over, Miss Lane? When are you coming back?"

"I am not coming back here."

She turned away her head; the tears were breaking forth again.

"Not coming back! Why?" he cried, quickly.

Her tears were flowing fast now. She looked at him with one swift glance of misery and reproach, and whispered brokenly:

"You ought to know why. Betty—Betty saw you!"

Harry sprung up on the step.

"What—that day when I—when I behaved like—like a cad? And you are going away because of me?"

The hasty, passionate nature of the lad was moved to a mighty impulse of remorse. She could only answer, pitying him and holding out her hand while she tried to smile through her tears:

"Never mind—never mind! I have forgiven you long ago. I—I—I only told you because you asked."

He had seized her offered hand, when the guard came up to shut the door.

"Going, sir?"

"Yes!" cried Harry, carried away by the impulse of the moment.

He jumped into the carriage, the door was locked, the train was in motion, and he and Miss Lane had started together for London.

CHAPTER V.

That night there was consternation at the Grange—Harry had not returned. His horse, which he had left in charge of a man he knew at the station, was brought back late in the day to Garstone, with the intelligence that his master had gone by the London train. The man said he thought it must have been a sudden determination of Mr. Braithwaite's, who had only said, when he left the horse in his care:

"I shall be back in five minutes, Tom. He'll keep quiet enough; he doesn't mind the trains."

Such a freak was not at all an unheard-of thing among the Braithwaites, and little more was thought of it after Sir George's return home that evening, for he looked upon it as an escapade which would end in the truant's return the next day with an empty pocket and the appearance of having been up all night.

But, when a week passed, and still no tidings were heard of him, and when, moreover, it came to be known that the late governess of the Mainwarings had left Beckham by the same train, and, as appeared later, in the same carriage, then the people of the village and the people in the town began to chatter, George to swear, and the Vicar of Garstone to look very grave. Mrs. Mainwaring wrote to the aunt to whose house Miss Lane had said she was going, and received in answer the news that the girl had not arrived, but had written, without giving her address, to say she was in lodgings in London. And Mrs. Mainwaring repented her abrupt harshness most bitterly, and did not need the reproaches of her husband, who blamed now his own inaction in allowing the young girl-governess' abrupt dismissal. Joan and Betty ceased their snappish comments on her, and talked together in whispers about her. And at the Grange they wondered how Harry was getting on without any money, for they knew he had only a small sum with him on the day he left Beckham.

Then came a letter from a friend of Sir George's, saying that Harry had been seen in Paris, where he seemed to be enjoying himself very much. And then an event happened which, for the time, turned all thoughts away from the truant son.

Sir George, who passed most of his time on horseback, was riding home one afternoon on a horse which had carried him safely through many a hard day's hunting, when, in taking a fence, with a ditch on the further side, over which they had gone easily time after time together, the horse slipped on landing, and rolled into the ditch on the top of his rider. Sir George tried to rise, but found that he was too much hurt to do so; he called for help, but fainted with pain before any came. At last a man who was passing with a cart saw him, and brought others to the spot by his shouts. They carried him home to the Grange, the doctor was ridden for with all speed, and, before night came, all Garstone knew that the baronet's life was in danger. Day after day he lingered on, though the hope of his recovery grew slender; hour after hour he lay conscious, but silent to all. The only person he asked for was the missing Harry. Every morning he asked the same questions.

"Has Harry come back? Has any one heard from him?"

And every morning the reply was the same. There were no tidings of him.

At last one evening George entered his father's room with a face dark with ill news. Sir George knew that something had happened which his son scarcely dared to tell him. His eyes brightened with stern eagerness.

"Well, speak out. You have heard news of Harry—bad news?"

"Yes, bad news."

"Is he dead?"

"No."

"Worse?"

"I—I think so; I am afraid so."

"Go on. I am not afraid to hear."

"I have just received a letter from Stanmer & Lloyd."

"Ah"—the sick man drew a sharp breath—"the bankers! Well?"

"They wrote about a check which——"

"Was forged?"

"They think so. It was in your name, and for three hundred pounds."

There was a long silence. When Sir George spoke again, his voice was changed.

"It must be hushed up. And you must find out the boy and bring him back to me. If—if I were well, it might be different; but I must forgive him now. You will find him out, George?"

"Yes, father."

Sir George lay back again in silence; but his face was still very stern; there was remorse for his own conduct as well as shame for his ill-brought-up sons in the expression it wore.

George went up to town the next day, and fulfilled the first part of his father's commission, that relating to the check, without much difficulty; but he failed to find a clew to his brother's hiding-place, if he were in hiding, which George doubted. It was more characteristic of the Braithwaites to do wrong and brave the consequences openly; and this course, while apparently favoring detection, often proved the safest.

Then a suggestion occurred to him for tracking the runaway. He wrote to Mrs. Mainwaring for the address of Miss Lane's aunt, and, on the day he received it, he knocked in the afternoon at the door of a very small semi-detached house a few miles out of London. The door had figured glass let into it in place of the upper panels, and he saw a face pressed against one of these in doubtful contemplation of him some minutes after his second ring. His hand was on the bell for the third time, when the door was opened, and a little servant with a very small and very dirty face asked what he wanted. He had not got further than to ask doubtfully if Mrs. Mansfield lived there when she turned round and abruptly left him standing at the entrance of the most pretentious "hall," for its size, that he had ever seen. For it was esthetically papered, and had an inappropriate dado, while a pair of ugly China monsters left scarcely room for the stranger to pass between them and the umbrella-stand. It was so small that he could distinctly hear the conversation which followed in the backyard.

"It's a gentleman, ma'am, who wants to see you—such a nice gentleman, in a great long coat!"

"Did you show him into the drawing-room?"

"No, ma'am."

"Show him in at once, and then you hang up the rest of the stockings. Say I will be with him in a minute, and take the pin out of my gown behind." Then, in a severe tone, "You dirty little thing, you are not fit to speak to a visitor!" And indeed this domestic did not harmonize well with the dado.

The small servant showed George into a tiny room, the furniture and arrangement of which told more of its owner's history than the hall had done. For it was a room which belonged to an anterior period of civilization. The carpet was of the aggressive kind, with old fashioned impossibly-colored roses. There was an inlaid round table, much too big for the room, jutting a long way out of one corner; the piano was worn and old-fashioned, the chairs were evidently relics of two or three different suits of furniture. The books were suggestive too—the "Pilgrim's Progress," with much gilt on the binding, odd numbers of the *Sunday at Home*, and the current number of the *Quiver*, two or three *Keepsakes*, some little-used volumes of miscellaneous poetry, which looked like school-prizes, *et cetera*. But the ornaments spoke more plainly than anything in the room—large, blue-glass vases on the mantel-piece, crochet antimacassars, each of a different pattern, over the chairs; and every ornament stood on a wool mat.

He had to wait some time; he heard Mrs. Mansfield go softly past the door and up the stairs, and the small servant follow her with hot water, as he could tell by her spilling it as she went along. Presently the door opened, and a woman of about forty, dressed in rusty black, much covered by trimmings which enhanced the shabbiness they were meant to hide, came in and apologized more than was necessary.

He stated the object of his visit as soon as he could. He had come on behalf of his mother and some other friends of Miss Lane, to find out her address.

"I could not have given it you myself before this morning," said Mrs. Mansfield. "She has written twice to me since she left Garstone; but it was only in the letter I received to-day from her that she put any address. She is lodging in London by herself, and trying to get daily pupils."

"Are you going to see her?" asked George.

"No, I have no time; she knows that herself, and doesn't expect me."

"Do you approve of her plan of living by herself? It seems a strange one for such a young girl."

"Indeed Annie doesn't trouble herself about my approval. I can't say I think it a proper thing for a girl to do who has been brought up like Annie; but she is so obstinate—just like her mother, my poor sister."

"It is a great pity that she does not consult you more," said George deferentially. "Having no mother, she ought certainly to defer to you as her representative."

"That is just what I say!" cried Mrs. Mansfield, growing confidential. "I have begged her to come and live here; the house is certainly smaller than she is used to, but still it's a home, and she would be more comfortable, or she ought to be"—this with some asperity—"among her own relations."

"Certainly," said George, with conviction. He had just caught the sound of children quarreling and screaming up-stairs, and his thoughts hardly went with his words.

"She might go backward and forward to town for her music-lessons from here quite easily; and why should she not get daily pupils about here as well as in town, if she has made up her mind to that? Then she would have the comforts of a home to come to in the evening, and she might amuse herself in her spare time by helping me to teach my own children."

"It would be a delightful arrangement," said George, with fervor; then, growing bold—"And, as she is a nice, lady-like girl, I have no doubt she would soon find a husband among her own friends."

Mrs. Mansfield shook her head, with her lips drawn tightly together.

"I am sorry to say, Mr. Braithwaite, that Annie considers herself too good for my friends. I don't wish to say anything against one of my own blood; but I must say I don't think such high-and-mighty airs becoming. It is not as if she was living now as she did when her father was alive, and when nothing was too good for her."

"Her father was well off, I believe?"

"Oh, yes; and, if he had been prudent, instead of spending heaps of money upon her education, he would have left her a little to live upon!"

"It must be a hard change for her, though. She is so young, and of course it is so natural to spoil a beautiful girl."

This rather rash speech caused Mrs. Mansfield to draw herself up.

"Well, I can't say that I see her beauty myself! I don't say she is a bad-looking girl; but I don't think her face is likely to do much for her: and in my young days gentlemen looked for something more than a pretty face in a wife, though to be sure they liked a pair of fine eyes too!"

George gathered from her manner of saying this that she judged her own vacant, round, bead-like eyes to be handsome; and he smiled a compliment, which brought a gratified but not becoming blush to her particularly plain face.

Before long he succeeded in getting from her Miss Lane's address, in one of the streets off Regent Street; and, pondering this choice of a rather expensive locality, he left Mrs. Mansfield's domestic paradise, and returned to town. At his hotel he found the following telegram:

"Come back at once. Sir George much worse. Harry has returned."

That night he was again at the Grange—not a minute too soon. They told him, on his arrival, that his father was not expected to live till morning, and he went straight up to the sickroom. Harry was there on his knees by the bedside, very still and grave and unlike himself. Sir George opened his eyes as his eldest son came in.

"George," said he, with difficulty, "I have forgiven him. Don't let it be mentioned again. I cut him out of my will a week ago; it is too late to alter it. Promise me to provide for him."

"I promise," said George, in a low voice.

"Call the rest. It's near now."

And they came one by one softly into the room. An old hound, a great favorite of his, slipped in too, slunk up to the bed, and wagged his tail at the master he had missed for days.

"Hallo, Diamond, come to say good-bye to me?"

And the hound, thus encouraged, licked his master's hand.

"Have you forgotten the old days, Diamond? They are over for me as well as for you now, my old beauty!" Then, gathering a remnant of strength, he gave a ringing "View-halloo!"

The hound bounded away in great excitement among the silent figures in the room, then came back, and once more licked his master's hand. But he got no answering caress, for the hand was still forever.

The days which followed between Sir George's death and the funeral were an awkward time for Harry and his eldest brother. The younger purposely held aloof, and avoided any private conversation with the present head of the family. Only once did George catch him alone, and instantly took advantage of the opportunity.

"Don't go," said he, laying his hand on the arm of his brother, who was going to leave the stable as he entered it. "I have been waiting for a chance to speak to you. Our father left your future in my hands, you know," he added, in a tone which, if he chose, the other might take as a warning.

"Well, what is it?" asked Harry, impatiently.

"Don't be so fidgety. It is nothing unpleasant. I only want to know if you can tell me where to find the Mainwarings' late governess, Miss Lane?"

"And you said you had nothing unpleasant to say! I call it unpleasant— confoundedly unpleasant—to ask me such a question! As if I had anything to do with Miss Lane! What do you want to know for?" His manner changed from sullen to fierce with this question.

"Your manner is a little inconsistent. If you know nothing about her, why are you so angry when I ask you if you do?"

"I don't care to be put through my catechism. You ask more questions than my father did."

"Then he spoke to you about this matter?"

"What if he did?"

"And you told him the truth?"

"Yes, the truth. I swear it! But I am not bound to answer your questions, and I won't. Take your hand off my arm; do you hear?"

"Only one question. When you have answered it, I won't bother you again. Do you know where Miss Lane lives?"

A light suddenly came into his brother's eyes, and he answered readily:

"I haven't the least idea where Miss Lane lives; I swear it!"

His brother took his hand sharply off his arm and turned away. He thought it was a lie; but he had no means of extracting the truth. He was more interested in Miss Lane than the younger guessed, more anxious for the interview he was about to seek with the prim little girl than he had ever been before about a meeting with a woman.

He had to keep his impatience in check until the funeral was over; but on the very day after, the young baronet went up to town and to the address Mrs. Mansfield had given him.

"Is Miss Lane at home?" he asked of the servant who opened the door. "Ask if she will see Sir George Braithwaite," he added, as the girl did not answer.

She left him in the hall while she went up-stairs, and then returned and asked him to walk up. And in the sitting-room into which he was shown sat Miss Lane—but not the downcast little creature of Garstone Vicarage days—a little, smiling fairy in cream-colored muslin, with a rose at her throat, and a small hand put out in welcome. After the first greetings, her glance fell on his deep hatband.

"My father is dead," said he.

She looked grave and sorry at once, but not so much surprised as if the fact of his illness had been unknown to her.

"You had heard of his accident?"

"Yes, I saw it in the papers," she answered, blushing, and not looking at him.

He looked at her searchingly. Who could have told her all about it but Harry?

"Were they all there when he died?" she asked, softly.

"All the family were there—yes. Didn't you know?"

"How could I know, Sir George? I have not kept up correspondence with the Mainwarings. They do not care enough about me."

"But you left others behind you at Garstone who did," said he, more hurriedly than he generally spoke such speeches, for his heart was beating faster.

He had never yet looked on a woman who so completely fulfilled his ideal of a beautiful and graceful lady. A passionate wish sprung up in him that he might be mistaken in spite of all, and that his brother might have no interest for her. He glanced at her hands; they were ringless. He would fain have convinced himself that the very glance of her steadfast brown eyes proved her to be innocent of any evil. Yet these rooms, this dainty dress, did not proclaim the struggling governess out of work. For the first time it flashed across his mind, as he looked at her, that, if only she could convince him that she was as free and as pure as he would fain believe, he, Sir George Braithwaite of Garstone Grange, would be ready to marry the little governess out of employment.

She had noticed his compliment only by a short, sharp breath, and asked after the vicar's family to divert the conversation.

"I am sure I shall like daily teaching much better than my life with them," she went on quickly.

"You have some pupils then?"

"Not yet. I—there have been difficulties in the way of my getting any before now; but I hope to do so soon," she said, hurriedly.

"And you don't find this life dull?" said Sir George, his jealousy awake again.

"Oh, no!"

"I suppose your friends come to see you very often?"

"No; I don't have many visitors."

"Perhaps they don't know where you are. You know you promised to give me your address; but you never did. You left me to find it out as best I could for myself."

"It—it is very kind of you to come," said the girl, flushing, "How did you find me out?" she asked, anxiously.

"I asked Mrs. Mainwaring for your aunt's address, and went from Garstone to her house."

"You went all the way to my aunt's!"

"I would have gone to the world's end to find you!" He left his seat and stood by the mantel-piece, bending over her. "Didn't you know I loved you? You were kind to me that day at the flower show. You promised me your address, you told me the train you were going by." She was trying to stop him; but it was out of her power now. "Then, when I said I would see you off, as your own words had given me the right to do, you gave me a cruel snub. And then you let Harry see you off, and—and travel up to town with you, they say."

She had risen, and was confronting him with bright, eager eyes.

"I did not let him—I did not expect him. He came, and I could not prevent it."

"Is that true, my darling?" cried George, passionately. She was standing, with upturned face, close to him. He threw his arms round her.

"Then you don't love him! You have nothing to do with him and his forgeries?"

"Forgeries?" she cried, paralyzed even while she tried to free herself.

As they stood, he with one arm round her, she still with horror, Harry came in. He sprung upon his brother and tore the trembling girl out of his arms.

"Oh, is this true? Is it true? You heard what he said!" she cried, with a shudder.

"Is it a time to accuse me when I find you in another man's arms?" he cried, fiercely.

"And by what right do you object to her being anywhere she pleases?"

"Pleases?"

"Yes. You swore to me two days ago that you did not know where Miss Lane lived. It was a lie!"

"It was not a lie. There is no such person as Miss Lane. This is Mrs. Harry Braithwaite, my wife!"

CHAPTER VI.

When Harry uttered the words "My wife!" his brother looked from one to the other for a few moments without a word; then, in a low, sullen voice, he said:

"You have tricked me and deceived me, both of you. It was very clever—very clever indeed, but hardly wise. I won't take up your time any longer now." Then, turning to Annie, he continued, "I am much obliged to you for your kind welcome. I must apologize for having brought down your husband's anger upon you; but, you see, you left me rather in the dark." Then to Harry—"You will hear from me in a day or two. Our father made me promise to provide for you, and I have a proposal to make which I don't think you will find ungenerous. Send me an answer as quickly as you can."

He shook his brother's hand and then Annie's and left the room. Harry turned to his wife, looking rather anxious.

"He is going to do something nasty, Annie—I am sure of it. I know George's manner when he is spiteful, and our chances look very bad, darling. No more Paris, no more pretty gowns, for the present, at any rate!"

But Annie did not answer. With trembling fingers she was pulling to pieces the flower which had fallen from her throat.

"Why, Annie, what is the matter? You look ill—you are crying!"

"I am not ill," said she, repulsing him. "I am heart-sick, miserable."

"But you mustn't give way like that, my darling. George will have to come round. He sha'n't make my wife spoil her pretty eyes."

"It is not George," she said, with fire. "Do you think I am such a coward as to mind not having pretty dresses? What was that he said about forgery?"

"Oh, nothing to make such a fuss about!" answered the young fellow sulkily. "I was hard up, I had no money for our wedding trip, and I couldn't help it. It wasn't as if I committed a crime, and copied somebody else's name, it was my own father's. I knew it would be all right, and so it was. He hushed it up directly, and said hardly anything about it."

"You call that nothing!" said Annie, raising her eyes wide with horror to his face.

"Of course I know it was wrong," replied he impatiently; "but there was nothing else to be done. I could not have married you without, or you would have had to pass your honeymoon in an attic."

"I would rather have passed it as a tramp on the high-road than as we did, if I had known."

"Well, you are an ungrateful little cat. When I thought of nothing but pleasing you and buying you pretty things from morning till night."

"Pretty things that were bought with stolen money!"

"How dare you say such thing to me?" he shouted. "Don't you know I'm your husband; and do you suppose I am not the best judge of my own conduct? Do you suppose I should ever do anything a gentleman need be ashamed of?"

"I think you have done a thing a beggar would be ashamed of."

"Thank you, thank you! You call me a beggar and you call me a thief. I shall be a murderer next, I suppose; and, by Jove, it would serve you right if I were. Haven't I behaved well to you? Didn't I come to London with you just to stop you from crying? And didn't I marry you when I knew very well that all my family would disapprove of it?"

"Oh, yes; you made a noble sacrifice. I am deeply grateful to you for throwing yourself away. It spoils the look of it a little, though, that your elder brother was willing to do so, too, if you hadn't been beforehand with him."

"You may say what you like; but it is a sacrifice of a man's liberty to marry at twenty. As for George, I believe you like him better than me all the time. Answer me—do you—did you ever care for him?" demanded he roughly.

"I shall not answer your insulting questions," said the young wife, in a very calm voice; and, as quickly as she could, she left the room. For she felt as if her heart were breaking; this sharp wrangle had made her almost hysterical, and she did not want to break down before the husband whom, for the time at least, she despised and all but hated.

Already during the few weeks of their wedded life, it had needed all the strength of his outbursts of demonstrative affection, all the bright contentment she felt at her release from schoolroom drudgery, to cloak the fact that they had not one taste, one sympathy in common; that their tempers were ill suited to each other, and the moral standard of the wife as different from that of the husband as light from darkness. This crime, which Harry had made light of, tore down the last shred of illusion from before the eyes of the wife of eighteen. She had made an awful mistake. Carried away by the passionate pleading of a headstrong boy at a time when she felt herself to be utterly friendless, and when his impulsive remorse had seemed to her to show a high and generous nature, she had bound herself by a tie which would last her life to an ignorant, uncouth, unprincipled lad who did not even love her. For already the sensitive woman felt that his caresses were growing careless;

and she knew that no husband of a few weeks could have used the words Harry had used to-day to a woman for whom he cared deeply.

Harry had gone out; and for three long hours Annie knelt on the floor by the bed pondering what she should do with her life, and praying for help to show her where her duty lay. She came to a resolution strangely wise for so young a woman; and, when her husband returned, she was as nearly her usual bright self as she could manage to be. Harry, of course, did not appreciate the struggle she had gone through before she could do this, but came to the conclusion that she saw how silly she had been to make such a fuss about a trifle which did not concern her, and thought it was time for him to show a little just indignation at finding his brother's arm round her.

But she stopped him with surprising promptness, as if his remarks were beneath argument. He began to bluster a little.

"Do you really doubt the propriety of my conduct?" she asked, coldly.

"Well, it is not a usual thing, is it, to find one's wife—er—er—like that?"

"Is it a usual thing for a wife to be requested by her husband to conceal the fact that she is married, especially from his relatives?"

"Why, no, of course not! And it doesn't matter now, you see, since I told my father all about it," said Harry, trying to speak more good-humoredly, since he saw by the steady look of his wife's eyes, as he had seen before in less serious discussions, that, if the argument went on he would get very much the worst of it.

So the peace was kept between them, though the warmth of their feelings for each other was getting rapidly less. An incident happened a few days later, however, which revived it for a time. George's promised proposal came, and Harry had scarcely read it before he was at his wife's feet, pressing his lips to her very dress with all the enthusiasm of a few weeks back.

"He wants us to go to the Grange—not for my sake, though; but to get you there; but he sha'n't! I'd sweep a crossing rather than let you go there! My generous brother—hang him!"

"To go to the Grange! To live there?"

"Yes; that is his way of fulfilling his promise to our father. He says there are too many burdens on the estate for him to make me a suitable allowance, unless we go and live there. But I wouldn't let you go there for the world!"

"But, Harry, I should be quite safe with you. You speak of your brother as if he were a savage."

"So he is. We are all a set of savages; and, being a savage myself, you see, I know how to trust the rest. I tell you you shall not go; and, if you try to persuade me, I shall think you don't love me."

He flung his arm round her, and looked up into her face with an air of boyish authority which she did not attempt to resist, though it made her smile. A few months of self-dependence had made her so much older, so much wiser than this spoiled child who was her lord and master.

She knew he could not live long in defiance of his elder brother; she knew he had no money of his own, and no capabilities of making any, or that, if he had any capabilities, he had no intention of using them. He had indeed most of the qualities necessary in a groom and some of those wanted by a jockey; but, being a gentleman, though he could copy their manners and share their tastes, he could follow their occupations only as an amusement. He had given her money so recklessly at first that she, though inclined to be extravagant, had, without saying anything to him about it, put some by in case of an emergency; so that, when his supplies to her stopped rather suddenly, she was able to go on paying their weekly bills without running into debt. But this could not last long; and she began to look out for some music-pupils, still without saying anything to her husband, whose pride would have cried out at the idea of his wife working for her living and his.

It was easy enough by this time to leave some hours in the day unaccounted for. Harry had met some acquaintances in town and picked up some others, and spent but little of his time with his wife, who, he complained, did not take as much trouble to amuse him as at first, and who could always amuse herself with a book—a most unaccountable taste in his eyes, so that she could publish an advertisement, answer others, go for the few replies she got to a neighboring stationer's, and give a lesson three times a week in Onslow Square without exciting his suspicions.

She knew that Lady Braithwaite and her daughter were now in town, staying with a sister of the former's at Lancaster Gate, but, as she would have thought nothing less likely than that they should take any notice of her, she stood for a moment in the doorway in silent astonishment when, coming into her sitting-room, after having given a music-lesson, she found Lilian, looking superbly handsome in her deep mourning, walking about examining the pictures and ornaments.

"I think you must be very comfortable here," said she, coming forward and kissing her, as if they had been affectionate friends of long standing.

Lilian's manners were charming when she chose, and she was at her best this afternoon—always queenly, but smiling and willing to be pleased with anything. She drew her tiny sister-in-law on to the sofa and sat down beside her. Annie, very glad of this visit, yet hardly daring to believe that Lilian could have heard of her marriage, scarcely knew what to say; but the other saved her the trouble of finding a remark.

"I wish we lived like this. These rooms are neither too large nor too small, while Aunt Constantia's big rooms are so big that you lose your way in them, and the small ones are so small that, if the door opens inside, it scrapes the opposite wall. I am supposed to be still a child, and therefore of no consequence; so I am put into a nice little cupboard, so compact that Jennings has to open the door and stand in the corridor to brush my hair."

Annie laughed at the picture of self-willed, spoiled Miss Braithwaite as a victim to neglect, and then asked after Lady Braithwaite.

"Oh, she is quite well, thank you, though of course she hasn't got over poor papa's death yet! You heard all about it from Harry, of course?"

"Yes," said Annie, wondering at the easy way in which her proud sister-in-law thus alluded to their new relationship. She was still more surprised when the other continued:

"It seems so strange to think of Harry as a married man! I suppose he will think I ought not to box his ears any longer now; but you will let me, won't you? I can't keep him in order in any other way; but I suppose you can."

Annie laughed—not very heartily.

"I haven't tried that plan, certainly. It wouldn't do for such a little woman as I am; I think I am too small for him," she added, as if this really had struck her suddenly as a grave objection.

Lilian burst out laughing.

"What an odd little creature you are! I have always heard that a little woman can make a big man as submissive as a dog, and rule him with a rod of iron, while he thinks all the time that he is the master. I am sure you would not condescend to obey Harry."

"Yes, I do," said the young wife, seriously—"at least; I do the things he tells me to do; but he doesn't tell me to do many things." And the thought flashed through her mind, "He doesn't take enough interest in me to mind what I do."

"And you don't ever want to do anything he doesn't wish you to do?"

"When I do, I do it without telling him about it."

Lilian was delighted with this speech, which Annie rather regretted having made.

"I am glad you are not so superhumanly good as I was beginning to fear. Don't you find him very dull company? He can hardly write his own name, he can't spell a bit, and he can talk about nothing but horses and guns."

Annie would not own that she had not enough of her husband's company to mind it.

"I don't want him to read when he is with me, and I haven't asked him to spell much. And I like horses myself, though I don't know much about them."

"Well, your life is not so dull as mine, at any rate," declared Lilian. "You are a married woman, and can go where you like and with whom you like; I wish I could," she added, petulantly.

"But I have nowhere to go and no one to go with except, of course, Harry," Annie added, hastily.

"You have got over the silly stage of newly-married life very soon," said Lilian, amused, but rather surprised. "Now I want to go to a hundred places I can't go to. Aunt Constantia looks down at my black gown and says, 'Too soon, my dear, too soon!' And she and mamma both disapprove of all the persons I like. I never was so wretched in my life—just when I am in mourning too, and want cheering dreadfully!"

"Well, you will soon be able to go out more, and then you will certainly leave off envying my quiet life."

"Oh, but there will be far worse trials for me then! Now that we are in mourning, at least no one can find fault with my dress; but, when we begin to go out again—and I am to be presented next season—I shall want money; and George is so mean—he says he is so poor, but that is nonsense!—that I know he will open his eyes and say that a hundred a year ought to buy me everything I want, and the same day he will send a groom up to Tattersall's to buy him a couple of hunters, and wonder at the selfish extravagance of women! It is so silly, too; for the very best thing he can do is to get me well married as soon as possible; and who will see me if I never go out, and who will look at me if I am dressed 'with tasteful economy?' As if economy was ever tasteful—as if I did not do my dressmaker credit, too! I assure you I look quite nice when I am well-dressed."

She threw back her graceful head and smiled at Annie with playful insolence, which was charming in such a beautiful girl; and, having got, for a time, to the end of her grievances, she gave a plaintive sigh, and then laughed at herself.

"I have been taking the privileges of a relative in boring you to death; but really my wrongs were getting too heavy to be borne in silence. It is very good of you to listen without yawning."

"Oh, you don't know how glad I am to see you and listen to you! I was afraid you would be so angry about Harry's marrying me."

"I won't pretend we were glad to hear of it; but everything else was swallowed up in papa's death. I don't think mamma has quite forgiven either of you yet; but she will come round in time. And, you see, as I told her, if Harry hadn't married you, George would have done so."

Annie started, and the color rushed to her face.

"Oh, you need not look surprised! I am sure of it. He was much more in love with you than Harry was; and, to tell you the truth, when you had left Garstone, and nobody could tell what had become of you, I thought George was more likely than Harry to know where you were."

She rattled on without taking much notice of Annie's continued agitation. After a minute's pause for breath, she added:

"And I did credit to your being a good little thing and a clever little thing, for George has far fewer scruples and far less sense of honor than even Harry, I can tell you. Harry is not a bad fellow at heart, though he is such a lout; there is no other word for him. Will you forgive my frankness? I am a pretty good judge of my brothers, and my knowledge may be useful to you."

She rose from the sofa and took Annie's trembling hand.

"I have frightened you, worried you. You won't let me come again. But you will, won't you?" she added, in a coaxing tone—"for I am so dull. May I come on Thursday, the day after to-morrow, and we will go to the Academy together? It will soon close now, so it will be full of country bumpkins; but I will brave them, if you will. Mamma and Aunt Constantia find it too tiring for them. May I come?"

She asked quite restlessly and anxiously; and Annie, surprised, begged her to come, and promised to be ready at whatever time she pleased.

When Harry returned home, and his wife told him of his sister's visit, he was even more surprised than she had been.

"Well, she is a queer girl; but I think this beats any freak she has had yet," he said. "You should just have heard her go on at me—and at you—at Garstone, when she first heard about it—just after our father's death too. I told her if she didn't hold her tongue, I would turn her out of the room." And presently he broke out again, "I wonder what she is up to now?"

Without suspecting any deep-laid plot under Lilian's friendliness, as her husband seemed to do, Annie was more surprised than ever when Thursday came and Miss Braithwaite drove up in a hansom very punctually, to see how excited she seemed to be over such a simple diversion as a visit to the Academy with her sister-in-law. She was looking radiantly lovely. The mourning, which did not at all set off Annie's brunette beauty, was the most perfect setting possible for Lilian's bright, fair complexion and chestnut-brown hair. She was in good spirits too, and so anxious to start that she gave Annie doubtful help in dressing with her own hands. Then they got into the hansom which was waiting outside, and were at Burlington House in five minutes.

Lilian did not care a straw about pictures, and gave most of her attention to the curious crowd which may be seen at the Academy every year during the last week of the season. They had been through two rooms, and were entering a third, when a gentleman came up to them, and the color deepened on Lilian's face. He was a tall, strikingly handsome man, of slighter build than the Braithwaites, and much better carriage. Lilian introduced him to her companion as "Colonel Richardson."

Then they all went on together. Miss Braithwaite, being in a brilliant mood, did all the talking; and, as her talk was chiefly addressed to the new-comer, Annie gradually fell behind them and gave her attention entirely to the pictures. As she noticed how happy Lilian looked, how evidently she was taking pains to please, and how attentive Colonel Richardson was to her, it occurred to the quiet little woman behind that this meeting was not accidental; she was not surprised at their pleasure in each other's society, and thought to herself what a handsome pair they would make. When they had nearly finished their inspection of the pictures, which had become a very transparent pretext to Annie's eyes, they turned to her, and Lilian dropped out of the conversation to allow Colonel Richardson to talk to her companion. He could talk about the pictures very well, she found, though he had ignored them a good deal that day; and, when he presently asked permission to call upon her and lend her a book with valuable engravings which he had brought from Italy, she could not easily refuse.

So, two days later, he called and brought the book; and while he was there Lilian came in, and they both stayed to tea. Annie, who was always rather overpowered by the brilliant and rather exacting Miss Braithwaite, was a sweet and gracious little hostess, but listened more than she talked. And Colonel Richardson called after that very frequently. It generally happened that Lilian was there; but that did not seem surprising, for she had got into the habit of spending a good deal of time with the gentle little sister-in-law who made such an amused and therefore amusing listener to her chatter. Sometimes Harry was there; and the influence of the elder man—Colonel

Richardson was between thirty-five and forty—upon the younger soon became very strong. The latter worshiped his new friend, and would follow him about like his shadow when he could, so that the colonel had to get him a mount or a seat on a drag to get rid of him.

One evening Harry came home from visiting his aunt and his mother with "a good joke" to tell his wife.

"Aunt Constantia and my mother have found a mare's nest," said he, with his usual elegance of speech. "They have discovered that the colonel is a most dangerous man, that he comes here not to see me, who can talk about horses and shooting and all the things he likes, but to make love to you and Lilian! Why, he never speaks to either of you if I'm here! He has too much sense to go dangling after any woman. I told my aunt I could look after my wife, and Lilian could look after herself. She is not the girl to throw herself at any man's head."

"But there is no reason why she should not accept his attentions."

"No reason! What—is his wife no reason?" asked Harry, sharply.

"His wife! Is he married?" cried Annie, in a low, frightened voice.

"Of course he is. Been married for the last ten years!"

CHAPTER VII.

The announcement that Colonel Richardson was married entirely changed the aspect in which his attention to Lilian had appeared. Annie understood now that she herself had been used to cover a friendship which the girl's relatives disapproved of, and the young wife's heart beat fast with excitement and dread of the scene she had to go through when she next heard Lilian's footstep outside her sitting-room door. She was doubtful how to open the subject; but her companion soon paved the way by asking if the colonel had brought a book from Mudie's.

"He called; but I had told Lydia to say I was not at home."

Lilian's face instantly wore its haughtiest expression.

"You sent such a message as that to Colonel Richardson?"

"Yes."

"Why?" Her beautiful gray eyes were fixed in indignant astonishment on her companion's face.

"I have decided that I cannot receive his visits any longer."

She was trembling. Lilian mistook this for a sign of fear.

"Do you not consider my introduction a sufficient assurance that a gentleman is worthy of the honor of your acquaintance?"

"Not in this case," said Annie, looking at her steadily.

"Explain what you mean."

"Certainly. I have the strongest reason for believing that you introduced Colonel Richardson to me and led me to think he was unmarried, because your friends, who knew more about him than I, disapproved of the acquaintance for you."

Lilian rose quickly from her seat, and seemed to be attempting to quell the smaller woman by her dignified appearance.

"You have insulted me grossly—shamefully! I suppose I have deserved it for condescending so far to you as I have done."

"You forget," Annie said, simply, without any show of either timidity or arrogance. "Two months ago you might have talked to me of condescension, for I was then only Miss Lane, the governess. Now I am Mrs. Harold Braithwaite, your brother's wife, your equal, and your superior—for the present—as a married woman."

"My equal—my superior!"

"Yes; that is not a matter of argument, but of fact. You cannot suppose for a moment that I wish to presume upon it. You made the first advances toward friendship with me, when I was rather lonely here and grateful for your society and that of the gentleman you introduced to me. Now I know your friendship was offered only that I might innocently help you to deceive your friends, and I am quite as ready to draw back as you can be;" and her brown eyes met the brilliant gray ones steadily.

Lilian was defeated, though she would not own it.

"You have caught up the grand manner very quickly," said she, patronizingly.

Annie smiled; such a sneer could not hurt her. Lilian left the room majestically; and it was only then that the features of her hostess assumed an anxious look. Would this headstrong girl give up her dangerous acquaintance simply because another difficulty had been put in the way of it? It was not likely. She had known quite well that Lilian, looking upon her only as a useful acquaintance, not as an ally, would not listen to any entreaties or remonstrances from her; therefore she had not tried any; but she almost reproached herself now for not having made the attempt.

She did not say anything to her husband about this interview, as that would have entailed the confession that she had refused to see his friend, which would have drawn down a useless fury of reproaches upon her own head.

She felt rather awkward therefore when Harry, after complaining and wondering that the colonel did not call, brought him home in triumph to dinner one evening, about a week after the scene with Lilian. He was sharp-sighted enough to notice a slight constraint in his wife's greeting of their guest, a slight diffidence in that of the colonel. While Harry dressed for dinner, the latter came nearer to Annie and said, in a low voice:

"I am in a difficult position, Mrs. Braithwaite. I have had the misfortune to offend you in some way; but, when your husband invited me here this evening, and I hinted that I was afraid you would not care to receive me, he would not listen to my objections, and insisted upon my coming."

"Pray do not think I wish to be discourteous," said Annie, fearful of being ungracious to a guest—one, too, whom she could not help liking.

"I am sure you do not, therefore I know I must have been guilty of some most unintentional offense to be punished with the severe snub I received last week. May I know what I have done?"

He was gently putting her in the wrong, and she felt uncomfortable and inclined to be remorseful. It was Lilian who had introduced him, and she herself had welcomed his visits. She answered deprecatingly:

"You have done nothing to offend me; it was on account of Lilian."

The words might have been dictated by a feeling of jealousy; but the tone in which they were spoken precluded that idea. Colonel Richardson did not pretend to misunderstand her.

"I see," he said, after a short pause. "But I think I have been rather hardly dealt with. I am forced by circumstances to remain in town when most of my friends have left it, and my wife, who is an invalid, is staying at Bournemouth. At the house of a common friend I make the acquaintance of a charming girl, whose relations, being in deep mourning, receive few visitors. She, finding me rather forlorn and friendless, offers to introduce me to her sister-in-law, an equally charming lady. I accept the offer eagerly—trespass perhaps too much upon the kindness of both ladies in coming whenever I have a chance to see them, and am rightly punished when——"

"Oh, no, no—forgive me!" cried poor Annie, overwhelmed with remorse at the apparent strength of the case against her. "I would not for the world have risked wounding you but for Lilian. You know how harsh the world is to such a beautiful young girl, and the pleasure we both took in your society has been already misconstrued in her case and has alarmed her friends. I have been very frank—perhaps too frank; but I think it was better, was it not?" she added pleadingly.

Of course he forgave her readily enough; and Annie, who felt that her husband would not be above listening at the keyhole, if he thought anything interesting was going on on the other side of the door, hastened to drop the confidential tone of their conversation.

Lilian being now offended without remedy, there was no reason to put any further check upon Colonel Richardson's visits. He did not call so often as before; but Annie was most grateful for the breaks he afforded in her monotonous life.

They spent most of hot August in London, for the most hopeless of reasons that they could not afford to go away. Harry got a little money—she did not know how, and was afraid to ask; but even he saw that they must be careful with it. However, in the last days of the month they got an invitation to go for a voyage in a yacht, and the five weeks they spent in that way were the happiest Annie had ever known.

There was only one other lady on board, the wife of the owner, and a much older woman, so Annie was a little queen for the time and received unlimited attention from every man but her husband, who showed however to greater advantage in her eyes than he had ever done before, for he knew how to manage a yacht as well as he knew how to manage a horse, and was, in fact, the best sailor on board.

By the first of October they were again in London, Harry more sulky, his wife more reserved than ever. This could not last long.

One morning at breakfast he threw a letter in a shame-faced sort of way across to his wife. It was from George, and contained a renewal of his offer to receive them at the Grange. The poor little wife had reason to dread this arrangement now, for Lady Braithwaite and Lilian, both of whom disliked her, the one for receiving Colonel Richardson and the other for dismissing him, were at the old home at Garstone. She read the letter and gave it back.

"Are you going to accept?" she asked simply.

"Well, I don't see what else there is to be done," he answered, without looking at her. "It is only fair that he should help us, and perhaps it is true that he can't spare enough just now to give me my due and let me go. We might go there for a month and try it. There would be some shooting now and some hunting later on, at any rate. And you would be more comfortable with Lil and mother than here by yourself, I'm sure."

Annie did not try to undeceive him on that point. She saw, by the eagerness with which he alluded to the country pleasures he was going back to, that nothing she could say would alter his determination to accept his brother's offer. She had known it must come to this, so she heard his decision quietly, and prepared with a heavy heart to go back to Garstone, a place full of bitter memories to her, for it was there she had been dismissed without a kind word by the cold Mainwarings, and it was there she had met her husband, who was, she felt already, to be a burden crushing down her life and robbing her of the career she had been fond of picturing to herself. For Annie was too high-principled a girl to try to undo her own act by leaving the three-months-wedded husband who already neglected and, in fact, bored her. She was useful to him in a way; he was a trifle more orderly in his mode of life since his marriage; she wrote his letters or told him what to say and how to spell the words. She did not care enough about him to put any irksome restraint upon him, having seen early that her reproaches only made him drink more and spend more of his time with his inferiors; but, on the whole, her influence improved his habits somewhat. She said to herself, with a bitter smile, that, by marrying, she had taken only a rather harder situation as governess, with none of the comforts of home and a precarious salary. She packed up her things, gloomily, for their journey, and her heart sunk lower and lower as they neared its end.

Harry, on the contrary, grew more and more excited and light-hearted as the train approached Beckham. His happiness at finding himself again on the way to his beloved dogs and horses found vent in a burst of affection. He bounced into the seat next to his wife at the last stopping station but one, when, two passengers having got out, they were left alone in the carriage. Then he treated her to a rough embrace.

"Aren't you glad to have left that smoky hole behind you and come into the air again—eh, Annie?"

But Annie was not, and a furtive tear told him so. He kissed her pretty little face that the yachting trip had bronzed.

"Don't cry, dear. Do you remember our last journey on this line, Annie, when you were so frightened because I jumped in, and wanted me to get out at the next station? And what a long time it was before I could make you leave off crying! But you have nothing to cry about now, you know, and I want you to look your best when we get to the station, that everybody may say what a pretty little wife I've brought home."

But there was nothing in this speech soothing to Annie, who looked anything but her best when they did steam into Beckham station. Sir George was on the platform to meet them, with a dog-cart waiting outside, and Harry felt disgusted and angry with his wife, when logically he should have felt glad, as he saw by his brother's first glance at her that he thought her appearance much changed for the worse. George drove, and Annie sat beside him, while Harry got up behind with the groom. She was not very entertaining to-day, though she tried hard to be so; but there was something pathetic to George in her attempts to be lively, and the very tones of her soft voice had a charm in themselves to him, so that he was touched, and listened to her with a quiet kindliness in his manner which made much greater impression upon her than the compliments and tender tones he had used to her before her marriage.

"I hope you don't so very much mind having to come and live at the Grange. We will all try to make you happy," he took the opportunity of saying when Harry's voice, in hot argument with the groom, rose loudly enough to drown the *tête-à-tête* in front.

She looked up at him gratefully, with the too ready tears in her eyes.

"Thank you; I am sure you will," she said, gently.

Words better left unsaid to the heartsore and neglected little wife rose to his lips; but her straightforwardness and a lull in the conversation at the back checked them—for the present.

She treasured up those few words of kindness and welcome, all the more carefully that the greetings she received from the rest of the family were cruelly cold. Lady Braithwaite and her daughter held out icy hands to her; Stephen had evidently taken sides with them; Wilfred was kind, but rather indifferent; and William, the youngest, was restrained by a very needless fear of exciting Harry's jealousy from showing the warmth he really felt toward the sad-looking little lady who had made such a delightful play-fellow.

The fatigue she felt after such a long journey excused her from talking much. She sat very quiet during dinner, feeling scarcely awake, and hardly catching the sense of the talk going on around her. Lilian did not know very much about the odds for the great races which were under discussion; but she liked to think she did, and joined in the conversation confidently. Lady Braithwaite listened with interest to the sort of squabbling laying down of the law on their favorite subjects to which her sons had accustomed her for years.

Harry was rampant, rejoicing to find himself once more able to hold his own in the talk around him; he drank more than usual, contradicted everybody, and, as George quietly said, did his best to make his unobtrusive presence felt.

Annie alone took no part in it all, but sat dreading the time when she should have to accompany the other ladies into the drawing-room and be at their mercy.

At last the moment came. She followed them quietly, receiving a parting chill at the dining-room door from the steady way in which crippled Stephen, who liked to show his activity by jumping up to open the door for them, though he was not the nearest to it, looked on the ground, and not at her, as she passed.

It was not so bad as she had expected, after all. Lilian had no pettiness, and did not descend to small persecutions. She did not show much cordiality, but hunted out all the newest songs from among the music for Annie to try, and then left her to amuse herself. Annie was grateful for this; it took her out of the range of Lady Braithwaite's disapproving eyes, and the occupation of trying new music kept her own tears from falling. She could defend herself or even attack boldly in argument or dispute, but this armed coldness took all the spirit out of her; she could retreat behind her natural reserve and seem not to care, but there followed a bitter reaction when she was alone.

It was a long time before the gentlemen came in to break the silence in the drawing-room. Lady Braithwaite was dozing, Lilian was sitting on the hearth-rug, playing with a retriever pup, Annie was softly trying over songs at the piano at the other end. Sounds of high voices and loud laughter came from time to time across the hall; at last they heard the dining-room door open, and Harry's voice above the rest in tones of high excitement.

"I tell you I can prove it, I can prove it!" he was saying to George as they two came in first; his face was flushed and his gait unsteady, and his manner more dictatorial than ever.

"How can you prove it?" asked George, who might have been drinking as much, but who showed it less.

"By a paper I've got somewhere. Annie," said he to his wife, scarcely turning toward where she sat at the piano, "where is that American paper the colonel gave me, about the trotting-matches?"

"I packed it with your papers. I can find it if you want it."

"Yes, yes, I want it. Then I'll show you I was right," said he, triumphantly, to his brother. Annie had risen, and was crossing the room to the door. George interposed.

"No, no, not to-night. Don't you see she is tired? You can't ask her to ransack your portmanteau to-night for a paper of no importance. It will do to-morrow."

"No, it won't do to-morrow," said Harry, who was not in a state to brook contradiction. "I say I will prove it to you now, to-night. It is of importance, of great importance, very important! You said I was wrong; I say I'm right, and I'll prove it."

Before the end of this speech, the last words of which were spoken with halting gravity, Annie had left the room, gently insisting upon passing George, who would still have tried to prevent her going. Harry, luckily, did not see his brother's good-natured attempt to save his tired little wife a tedious search for an old newspaper. She went up to their room; it was Harry's old room, with a second little bed put up in it. His portmanteau had been unstrapped. She turned out the gas in trying to turn it up; so she opened the door and dragged the portmanteau into the corridor, under the burner outside.

Fatigue had dulled her faculties, and it was a long time before she found what she wanted. She was still searching when she heard heavy footsteps behind her, and looking round from where she was on her knees, she saw Wilfred leaning against the friendly wall.

"Let me help you," said he; and he knelt down beside her, not without difficulty.

She thanked him, though his assistance was not likely to prove valuable.

"Harry is a brute to you," he said, solemnly.

"Oh, no; he is only a little thoughtless!"

"Yes, he is," said Wilfred. "He is a brute, because he is a fool. But he will have to treat you better now he has brought you home. We'll see to that."

"Oh, I hope you won't interfere; it would only make it a great deal worse for me! He is not cruel to me, and I don't mind his neglect."

"I dare say you would rather have his neglect than his attention, and I quite agree with you. And now you have three nice new brothers, who will give you all the attention you want," said he, looking at her affectionately over the portmanteau, while he supported himself on his elbows on the edge of it.

"Thank you; you won't find me very exacting," said she, turning over some papers in search of the one she wanted.

But he would not go.

"You maybe as exacting as you like to me," he continued, monotonously; "I would do anything for you. You are a sweet, good little lady, and you may take me to church if you like."

She had at last found what she wanted, and rose quickly from her knees, while Wilfred slowly followed her example. She had shut the portmanteau and pushed it back into the room before he had had time to do more than offer to do so.

As she shut the door and was going down-stairs, he put his hand gently on her arm, and they went down-stairs together. In the hall he said, gently:

"You need not think I am offended because you wouldn't let me help you," and went off to the billiard-room.

Wilfred was the most notorious reprobate of the lot; but the instincts of a gentleman showed oftener in him than in the others.

Annie went on to the drawing-room, where her husband, reproaching her for being so long, seized the paper from her. But his hands and eyes were too unsteady to find what he wanted, and she had to find and read it out to him.

The passage, about the pace of a celebrated American trotting-mare, proved Harry to be right, and he triumphed loudly, not thinking to thank his wife for her trouble. Then he asked her to write to their late lodging for a pipe and pair of spurs he had left behind, and again she quietly left the room, and went into the study to do so.

This time it was William who interrupted her. He knocked softly at the door, and came in rather shyly.

"I thought I'd show you where the pens and paper are," said he; and he collected the writing materials for her and hunted for a stamp while she wrote.

Then, when she had directed the envelope, he put the stamp on and brought his fist down upon it with an unnecessary thump.

"What is that for?"

"That's to make it stick, of course."

For the first time that evening Annie burst out laughing. The boy threw his arms round her and gave her a sounding kiss.

"I'm so glad to hear you laugh again. You looked as if you would never laugh any more. And I'm so glad you're come, so jolly glad!"

She was laughing and crying together now, as she drew the boy's face to her and kissed his cheek.

"And I'm so glad you're glad. We'll have another game at shuttlecock to-morrow."

"Oh, no," he said earnestly; "I've got something better than that for you to-morrow. I've got a new terrier, the gamest you ever saw, and we'll have the most splendid rat-hunt you ever were at in your life."

CHAPTER VIII.

Annie did not find life at the Elms such a miserable affair as she had expected. That first evening the key-note was struck of the conduct of each member of the family toward her. Lady Braithwaite continued to treat her with distant coldness, or affected to ignore her entirely. Lilian followed suit, except at odd moments of capricious good humor, when she would treat her like a pretty child to be teased and caressed. George was kind, but instinct made her shun *tête-à-têtes* with him. She did not see much of Wilfred, who used to tell her that she made him ashamed of himself and promise to reform. He even went so far as to attend a temperance-meeting in the village, where, he declared afterward, that he heard a lot of things which were very true, and where he signed the pledge without being asked, in the hope of pleasing her; he was not quite sober at the time. When on his return home he went straight to the sideboard and mixed himself some whisky-and-water, Stephen reminded him of his vow; but Wilfred only said, softly: "Hang the pledge!" and went to bed in the same state as usual.

Stephen scarcely spoke to her. She soon found out that his admiration of Lilian, which she had noticed on her first visit to Garstone Grange, had grown into a mad passion which the object of it was not slow to make use of. He was her slave; she might snub him, torment him, hurt his sensitive feelings; nothing could change his devotion to her, which was very touching to Annie, who knew how hopeless his passion was, and that the handsome girl used her crippled lover only as a tool and a toy. For Lilian was a headstrong, willful girl, more difficult to manage than her mother and brothers guessed.

She had commissions to give her cousin which nobody else knew of, letters which she had to coax him to post, and answers to them which had to come under cover to him. And the poor young fellow never faltered in his allegiance, but, after a stormy war of words with her, which she knew how to end with a careless kiss brushed across his burning forehead, he always gave way; and her little secrets, whatever they might be, remained as safe as if no one but herself in the household knew of them.

One of these secrets, and perhaps the most important, had a narrow escape of being revealed one evening, however, when Annie and her constant companion, William, were standing still as statues in the large, wire-faced house where the rabbit-hutches were kept, amusing themselves by watching the mice play about, and finally run into the traps they had prepared for them.

This was a very favorite pastime, always ending in a friendly squabble, as William wanted to "drown the little pets" and Annie insisted upon letting "the dear little things have their liberty again." Finally half used to be drowned or given to the cat, and half let loose again; and, if there was an odd one, William tossed up for it.

It was about six o'clock on a November evening that they were standing breathless with excitement, straining their eyes in the dusk to see one cautious little mouse running round and round and all but into the trap, when they heard footsteps outside, but were far too deeply interested to look round. Presently they heard another sound, and knew by the noise of the crutches on the ground that it was Stephen who was approaching. They heard the footsteps of the first comer going to meet him, and Lilian's voice saying impatiently:

"What a long time you have been! I thought you were never coming! Is there one? Give it me—quick, quick!"

"There it is," said Stephen, sullenly. "What—aren't you going to give me a word of thanks, when I went out all the way to Beckham for you when I was in such pain? Oh, Lilian, have you no heart?"

William and Annie could not see the speakers, though they could hear every word—could hear too the impatient tearing of an envelope. Then Lilian's voice, in a soft, cooing, but only half-attentive tone, said:

"Yes, you are a dear, dear good boy, and my best—friend—in the world." Then more quickly. "Just let me finish reading this, there's a dear, kind fellow!"

There was a pause, and a heavy sigh from the cripple. Then Lilian spoke again more brightly:

"Now, I can thank you as you deserve. I feel as happy as a bird, and all thanks to you," she added, caressingly.

But Stephen was sullen.

"It is not thanks to me; it is thanks to the man who wrote that infernal letter! I wish I had died before I brought it to you!"

"Why did you bring it then? Why have you brought me a dozen from the same person, all under cover to you?"

"Because—because I couldn't help it—because I must do what you tell me, in spite of myself. Oh, Lilian, can you reproach me with what I do for you?"

"I am not reproaching you, you dear old, silly boy! I was thanking you, when you suddenly began to scold me. I trust you more than anybody else in the world; you know I do."

"Then why don't you trust me entirely, and tell me whom the letters are from? You know I would never betray you. You know that, whoever it was, I would do for you then all that I do now, and more—if that could be."

"Why don't you tear them open and see? They all pass through your hands."

"I would if they were any one's letters but yours. But your wishes are sacred to me—they are, indeed, and, if I were to do that, you would never speak to me again."

"Well, to judge from the way you reproach me, that would be a very good thing."

"No, Lilian, no, no! Be cruel to me as you like; but don't talk of casting me aside like that. What more can I do for you than I have done? What——"

They heard his voice in passionate protest long after the words themselves were lost, as the sound of the crutches, following Lilian toward the house, grew fainter on the pathway. The interest Annie and William had taken in the mice was quite gone. They still stood opposite to each other in the deepening dusk; but for some minutes after the voices had become inaudible they could not find a word to say. At last William broke the silence.

"I say, Annie, what on earth do you think Lilian is up to?"

"I don't know; I can't think!"

"It can't be all square, you know. I wonder who it is that is writing to her? However, she always was full of tricks, and it is no good saying anything. I shall just hold my tongue about it; wouldn't you?"

"Yes, certainly. We can't do anything to stop it, and we heard it all by accident. We should only make everybody angry with her and she——"

"Would swear we have told lies, and Stephen would back her up."

"And we shouldn't prevent her getting her own way even then," said Annie, sorrowfully.

She had a shrewd suspicion who the unknown correspondent was, and an incident which occurred a little later confirmed it.

Meanwhile the quiet outdoor country life she led, always driving, or walking, or playing some game of their own invention with William, had rapidly restored to her beauty the bloom that unhappiness and *ennui* had begun to rob it of. George took the most notice of this improvement, and Harry the least. Yet even the latter was not quite insensible to the change for the better in his wife's good looks, and told her one day, with rough good-humor, that married life seemed to agree with her, though she did not seem to appreciate what it had done for her. Annie answered with a rather ironical laugh. It seemed to her that the appreciation ought to be on the other side.

For he remained one of the most careless and selfish of husbands, while she fulfilled her duty to him with an exactness which got no thanks from him. She was his slave in little things, and never asked for the smallest service or attention in return. Perhaps Wilfred was right when he suggested that she would rather be without it. However that might he, he was as free to go where he pleased and do as he pleased as in his bachelor days, while he alone, of all these young men, never had to hunt for things he had mislaid, never had to cry out for a missing button, and had his scanty correspondence done for him much better than he could have done it for himself.

William once humbly expressed a wish that she would get the servants to look after his hunting-things as she did for Harry. But she only laughed at him.

"Well," said William, rather aggrieved, swinging his legs backward and forward from the gate on which they were sitting together, "I do ever so many more things for you than Harry does."

"Ah, but then he is my husband!" returned she, offering him an apple.

"I say, Annie, you don't like Harry, do you?" he asked, mysteriously, after a pause.

"Of course I do! How can you ask me such a question?" said the outraged wife indignantly.

"Oh, well, I don't believe you do, all the same!" said he, obstinately. "And I don't wonder! If I were you, I would let him run away, and then you could get rid of him and marry somebody nicer."

"Do you know what you are talking about?" asked Annie, haughtily, drawing herself up with as much dignity as the maintenance of her balance on the top rail of a five-barred gate would allow.

"Yes, quite well, Annie dear; I am saying it only for your good," said he, his boyish sense of humor peeping out in spite of his being really half in earnest.

And then they laughed themselves off the gate.

For this was how the *regime* of coldness and neglect on the part of her husband, mother-in-law, and sister-in-law had turned out. It had thrown Mrs. Harold Braithwaite upon the society of her youngest brother-in-law, and made of her a melancholy statue in the house, a happy hoiden out of it. The only thing she was careful of was to avoid the scenes of the daily walks of her late pupils during their out-of-school hours, as she told William it might have a bad moral effect upon them to see their late governess scrambling up banks, and in other undignified situations.

She was out of doors nearly all day, it not having yet occurred to Lady Braithwaite to torment her daughter-in-law, who was very submissive to her, by making her stay in to help to entertain chance visitors. She got two invitations, however, with the other ladies, and endured with them and George a dull dinner-party, and with them, without George, a duller afternoon tea, at both of which she was much admired and looked upon as a pretty child. Her style of beauty led to this mistake; she was so small, so low-voiced, had such fresh-colored, rounded cheeks, and such timid though pretty manners that nobody suspected the strength of will, and ambition, and other deep-seated qualities, of which their young possessor was herself scarcely aware. They lay dormant indeed just now. The uppermost side of her many-sided nature at present was a buoyancy of spirit which made a lad scarcely sixteen her favorite companion, and a wild delight in having escaped from the shackles of the schoolroom on the one hand, and of lodging alone with a sulky, ignorant husband on the other.

And, just when her heart began to cry out for something more than this, she made a discovery which sent her to her knees in utter joy and thankfulness to Heaven. No more *ennui*, no more repining now; even in the house the gravity of her little face gave place to an expression full of hope and sweetness, while, once escaped from silent submission and Lady Braithwaite, her eyes would dance and her lips break into soft song, till William declared he did not know what had come over her, and confessed one day, with a lump in his throat when she stopped to rest on a felled tree, that he believed she was going to die and go to heaven.

"And—and you seem to be glad; and—and it is beastly of you when you know how fond I——"

Here the lad gave way; and she laughed at him and made him sit by her, and told him he was talking nonsense.

"If I look 'so sweet' as you say, that marvelous effect is due, not to my being dying of consumption, but to the Garstone air, which is making another woman of me."

"Then why do you always want to stop and rest? You never used to."

"Because—because the cold weather is coming on, and that always tries me."

"But it oughtn't to; it ought to brace you up."

"Here come the Mainwarings! Let us get through the hedge," interrupted Annie.

And an undignified exit put a stop to the conversation. Annie told her secret to no one living.

That very day, when these two returned home just in time for dinner, they found that an unexpected guest had arrived. It was Colonel Richardson. Beckham was not in a hunting-country, but a journey of an hour and a half by train took the Braithwaites within an easy distance of the meets of a very good pack of fox-hounds; and it was at a hunt-breakfast that day that the three eldest Braithwaites had met him. Harry, delighted to see his idol again, had introduced him to his brothers, and Sir George had invited him to return with them to the Grange, to break the journey to Scotland, where the colonel was due. He scarcely recognized Annie, she was so much changed for the better. Lilian received him with an indifference which, to Annie's observant eyes, seemed rather overdone.

That evening, after dinner, when the ladies went into the drawing-room, Annie went as usual straight to the piano, while Lilian lounged upon a low seat in the corner near the entrance to the conservatory; her favorite retriever came to rub his head against her hand, and Annie thought, as she looked from the dog to its mistress, that she had never seen such a lovely woman. For Lilian had taken the utmost pains with her dress that evening; her black gown, cut square at the neck, set off the fairness of her complexion. She habitually despised ornaments, and could afford to do so; but to-night a few sprays of white azalea and white heath and delicate maiden-hair fern relieved the somber dress, and a very small bunch of azalea and fern was fastened by a gold-headed pin in her chestnut hair. And Annie saw the girl's face flush when they heard the dining-room door open and the gentlemen's voices across the hall; but when they all entered the room, Colonel Richardson came, in a few minutes, not to that seat near the conservatory, but to the piano, and told Annie that Schubert was his favorite composer. For it was a song from the "Schwanengesang," arranged for the piano, that she was playing.

Annie looked up with irrepressible surprise that he should recognize it. She was so used to an audience who considered all music above the level of Offenbach as a not unpleasant noise that her face beamed with pleasure at his very simple remark.

"I will play you another—my favorite," said she.

And, in her delight at being with an appreciative listener, she played better than usual, and at the end looked up naively for his approval. He gave it without stint; and she went on from these to other favorite pieces, which she knew well enough to be able to talk at the same time.

"You must lead an isolated life here, I should think, with no one to talk to?"

"So I don't talk," said she, smiling; "I run wild in the fields with William."

"Do you like the life?"

"Yes and—no. I like it when I don't think. I like walking so far and running so fast and jumping over so many ditches that I am too tired at night to do anything but long for bed-time."

"But you can't pass all your life like that."

"That is the worst of it. I hate the thought of coming back to semi-civilization when I am too old for my savage pastimes."

"You used to write a little, I think you told me. Have you given it up!"

"Quite. I could never make a great author now, and nothing less would content me."

He smiled; there was something of the simplicity of a child about this matron. To be a great author one had but to wish it and to be unmarried. And he lingered about the piano a long time, discussing authors and authorship, and now and then hazarding a remark made expressly to bring the indignant fire into her eyes and some speech to her pretty lips piquant in its severity.

At last Lilian could bear it no longer; she rose and, with heightened color, and a dangerous light in her eyes, walked to the piano.

"Won't you sing something, Annie?"

Her sister-in-law at once complied, and, before she had finished the first verse, Lilian had diverted the colonel's attention from all but herself. The song ended, Annie rose, and, her cheeks still flushed with the excitement of playing her best, slipped into the cool conservatory, murmuring the last words of her song still softly to herself. She had not been there two minutes before George joined her.

"You don't mind smoke, Annie, do you?"

"No; besides, I am going back into the drawing-room."

"Don't go yet. It is much nicer out here. And Harry has a quarrelsome fit on and would disgust you."

That instantly checked her steps. Harry's bursts of childish petulance were among her greatest trials. She turned with an impatient sigh again to the flowers.

"You played beautifully to-night, much better than you ever play for any of us."

"Colonel Richardson understands music."

"While we understand only drinking and fighting; that is what you mean, isn't it?"

"Oh, no, it is not! You understand a great many things which I know nothing about—how to tease a person to death, for instance," said she, with weary petulance.

"That is unkind," said George, quietly. "Never mind; I won't reproach you now, when you are tired and excited by your own playing."

She looked up at him with some surprise.

"It is astonishing that such a boor as I should have noticed that, isn't it, and that I should know the difference between the half-mechanical playing of pretty tunes and music full of passion and feeling, like that you gave Colonel Richardson to-night."

"I did not know you liked music," said she, in a low, troubled voice.

"You never took the trouble to inquire; did you? But even among the 'semi-civilized'—to quote some words I heard you use to-night—there may be capabilities for something better, may there not?"

Annie hung her head in confusion. He spoke quite gently, and looked down at her as if he were hurt, not angry.

"I am sorry—I spoke without thinking," she said, in an unsteady voice. "You were right; I am very tired, and that makes me cross and—and foolish. But I won't play mechanically to you again. I will find out what you like best, and learn to play that as well as I possibly can; and I'm so sorry you were hurt by my rude speech!"

She held out her hand to him, to see whether he had forgiven her; he took it, held it in the warm pressure of his, and finally kissed the little fingers two or three times before letting them go.

"You are a dear little creature, and I should like you to insult me every day for the pleasure of forgiving you. But that is too much to hope for; you won't do more than ignore me."

"Is that fair? You pretend to forgive me, and then bring another accusation against me in the same breath," protested Annie, who did, indeed, habitually avoid *tête-à-têtes* with him, but who, as usual, once brought to bay, was perfectly at her ease and able to defend herself.

"Well, I thought I had better state all my grievances at once, as I know it will be a long time before you give me another chance. Seriously, it gives me great pain to see you sitting silent in my house or slipping through the rooms like a snubbed and neglected child, only waking up into life and brightness when you are out of sight of—those who are longing to see you happy."

The tears were in her eyes. She was touched by the kindness of his words; but how could she tell him that his own mother and sister cast, by their coldness, a chill upon her from which, in their presence, it was impossible for her to escape?

"I will try to be more cheerful," said she humbly, and rather dismally.

"No, that won't do," declared George, impatiently. "I don't want you to pump up liveliness that you don't feel, or laugh when you feel inclined to cry."

"Then what do you want me to do?"

"Well, when anything amuses you, and you look stealthily at William with a perfectly stolid face but a laugh in your eyes, will you look at me, too? I can enjoy a joke as well as he."

"Did you notice that?" said Annie, wonderingly.

"Yes; you exaggerate my dullness enormously. Now, will you promise to share the joke with me?"

"But William is only a boy. If I were to laugh with you as I do with him, Harry would think himself shunted and be horribly unpleasant, as usual. I don't mean to say anything against Harry," she added, hastily. "He is your brother——"

"Do you think I feel so tenderly toward him, that I cannot hear a word of truth about him?" said George passionately. "Do you think I cherish any deep affection for the brute who first robbed me of the treasure I would have died to win, and then neglected her, crushed the brightness out of her youth by his boorish ignorance, insulted and disgusted her by his tastes and habits?"

Annie was frightened by his vehemence—moved too in spite of herself. He saw this, and seized his advantage.

"Annie," said he, bending down over her with his handsome face full of passionate tenderness, "it is too late now; but didn't you care for me a little once?"

With a long sobbing breath which was almost a cry, Annie bent her head instinctively to hide her face, and, springing away before he could detain her, went back into the drawing-room.

Sir George drew himself up again to his full height, and mechanically put his long-since-extinguished cigar to his lips. He was answered.

CHAPTER IX.

The next day Colonel Richardson went to Scotland, after taking a very warm farewell of Annie, who, so far as she herself was concerned, was extremely sorry for his departure. He was the only man to whom she had spoken since her marriage who had tastes in common with her, and whose views of life were not bounded by the stable, the kennel, and the dinner-table. George had indeed shown himself to be ready to enter into her feelings, but his sympathy she was afraid to encourage. It was true that she had felt for him, from the first time he had talked to her at the Grange dinner-table, a warmer sentiment than she had ever felt for Harry or any other man; and, though since her marriage she had stifled it without much difficulty, she could not but know his interest in her remained strong. She felt, however, that since last night's talk she would have to be more careful as to her conduct, and combine prudence with a little more graciousness. It did not prove so difficult, after all.

That very afternoon she had gone into the library to amuse herself among the old books that nobody else ever touched, but in whose very presence she delighted; and she was perched upon the ladder that stood there by which to reach the highest shelves, and had covered herself with dust in her endeavors to get at the dingy-looking volume whose only attraction lay in the fact that it was out of reach, when Sir George came in. She was surprised to see him, as she had never seen any of the brothers indulge in heavier reading than that which a sporting paper afforded.

"What are you doing among my books?" he asked, with severity.

"I don't wonder you are astonished to see any one reading them," said she, looking down saucily, with her dull discovery open in her hand.

"You think I don't know how to read, I believe."

"I am sure you couldn't read this, at any rate. It is called 'Extracts from the Sermons of the Reverend Thomas Dobbs, late Vicar of Garstone,' and it is dated 1844."

"Why, no; I indulge in that only on very special occasions! I don't think much of your literary taste."

"And I don't think much of your library. I can't find anything better."

"Oh, nonsense! Here's the 'Life of Knox,' and the 'Works of Josephus,' and 'Fox's Martyrs.' I remember my mother cured us of the vice of reading when we were youngsters by letting us have these entertaining works to read on Sundays. Have you ever noticed, Annie, that careless and irreligious parents are always very particular about what their children read on Sunday?"

"But I am too old to be cured in that simple manner. Find me something nicer, please."

"Come down, then, and sit by the fire, and I'll find you 'Clarissa Harlowe,' or something else as light and frivolous."

She came down and sat in the chair he drew on to the hearth-rug, while he brought one book after another, and, after dusting it carefully, placed it on her lap. Sometimes he would kneel by her side for a few minutes to look over one with her, and listen to her remarks upon it; and they got on so well together over this pastime that by the time the light of the December afternoon had faded, and the red glow of the fire was all they had to see by, the awkward barrier between them was quite broken down, and a friendly intercourse between them begun, which was to Annie merely a new pleasure, but which brought to the young baronet a delight which he knew to be full of peril.

After that day she avoided him no longer, but treated him with gracious gratitude for his kindness, which would have disarmed a man of better principles.

Lilian's coldness to her had grown into more open dislike since Colonel Richardson's fondness for music had kept him so long at her side on the eve of his journey to Scotland. But the girl could not do much to make her sister-in-law uncomfortable for fear of her eldest brother, with whom she jealously felt Annie's interest to be strong. Young Sir George was a harder and somewhat colder man than his father had been, and took the lead in the family of which he was now the head as much by character as by position.

It was getting very near Christmas when the baronet told his sister one day at luncheon that he wished to speak to her. They went into the library together, had a long interview, and, when the girl came out, her face was red and swollen with crying. She was very silent that evening, and Stephen watched her in wistful wretchedness. He had not been able to speak to her that afternoon; he could only guess at the reason for her unhappiness, and he sat brooding sullenly over George's cruelty in bringing tears to those proud eyes, and longing to be with her alone, that he might learn what her trouble was and comfort her. It was late in the evening before he got an opportunity of speaking to her in the morning-room, whither she had gone on the pretext of fetching some work, knowing well that her cousin would follow her. She broke into the subject at once.

"Mr. Falconer has proposed for me, and George insists on my accepting him."

Mr. Falconer was a rich gentleman of about forty, who had paid Lilian marked attention for some time. Lilian affected to look down upon him because his father had made his money in "cotton;" but the sneer was absurd, as her admirer was a man scarcely less stalwart and handsome than her own brothers, and as much their superior in intellect, character, and feeling as it was possible for a man to be.

Stephen leaned on his crutches, trembling from head to foot at the news. He had known very well, poor fellow, in spite of mad dreams after an occasional moment of her fascinating kindness, that she could never be his; but her marriage had been a horrible dread for the distant future, and, now that it proved a not distant reality, his heart sunk within him. She was touched by the utter prostration of this poor cripple, who would, as she very well knew, have given his life at any moment for her. She led him to a chair, and tried to cheer him with a sort of regal tenderness. At last he said, his lips trembling:

"But George can't force you to marry him, Lily."

"Yes, he can, practically. The money that ought to have been mine, of course, I shall never get from this spendthrift crew. George says it is impossible that he can give me what my father intended me to have, that the estate is so burdened that there may be a break-up before very long, and I am half inclined to believe him. So I am portionless, and ought to think myself lucky to get a husband at all, it seems."

"But, Lilian, that is nonsense! You are the most beautiful girl in the country; you will make a sensation in London, and marry a duke, if you like. You are surely never going to let George do what he likes with you, with your high spirit?"

The girl did not answer, but impulsively hid her face in her hands. A light came into Stephen's troubled eyes, and he shuddered as he looked at her.

"Lily," he whispered, "has George heard anything?"

"I think so," she answered, without looking up. "He just hinted, in a way that made me think he must have been prying into my affairs, that it would be better for me to do as he wished. But, after all," she cried, in a different tone, raising her proud head from the table as suddenly as she had cast it down, "I have done nothing wrong—nothing to be ashamed of. It is not my fault if I am so hunted and teased and mistrusted by my own family that I cannot see what friends I please, but must correspond with them secretly. For I won't give up my friends at any one's bidding!"

"But you saw him not long ago, and by your friends' invitation," said Stephen, in a low voice.

"What do you mean?"

"Do you think I didn't know at the first moment of seeing you with Colonel Richardson, that it was his letters I had been receiving for you? Oh, Lilian—and he is married!"

"And what if he is?" asked the girl, quietly. "I like him well enough to marry him if he were free; but I am not going to give up his friendship just because Aunt Constantia and mamma and Annie insulted him and me when I was in town by saying our acquaintance was improper. I shall have what friends I please—now and always; and, if I am to marry Mr. Falconer soon after Christmas, I will see Colonel Richardson again before then."

"Soon after Christmas!" echoed Stephen, in a low voice.

"So George says. And the sooner the better, for then I shall be free," said the girl, impatiently. "And now you must post a letter for me at Beckham to-morrow—just one more—the last," she added, coaxingly.

"To Colonel Richardson, under cover, as usual, I suppose?"

"Yes. And, as it is perhaps the very last service you will ever be able to do me, I am sure you won't tease about it, will you?"

"It is a very bad service I am doing you, Lily. If George were really to find it out, I think he would kill me, and perhaps you."

"Oh, the sense of honor is not so keen as you imagine in our family!" sneered Lilian. "He would bully us both, and perhaps strike one of us; but he wouldn't risk hanging on your account or mine."

"But what do you want to say to Colonel Richardson?"

"I want to tell him to come and say good-bye to me before he goes away, for he has been ordered abroad. George won't invite him here again, I know; but I must see him, and I will."

"But how can you——"

"He must come on Christmas Day, in the evening. You know how my brothers will celebrate Christmas by drinking more than usual, and then quarreling among themselves. They will soon give me an excuse for leaving their society, and I will meet Colonel Richardson at the gate at the bottom of the garden—the one that leads to the short cut to Beckham."

"You would risk that? Think what you are doing, Lilian. Colonel Richardson would never consent to put your reputation in peril like that."

"He will put himself in peril too, with my wild brothers about; so he'll risk it. And I know how to make him come. I'll tell him, if he doesn't come down here, I'll come up to London to see him."

"Lily, are you mad? I will not help you to do this."

"Very well, then; I'll risk it without your help—post my own letter, receive the answer, and you may betray me to George if you dare. I believe I am mad, I am so miserable!"

"And all for a man who doesn't appreciate you, who likes Annie better than you?"

"It is not true," said she fiercely. "If I believed that, she should not stay in the house a day longer—I would not rest until I got the little hypocrite turned out! But it is not true—it is not true! Now, will you desert me at the last just when I am so wretched, and have nobody to help me?"

"I will serve you to the end, for good or for evil, as I have always done, Lily; you know I live only for that. When you are gone, whether Mr. Falconer marries you or somebody else, my wretched life will be no good to me, and I don't care how soon I lose it. No one will ever worship you as I do, Lily, nor for so little thanks."

But she soothed him with sweet words and kind eyes. She did indeed feel the strength of his devotion, and, moreover, he was too useful an ally not to be worth a few kind speeches.

So the letter was sent, and the answer came—and the secret was safe.

Since the regular hunting-season had begun, Harry's neglect of his wife had not only grown more open than ever, but had been supplemented by sneers at her "refined tastes" and "poetry, prunes, prism" manners. She could not tell the cause of this change, and went on quietly in her own way, dutifully caring for his small comforts, and accepting his coarse snubs with the same placid indifference with which she had formerly taken his scanty thanks.

When Christmas Day arrived it was spent just as Lilian had predicted. In the morning the ladies went to church, accompanied by Stephen and William. As there was no hunting, and Lady Braithwaite had insisted upon the grooms having a holiday, the other young men spent the afternoon in the stable and the billiard-room, wrangling more than usual. Wilfred had already remonstrated with George for teasing Harry.

"You are always saying things to put his back up now. What do you do it for?" he asked.

"I don't care a straw what he says!" cried Harry, sullenly, who was flushed and excited long before the afternoon was over. "And, as for my not being 'a person of authority,' as he calls it, I have as much authority as anybody here."

"Over whom or over what, pray?" said George, tauntingly. "I don't say you can't manage a horse as well as—an hostler; but show me the man or woman on whom your word or your opinion has the slightest effect."

"Well, I like that!" burst out Harry, his face twitching with passion. "Don't I manage my own wife—doesn't she obey me, and quickly, too? Do you ever hear her contradict me or differ from my opinion? Answer me, or, by Jove, I'll make you!"

"Your wife doesn't think your opinion worth differing from, and she obeys you as the shortest way of getting rid of your presence. Everybody knows that."

"I say, George, do shut up!" broke in Wilfred. "Can't you see you are only irritating him against his poor little wife, who has quite enough to put up with from him already? What on earth are you driving at? Can't make you out lately!"

"Don't interfere with your infernal preaching!" shouted Harry. "So my wife has enough to put up with from me already! Very well, she'll have more than enough, then, before long, if she doesn't get rid of her confoundedly cold tragedy-queen airs, I can tell her! I'll show her and you too if I'm not master of my own wife!" And Harry flung away the cigar-end he had been biting, and swung himself out of the yard, unable to control himself any longer.

Wilfred turned to his brother.

"Why the dickens did you badger the boy like that? He'll only go and let off his ill-temper on poor little Annie, and perhaps take to proving his authority with his fists or his boots, the hulking bully!"

"Well, the sooner he does, and disgusts her thoroughly, and makes her throw him over altogether, the better for her."

Wilfred looked at his brother keenly.

"I say, George, you're not playing square."

"Yes, I am; you don't know the game;" and the baronet lounged out of the stable-yard with his hands in his pockets, but with teeth so firmly set that he bit his cigar in two.

Dinner that evening began quietly enough. There was a lull in the hostilities between the young men, Harry being sullen, Wilfred rather sleepy, and George giving all his attention to Lilian, who was in her most brilliant mood, talking, laughing, teasing her eldest brother, and delighting him by her archness; only one person at the table noticed how feverishly bright her eyes were, and the nervous play of her delicate fingers when she was not speaking. For Stephen never took his eyes off her; he drank scarcely anything and ate nothing. Annie was pale to the lips, and the sound of Harry's voice made her start. Only Lady Braithwaite and William were quite their usual selves.

"So this is the last Christmas I am to spend as Miss Braithwaite!" said Lilian. "I wonder how I shall like married life."

"Ask Annie how she likes it," suggested George.

The young wife did not look up; but all could see that a shiver passed over her slight form. Harry made a restless movement on his chair.

"Confound her!" William, who sat next, heard him mutter; and the boy's blood took fire. Wiser than George or Wilfred in the interests of his play-fellow, however, he said nothing, and clinched his hands together under the table to keep himself from punching his brother's head. Such acts as that had not been unknown in past times at the Grange dinner-table, and a repetition of them seemed perilously near.

When they at last came into the drawing-room after dinner, after sitting an unusually long time over their wine, Annie was seated—it almost seemed that she was hidden—in the shadow of one of the window-curtains close to the conservatory. Lady Braithwaite was happily dozing as usual, and Lilian was flitting about the room, more animated, more restless than usual. She looked at her brothers searchingly as they came in, they were all talking and laughing loudly and discordantly. Stephen was the only one perfectly sober, and he, white to the lips and silent, was more excited than they. He watched Lilian with glistening eyes full of fear and anxiety.

She had scarcely listened to half a dozen sentences of her brothers when she left them and crossed the room.

"Where are you going? We want you to play something."

"I think you can amuse yourselves better without me to-night," she said, with playful insolence—"at least for the present. I'll come down presently, when I've finished my letter to Aunt Constantia, and give you 'John Peel.'"

She calculated upon their having found some other means of passing the time long before they thought of her again; and, before they could stop her, she had left the room. The little black figure in the shadow of the curtain sprung up, and was at the door to follow her example, when Harry's voice thundered:

"Annie, stop where you are!"

But for once she took no notice, and she was turning the handle when he sprung forward and stumbled over a footstool. George laughed. William darted across the room to Annie, and, holding the door open, said:

"Go, dear—quick!"

But the power to do so had gone from the frightened woman's limbs. She hesitated. In that one moment Harry had recovered himself, and, just as William was giving her a gentle little push, her husband reached them, and, seizing Annie's arm roughly, swung her round into the middle of the room again.

There came a sullen imprecation from the lips of every other man in the room, and William, with a howl of rage, felled his staggering brother like an ox to the ground. Wilfred, sober for the moment, turned to the wife, who had clasped her hands in fright as she saw her husband fall.

"Go, my child, go!" he said earnestly. "He isn't hurt. For Heaven's sake, go before he gets up!"

They were all between her and the door now, swearing, fallen husband and the rest. She turned, fled through the conservatory, and out into the garden; she ran, ran—over the steeply-sloping lawn and down into the shrubbery at the bottom, too much scared to stop herself. She fancied she saw a tall, black figure among the trees in front of her, and called "Lilian!"—but there was no answer. Then, having reached the path that ran between the trees all around the garden she leaned against a tree to get back her breath. The next minute she heard a man's footsteps coming hurriedly down the walk. Her excited fancy told her it was her husband come to wreak his disappointed fury on her; she tried to get behind a tree, but there was a wire fence which stopped her. She crouched down on the ground with her face hidden, until the footsteps came quite close and stopped.

"Don't, don't! I can't bear any more!" she said, hoarsely.

But an arm was put round her very gently, and tried to raise her from the ground.

"My darling, it is not your brutal husband. Don't you know who it is?"

"Oh, George!" she cried, with a gasp of relief, as he raised her from the ground.

She hung on his arm, quite still, except for a convulsive trembling from time to time, for a few minutes, until her shaken sense began to return; then she tried to stand alone.

"I am better now, thank you, George. But, oh, I was so frightened!"

"Lie still in my arms, my darling," said he, his voice shaking.

He drew her more closely to him, and she could feel the quick beating of his heart against hers.

"Let me go, George; I am quite well now. You frighten me too!" she said, piteously, imploringly, trying to unlock his hands with her slender fingers.

He held her more closely at once.

"I frighten you, Annie! I would not hurt a hair of your beautiful head for the world. Oh, my darling, my darling, tell me you are better! Look up at me, Annie."

She raised her eyes timidly to his face, then dropped them again, as his passionate gaze met hers.

"I am much better. Let me go, George, please. Won't you do what I ask you? I am tired; I want to go in—to bed. Oh, George, if you are really sorry for me, let me go in, or I shall die out here in the cold!"

"You shall not die; you shall not be cold in my arms. Do you want to go back to the husband who is waiting to bully you, perhaps to strike you, away from the man who loves you with all his soul?"

Annie gathered all her strength and gave one ringing cry:

"Harry!"

The bare branches of the shrubbery-trees rustled and cracked as a man sprung into the pathway and tore the trembling woman from the unprepared George. She looked up.

"Thank Heaven! Colonel Richardson!"

George looked at him, too, dumb with surprise. But his eyes saw what Annie's did not. From the opposite side of the path Lilian's handsome eyes were flashing in the moonlight in jealous anger at the woman who lay unconscious in Colonel Richardson's arms.

CHAPTER X.

Careless of herself and her own secret, in the burning desire to be revenged upon Annie, Lilian sped back to the house, not knowing that George had seen her, and found Harry with the rest in the billiard-room, still quarreling hotly about the scene in the drawing-room, of which she had not yet heard. Stephen had been forbidden by her to leave the house that night, and he had been tortured with anxiety on her account ever since he saw Annie go into the conservatory, and then noticed a few minutes later that George had also disappeared.

Lilian beckoned Harry imperiously out of the room.

"I have something important to say to you."

Her wide, glistening eyes, panting bosom, and resolutely subdued manner, checked his oaths at this interruption. He followed her into the hall.

"George and Colonel Richardson are in the garden, in the copse at the bottom, quarreling over your wife. I am sorry if I have startled you; but I thought you had better know."

"She is the blight of my life," hissed out Harry, with a bitter imprecation, trying to steady himself.

"Hadn't you better do something more than stand here and abuse her?" asked Lilian, dryly.

She turned in disgust from the infuriated lad, and went into the drawing-room. He was on the point of following her, when Annie came into the hall from the garden by another door. There was not a trace of color in her face; she crept slowly, and it seemed to her drunken husband guiltily, toward the staircase.

"Stop!" growled Harry. "You have something to say to me now. Where have you been?"

"In the garden."

"Whom were you with?"

"With George."

"And Colonel Richardson?"

"Yes."

She spoke wearily, all spirit seemed to have been taken out of her by the scenes she had gone through since Harry's first bullying that afternoon.

"What were you doing there? Tell me at once."

"I was doing nothing to be ashamed of; you know that perfectly well. I will tell you all about it to-morrow. It would be of no use to try to make you understand now," said she, glancing up at his flushed face with an involuntary shudder of disgust.

"You will tell me now, whether I understand or not—that is my lookout," returned he, doggedly. "I've had enough of your infernal airs of superiority, and I mean to show you I'm master. You go about with a long face, telling everybody you are too good for me, when all the while——"

"Take care what you say!" she broke in, with sudden spirit.

"What were you doing in the garden, then?" thundered he. "What was Colonel Richardson there for?"

She did not answer. It was not so much to shield Lilian as from fear of another and worse quarrel between the brothers that she was silent; and excitement, fatigue, and disgust were making her reckless.

"Do you intend to answer me or not?" asked Harry, laying a heavy hand on her shoulder.

His touch made her defiant.

"Not now."

He raised his hand and struck her. It was not really a severe blow; but it was enough to throw the fragile little creature to the ground.

"You brute, you cruel, cowardly brute!" she cried, in a low, sobbing voice, looking up at him with passionate dark eyes full of hatred, from where she had fallen. "You may have killed your child!"—and her head fell back upon the floor at his feet, while he stood still in stupid, dumb bewilderment.

Only for a moment. The rough, drunken fellow was not heartless. When his dim, dazed eyes saw clearly the white, senseless face at his feet, and his dull ears began to admit a suggestion of her meaning, he flung himself down beside her and gathered the unconscious woman into his arms in a passion of loud, demonstrative remorse.

"I have killed her—I have killed her!" bemoaned to the group of frightened people from the drawing-room, billiard-room, and servants'-hall whom his cries brought quickly into the hall. "Heaven forgive me, she is dead! My poor, pretty little wife! Oh, I am a brute, a beast! Annie, Annie! She will never speak to me again!"—and the slight frame he held in his arms and pressed to his convulsed and swollen face shook with the violence of his sobs.

It was a genuine grief that prompted this outburst; but it was the grief, not of a man, but of a child who in a fit of thoughtless anger had taken the life of a pet dog or bird.

They took her from him with difficulty, assuring him that she had only fainted; and George and Wilfred led him away, while the women tried to restore her to consciousness. It was a long time before they succeeded; then Lady Braithwaite came into the billiard-room where the young men were.

"She must have a doctor. Somebody must ride to Beckham at once," she said.

"I will!" cried Harry, jumping up.

"Nonsense; you are not sober enough," said George curtly. He was bearing his share of remorse at the result of the day's work.

But, before he had reached the door. Harry passed him with a rough push and an oath. The shock had sobered the lad for the time; but he had been drinking since to drown his remorse. However, he was so familiar with the stable as to be able almost by instinct to find what he wanted; he put saddle and bridle himself on to the fastest horse there, and, once in the saddle, he was all right, for, drunk or sober, Harry could ride.

He got back before the doctor, and ran, all breathless, heated, and splashed, up the stairs to the door of the room, into which Annie had been taken, knocked as softly as he could, and opened the door. She was lying on the bed, and his mother and the housekeeper were with her. They made gestures to him to go back; but he stood there, his face all quivering with wistful anxiety.

"Only let me just say one word to her," pleaded he, hoarsely. He was panting still from the speed with which he had come.

Annie, who had been lying half-unconscious, opened her eyes and turned to Lady Braithwaite with a low cry:

"Don't let him come near me!" she whispered.

But Harry heard; and he slunk out of the room, stunned as no physical blow could have stunned him.

Annie lay ill for weeks, and in all that time no messages, no entreaties would induce her to see her husband. The only glimpses he got of her were by stealth, when she was asleep. For the sweet hope of being a mother, which had made her secretly, silently happy under all his neglect, had now been taken from her, and she felt that it was his brutality which had snatched away the one joy her wretched marriage had brought her.

Lady Braithwaite tried to soothe her mind and induce her to forgive her husband. But the submissive daughter-in-law was strong in her weakness; and no persuasion on the part of the elder lady, who had now grown as kind as she had formerly been cold, could extract more than:

"Tell him I forgive him; but don't let me see him."

She was so obstinate in this decision that, even when she was well enough to be carried down-stairs, she refused to move from her room, and the women about her knew that it was the dread of meeting her husband which kept her a prisoner. So that Lady Braithwaite had to make her way to Harry's room one night, and persuade him to go away for a time. It was a difficult task for a mother, for the lad's passion broke out vehemently in alternate fits against his wife and of fondness for her. First he said he would go to the ends of the earth, if that would do her any good, and the next minute he swore she was a hard, ungrateful little vixen, and deserved to have her ears boxed.

However, at last Lady Braithwaite carried her point; and he agreed to go away for a fortnight to some relatives of hers in Leicestershire—no very great hardship, in truth, as the hunting-season was not yet over.

So one morning, before Annie was awake, he stole into her room with elaborately clumsy movements expressive of his intention not to make the least noise, all ready for his journey, except that he was without his boots— he had left them outside the door for fear of their creaking. He stood looking at her wistfully for a few minutes, and then crept close to the bed and softly kissed her. She did not move or wake. Then he took out of his pocket a letter, directed, rather quaintly, to "Mrs. Harold Braithwaite, Garstone Grange, Lancashire." He had first written outside it simply, "Annie;" but then it had occurred to him that the dignity of the offended husband required the full title. This letter he tucked gently under her shoulder, as he did not want anybody else to see it. Then, with another kiss and the murmur, "She doesn't deserve it—I'm blessed if she does!" he left the room.

When he got outside the door, he hesitated a moment.

"Wonder if it would hurt her to wake her? She might just say good-bye. Oh, well, it is only for a fortnight!" and he put on his boots and went down-stairs.

Only a fortnight—so he thought!

When Annie woke that morning, she found the letter. It was badly written, strangely spelled, not punctuated at all, an authentic uninspired document evidently:

"MY DEAR ANNIE,—I ought not to have to write to you at all as a husband ought to see his wife whenever he likes and she ought to think it a compliment but you are ill though I believe you are nearly well now and I say no more. You don't know how sorry I am about it all or you would be kinder for I can not ride or sleep or do anything hardly for thinking of you. Then all say I am silly to go on like this just for a woman and I dare say they are right in the abstrackt but they don't know how much a man feels this sort of tretment until they are married themselves which I hope they won't be till they are older than you and me for a man should not marry until five-and-twenty I am sure of that now. I do not say that to reproach you for it was not your fault, and it is nearly as bad for you as for me and it will all be different in a fortnight when I come back for I will be very gentle and kind to you and I want you to promise that you won't say any more about it nor throw it in my face afterward when you are angry with me and that you won't always be so dredfully quiet before people as if you were afraid of me. I know I am not good enough for you and everybody is always telling me so and it is not at all a pleasant thing for a fellow and I think if you were a little less good it would be better. I would as soon you gave me a slap in the face than obey me in the way you do like a statue or a martyr which you are not. Don't think I want to say hard things to you for everybody will tell you how wretched I have been and I will say a lot more to you when I see you but now as the dog-cart is round and I have not had my breakfast I will say good-by and if you are not awake I will put it under your pillow. Your affectionate husband,

"HARRY."

As Annie read this letter, it struck her for the first time that she had not appreciated the extreme youthfulness of her husband, who was much younger at twenty than she was on the eve of being nineteen. The letter, in its boyish simplicity, amused and touched her; however, it did not alter, but rather strengthened, a resolution which she had been busily forming and developing during those quiet weeks of illness.

On the day following Harry's departure for Leicestershire she was led downstairs, being strong enough to walk now, and enthroned in the drawing-room as a special pet and sovereign. She was rather shy with George at first; but he knew how to be so quietly kind as to put her at her ease. William danced wild hornpipes of joy round her, until they threatened to turn him out for being noisy, upon which he instantly subsided, and fell into the opposite extreme of speaking only in a thick whisper. All the rest were kind, Lilian rather ashamed of herself, but grateful to Annie for not having mentioned her name to indiscreet Harry on that eventful Christmas night.

George, after another stormy interview with his sister in the library, in which she had been in a position to give him back taunt for taunt, wisely agreed to bury all allusion to that night's events, and merely used the power they gave him to insist on her marrying Mr. Falconer sooner than she wished. It had been a miserable business, that moonlit scene in the copse, requiring hushing up all round, but especially on Lilian's account; so her eldest brother and Colonel Richardson had had to content themselves with an exchange of hard words, and the latter had returned to the station and the former to the house, each with an uneasy consciousness that he had never appeared to less advantage in his own eyes in his life.

By the time Annie came down-stairs for the first time, the preparations for Lilian's wedding were already in progress; and, when Annie suggested to Lady Braithwaite that she thought she wanted change of air, the latter offered to take her away to the seaside as soon as Lilian was married, saying she could not leave home before. But Annie thanked her, and said she would be well enough to travel by herself in a day or two; and she wanted to go as soon as she could to her aunt's, she thought.

When George heard of it, he begged his sister-in-law to wait until after the wedding, when he himself would take both her and his mother to Southport. She thanked him, but without accepting or declining the proposal.

On the very day before Harry's expected return, however, George having left home early in the morning for a day's hunting, Annie came into the morning-room—where Lady Braithwaite and her daughter were inspecting some newly arrived wedding presents—dressed for a journey.

"I knew the obstinate little thing would go off by herself, after all," said Lilian, rather glad of her sister-in-law's resolution.

The elder lady was completely taken by surprise.

"What about your luggage? You can't go away without any," she said.

"I packed it all last night, and ordered a cab from Beckham yesterday—at least, it was I who sent the order. The cab is at the door now."

"But you can't go off in that way; people would think it so strange! Wait until after dinner, and I will take you."

"Thank you. William is going to drive me. The dog-cart will be round in a minute."

This diverted Lady Braithwaite's thoughts.

"That horrid dog-cart! You are going to let him take you in that! You will certainly be thrown out and killed!"

"I am not afraid," said Annie, smiling; and, hearing William's voice calling her from the hall, she bade them both good-bye and left the room, they following her to the front door.

Her manner was very quiet and composed; but Lilian was not easily deceived. She turned to her mother as the dog-cart disappeared down the drive.

"She does not mean to come back, mamma," she said, in a low voice. And one of the servants standing at the back overheard and nodded to another, whispering:

"I told you so."

William was in high spirits at driving his dear Annie again; but she was very silent, or talked without her usual brightness. He said nothing; but he thought to himself, "If she is so sorry to go away, she will be back all the sooner," and, when, at the station, he had taken her ticket—first-class, in spite of her directions—and found her a comfortable carriage, he got in and flung his arms around her affectionately, and told her he should count the days till she came back. Then, to his sudden dismay, she burst into tears. The boy's face fell.

"Annie, what is the matter?" Then, in a mysterious voice, "You haven't cut away from Harry, have you?"

Annie nodded.

"Don't tell any one at the Grange yet, William, there's a dear, good old boy. I will write and explain. But I'm glad you know. I couldn't bear it any longer. It was ruining both our lives; we never could have agreed, and we shall both be happier apart."

"But where are you going? What are you going to do? You are not going to be a governess again, are you?"

"I don't know. I am not sure of anything yet, only of this—that I shall be all right, and nobody need be anxious about me."

"But I shall be. Oh, Annie, don't go! Let me go with you and see you safely to your aunt's. I have some money with me—George gave me my allowance only this morning. Do let me go!"

"No, no; you must not think of such a thing," said Annie, almost laughing.

"And you were going to leave me just like the rest, without a word about your not coming back! Oh, Annie, when we've been such chums!"

The boy's reproachful face overcame Annie.

"Look here—I'll tell you what I haven't told anybody else, and don't mean to tell anybody else," said she, affectionately; and she whispered something into his ear.

"Oh, Annie!"

"Mind you are not to tell any one—ever. I have not even made you promise, you see."

"You needn't be afraid. Your brother-in-law is a gentleman," said William, gravely.

The express by which she was going stopped twenty minutes at Beckham; but now the guard was crying, "Take your seats!"—and William had to jump out. He got up on the step outside to see as much as he could of her at the very last, and said, in an important whisper:

"But I sha'n't know where to write to you."

"I will let you know. And mind, William, you are not to drink—at least, not like the others!"

"All right; I won't. I may smoke, mayn't I?"

"Oh, yes, you may smoke, and you may ride and fish and shoot as much as you like; only do try to read a little, and don't swear quite so much as Wilfred or Harry."

"All right. You don't mind my saying a big, big D—— when I get a bad fall just before the finish?"

"N—o, I'll pass that. Now get down; the train is going, and you will be hurt."

William jumped off, but dashed down the platform beside the moving train a minute after, panting out, as he threw his purse into the carriage:

"You must take it; I've taken out all I want, and you may want it. You know I took first-class when you said second. Write."

The last impression she carried away of her life at the Grange was the memory of the big, handsome boy standing looking at the disappearing train, with an expression on his face which threatened tears when he should be out of sight of the busy crowd around him.

When Annie's own tears had stopped, she picked up the boy's purse, which had fallen as he flung it, on to the opposite seat. It was a handsome purse and pocket-book, given him by his mother; but it had suffered from experiments made upon it with the various articles in his tool-chest. He had begun a diary in it when it was new, which had dwindled down to an occasional note of his transactions in rabbits. There were other boyish documents, a cutting from the *Field*, *et cetera*, and there was more than five pounds in money, a broken scarf-pin, and two used foreign postage-stamps. She had no scruples about accepting the money, which was a welcome addition to her not very large store, and the pocket-book she put in her desk later as a cherished *souvenir* of the being she cared most about in the world.

The boy's high spirits and frank pleasure in hers had won her from the first, and the only things she regretted in her life at the Grange were the walks and drives and barbaric sports of ratting and mouse-bunting with him as a companion.

When she got to London, she went straight to a street she had been told of, north of Oxford Street, well known for cheap lodgings. She took a furnished bedroom at the top of a dingy house, and then next day she returned to Euston Station to fetch her luggage, which she had left at the parcels-office there, for fear of the extra expense of driving about in a cab with it, in case she should have any difficulty in finding a suitable lodging. She was on foot; and, as she entered the station, a hansom passed her with a young man in it who quite startled her by his likeness to Harry. The resemblance was so strong that she stopped, half inclined to turn back and walk about for a little while, in case it should be, indeed, her husband, so that he might have left the station before she got there. But then she reasoned with herself that Harry was in Leicestershire, and was expected at Garstone to-day, even if he were not already there; so that she decided to go boldly on. Another feeling impelled her forward—an unacknowledged hankering for a last sight of her husband, or even for a look at the man who so strongly resembled him.

Annie did not love her husband—she had never really loved him; and since Christmas she almost hated him. But, now that she had left him forever, and that too without any farewell, a natural inconsistency prompted her to try to steal a last look at the handsome lad who had been her lord and master.

So she went into the station, and, leaving her luggage for future consideration, looked about cautiously for the man she had seen in the hansom. He was not to be seen about the ticket offices, and, growing bolder, she slipped in and out among the groups of people on the platform. A train was about to start for the North. Still with caution, but attracted in spite of herself toward that train, which, as she knew, would stop at Beckham, Annie advanced until she was nearly opposite to the doors of the refreshment-room. They opened, and a young man came out. Annie stopped, with the color rushing to her face; for it was Harry. He looked so handsome in his light traveling-suit, with his overcoat hanging loosely over his arm, that she felt quite proud of him, and stood there with her eyes fixed upon him, half hoping that he would turn and see her.

But he did not, for he was gazing eagerly in the opposite direction—so eagerly that he risked being left behind, as the carriage doors were being closed. Annie's eyes followed his, and found that the object of his evident admiration was a showily-dressed woman with bold eyes and impossibly yellow hair, who was tottering along the platform in boots which had long slender pegs instead of heels.

With a sigh of disgust, Annie turned away. It was years before she saw her husband again.

CHAPTER XI.

The first thing Annie had done on arriving at her London lodging had been to take off her wedding-ring and hide it away in a corner of her desk. She had given to the landlady the name "Miss Langton," which she had resolved to adopt for the future. These were her first steps toward cutting herself off from her past life; the next was a bolder one.

During these long weeks when she had lain ill in bed, she had pondered in her mind how she could live when she had left her husband, as she at the very beginning of her illness determined to do. One trial of the life of a governess had been enough for her, and she could not easily have re-entered it except in some sort under false pretenses. Besides, now that she had thrown herself upon her own resources, and stood once more alone in the world, her old ambitions had awakened within her, the old spirit cried out, the vague but strong consciousness of untried powers turned her thoughts to a career of art. One form of art alone seemed open to her—the stage. All that she knew, or almost all that she knew, of a theatrical life was distasteful to her, and her instinct would have led her to give herself up to writing. But she had already tried that, knew how hard it was even to get a hearing from the reading public, and cast aside the thought of literary distinction as taking too long to win.

Of course, knowing nothing about the stage, she fell into the common error of thinking that talent made itself more quickly manifest there, and utterly ignored the fact that it is about as easy for a woman of high principles, without either money or interest, to attain a good position in a London theater as for a drummer-boy to become a general. She knew she would have to wait and to work before she found her way to the front rank; but how long that weary waiting would last, or how dull that work would be, she had not the least idea. She had unbounded faith in herself, she had energy, a little patience, and she believed herself to have talent, and her heart beat fast with the thought that she was now free to measure her strength against the world.

As for the horror of her husband and the rest of the Braithwaites, if they ever came to hear of the step she had taken, why, she did not care for their opinion, and their disgust could not humiliate her. Besides, the fact of her having become an actress would effectually cut her off from them forever and prevent their trying to bring her back to them, a possibility too dreadful to be considered calmly.

For, now that they were over, yet still fresh in her mind, the trials she had suffered during those few months of married life seemed, in these first days of relief from them, even greater than they had really been. Harry seemed more brutal, more ignorant, more dissipated, Lady Braithwaite and Lilian more coldly insolent, George more selfish, Wilfred more drunken, Stephen more unkind; so that the stage held out attractions for her in the social oblivion it involved which it would have been far from having in her eyes in other circumstances.

Not once did the thought occur to Annie that she was doing wrong in thus leaving her husband without consulting him. From the first she had been too obviously his superior in judgment to set any value on his opinion, and now she only thought she was ridding him as well as herself of an intolerable burden in the simplest manner. She had tried hard to do her duty as a wife, and had succeeded only in exasperating him against her and in unwittingly irritating him to more than his customary excesses. In leaving him free she thought she was rendering him the highest service in her power; and in freeing herself she felt, with a throb of joy, that she was once more able to indulge in her old dreams of ambition and success.

But in this argument with herself she forgot one thing—namely, that she had not left Harry free. This forgetfulness was the natural result of the effacement she had suffered at Garstone Grange which had caused her to depreciate her duties as they had depreciated her rights. It did not occur to her to think that she, morally the stronger of the two, was abandoning her husband, in all the first heat of a singularly wild and passionate nature, to a life in which the innocent indulgence of the affections was no longer possible; for she looked upon him as a brute incapable of any but the lowest forms of love. As for herself, she did not think herself in danger—she was of cooler temperament and higher intellect; her imagination took fire much more readily than her heart; she had thrown herself into the prospect of a brilliant career, and the idea of leading a loveless life had few terrors for her at first, except in rare moments of depression.

But, though the future was full of charm for her, the present was not without great difficulties. How was she to enter upon her new life? She remembered that some years ago, in the old days when her father was alive, when she was still a school girl and theatrical matters had the charm of mystery, she had been with her father on one occasion when he had met and introduced to her an acquaintance of his who was a manager and an actor too, and whom she had wondered to find so exceedingly silent and grave when she remembered how he had made her laugh upon the stage. She now hit upon the bold measure of writing to him, and asking if he would see her; but a week passed, and her letter received no answer. She wrote again to his theater, and this time inclosed a stamped directed envelope, with an apology for doing so, and an earnest request for five minutes of his time. She received in reply a hasty note naming a day and hour when he could see her; and, more excited than she had ever been in her life before, she arrived at the theater at the appointed time. She had to wait a long, weary time, very much ashamed of herself, very much afraid her application would be in vain, very much wishing herself out of the group of shabby men—whom she mistook for actors—with whom she was waiting, when at last the manager came. As his eyes fell on her, she stepped forward, holding his letter and giving her maiden name.

As she had expected, he had long since forgotten her; but he asked her to follow him up-stairs, and gave her a courteous hearing at the back of the dress-circle. After some difficulty, he remembered, or said he remembered, their former meeting. He strongly advised her not to go on the stage, telling her that even great talent did not always command success, that it was a hard life, full of disappointments. Finding her resolution still firm, and for the sake of her father, with whom he had at one time been intimate, he agreed to let her make a very modest first appearance at his theater as a silent "guest." He did not much approve of lady amateurs, even in this humble capacity, but the girl was much in earnest, her pretty pleading was so touching, that he made this small concession, scarcely doubting that, if she went through all the rehearsals, after a few nights of a suffocating dressing-room and a draughty stage, she would appear no more, cured of her unfortunate whim.

The rehearsals were a hard trial, certainly. To stand about for three or four hours on a dark stage in the company of two or three more "ladies" who would have been scarcely refined enough for her to engage as maids, and then sometimes to be dismissed without having to go through her simple duty of walking across at the back of the scene with a shabby man who by day filled the position of a bill-sticker, was not work too exciting to leave time for some unpleasant reflection. When the piece came out things were a little better. Of the three girls who dressed with her in a large, bare room which seemed miles away, up at the top of the theater, two were illiterate but inoffensive, and the third proved to be one of the merriest little creatures who ever wished to be a great actress when nature intended her for a good washer-woman.

Going home alone at night frightened her dreadfully, and she never got quite used to it. Luckily there were omnibuses which took her nearly the whole way; but the short distance she had to walk before she caught one was a nightly agony, though nobody ever took any notice of the insignificant muffled up figure.

The piece was a failure, and did not run long; but she did duty again in the same humble capacity with the same companions in the comedy which followed, hoping for an opening to something more dignified and better calculated to show off her histrionic powers, if she possessed any. The opening came. It was a very small one, merely the opportunity of saying one line as a maid-servant; but the minutes before hearing her own voice for the first time in public were fraught with a terribly intense excitement which no important part in after-times ever called up in her with the same strength.

It was a few nights after this ordeal that on returning from the theater she was seized, for the first time since leaving Garstone, with a longing to hear what was going on there—how her departure had been taken, and how William passed his time without her. So she wrote to her brother-in-law, giving, as the address for him to write to, that of a stationer whose shop she passed on her way to and from the theater. It was not that she mistrusted the boy's word, or even his carefulness; but she did not wish to get him into trouble, as would certainly have been the case if any of the rest suspected him of knowing her real address.

In answer she got the following letter:

"MY DEAR ANNIE,—I thought you were never going to keep your promise and write to me after all, and you haven't told me much now you do write to me. For I want to know ever so much more than you say. You need not be afraid of anybody seeing your letter. For when I got it at Moss' I took it straight back and down to the willow-pond. I read it, and fastened it under the lining of my hunting-cap. So its all rigt. There was a shindy when they new you were gone. George went to your aunt and first he scolded mother and Lil and said they ought to be ashamed of themselves and your aunt dident know where you were. And Harry you should have seen him go on. You would have thought he was a good husbend and you a bad wife if you heard him. He had been to London and sold his hunting-wach and bougt you a dimand ring which I think you would have liked but of course you were write to go away and I said so and he punched my head and I punched him back. So he dident get much good by his interferring with me. They thought I new where you were and I said if they thought I did they migt just try to make me say thats all. So they lissened to reason and Harry drinks more than ever he is as bad as Wilfred evry bit. And he is allways hanging about Green's forge now. Susan Greens come back a pretty thing for a man married like he is now. I only tell you this becos I think you ought to know being his wife which is a great pity. They none of them know you will never come back except Lil who says you wont and that makes George very angry and one evening made Harry cry like a great baby insted of trying to find you. The place is beesly now you are gone and if I wasent going to uncle Geralds in Ireland I thing I should have to come and dig you out.

"Your afecsionate brother-in-law,

"WILLIAM FITZPATRICK BRAITHWAITE.

"P.S.—If you could see the black and white rabit now I think you would laugh for his legs are alright but so stiff that he hops bout as if he was made of wood. Jo bit the pups tail off a fortnight ago."

This letter made Annie thoughtful. The Rubicon was passed now; she could not have gone back, even had she wished to do so, with what they would have considered the contamination of the stage upon her. But what William said about Harry caused her to ask herself for the first time whether she had not done him wrong, whether she ought not still to have stayed and continued coldly to fulfill her wifely duty to the letter, whether there had not been more selfishness than self-sacrifice in giving him back his liberty. She felt not one whit more of affection for the drunken lad who had become the ardent admirer of the blacksmith's daughter, but this last fact was too significant not to awaken her self-reproach. She felt at the bottom of her heart an unacknowledged gladness that it was no longer in her power to go back, and in the cares of her present life she soon forgot again those of her past.

For the few shillings she received for her work at the theater were not enough to pay her modest expenses for food and lodging without her drawing upon the small sum she had brought with her from the Grange; William's money she had resolved not to touch except in case of utmost need. So she tried her strength by living too simply, while she passed, in spite of herself, at the theater as a "rich" lady, who "came behind" for a freak. She had clothing enough to last for some time, and before the end of the summer she was lucky in being able to sell a short story; and then, after being for a few weeks out of work and in debt, and almost in danger of absolute want, she got an engagement at a salary which was just enough to live upon, but with no chance of more than a few lines to speak.

And this was her life, with now and then a hope of something better to do, followed always by disappointment and sometimes by despair for nearly three years, at the end of which time she was still appearing at a fashionable comedy theater, where she had been figuring in the programmes for some months on the last line of the list of characters, thus—"Maid, Miss Langton."

And the brilliant future she had pictured once for herself seemed further away than ever. For she had by this time mastered some of the secrets of success on the stage. The highest success, she still knew, fell only to the highest talent; and this belief, which was directly against the creed of most of her companions, she held to the end. It was all luck, they said. It was chiefly luck, she thought too—the luck of being somebody's son or somebody's daughter, of having good looks and bad principles or wealthy friends, of being by chance on the right spot at the right time; and luck had been against her.

Disappointment, too, and weary, weary waiting had taken the bloom off her beauty, which was of a type depending very much on expression; and the look her face habitually wore now was that of a woman whom cares and failures and struggles with necessity had reduced to an automaton. Yet in some respects her position would not have been an unenviable one to a less ambitious woman. The conscientious care which had formerly made her a good governess, and later an almost too submissive wife to her careless husband, made her now fill her very unimportant *roles* with an attention to the most trifling details which obtained for her the consideration of the authorities in the theater, although it was of course not possible that her efforts to be artistic in her representation of monosyllabic maids should attract the attention of the general public or of the critics in front. And her salary, though not high, was now sufficient to keep her in comfort, which might have been greater, had she been more economical. So that the privilege of thinking herself a martyr was almost out of her reach.

She had not quite given up hope, though it was no longer joined to bright confidence in ultimate success, when a small part was intrusted to her which enabled her to show unmistakable signs of talent. It was such a very small part, and it would so undoubtedly have improved the piece from a dramatist's point of view to cut out the scene it was in altogether, that the critics took no notice, and the public did not seem impressed. But it drew the attention of her companions to her; and Annie, with her heart beating wildly, overheard more than one prediction that she would "get on."

With reawakened ambition, her old high spirits came back to her; the cloud of cold reserve which closed over her in spite of herself when she was unhappy, disappeared, and for the first time Annie found pleasure in her profession. The society afforded at that time by the theater she was in, was some of the pleasantest in London. It included men and women who were among the world's recognized pets—women of beauty and men of wit, handsome actors, and two actresses of whom Europe had acknowledged the genius. Annie felt the charm of this brilliant circle, which was indeed, as theaters so seldom are, as attractive as the outside world imagined it to be.

She was sitting in the green-room one evening, between the acts, when two of the actors came in, discussing the beauty of a lady who sat in one of the boxes nearest to the stage.

"I'm sure I've seen her in the Park," said one; "and I've been told her name; but I forget it."

"Is that her husband behind her—the tall man with the eye-glass?"

"Don't know, I'm sure. Should think not."

The other laughed.

"She is the handsomest woman we have had in front for a long time—much better-looking than any of the professional beauties. Perhaps she is a professional beauty—eh?"

"No—too good-looking."

It was the other's turn to laugh; and, when they were called on to the stage, they were still criticising the unknown fair one and anxious for another view of her.

Annie's curiosity was excited, and, contrary to her custom of devoting her attention entirely to what was going on on the stage, she managed, on her next appearance to say a few lines, to get an opportunity of looking toward the box the two speakers had indicated. And she gave one of the slightest, most imperceptible of starts, for the lady was Lilian, exquisitely dressed and looking handsomer than ever. Annie could not see the face of the man behind her in her glance at the box; but she was anxious to know who it was, and later in the evening she was satisfied; for a young actor named Gerald Gibson told another in her hearing that the lady was Mrs. Falconer, that he had been to a dance at her house two nights before, and that "the tall man with the eye-glass," who was one of the other occupants of the box, was a Colonel Richardson, who had just returned from abroad.

All this filled Annie with excitement and anxiety. Had Lilian recognized her? Who were the other people in the box? Had Colonel Richardson really only just returned from abroad? These and other questions concerning her sister-in-law and the rest of her husband's family kept her awake that night in a fever of newly awakened interest in the Braithwaites. The remembrance of her life at Garstone occupied her very little now, the long, solitary hours of daylight, when she was not engaged in rehearsal, she filled by writing, her old taste for which had revived to console her for her otherwise monotonous life. After the exchange of a few letters with William, she had heard no more from him, and it was now more than two years since she had received his last. During all this time no news had reached her, of her husband or his family. She had said of late bitterly to herself that, if they had cared to do so, they would have found her out long ago, and she had begun to wonder whether she would ever see any of them again, when this unexpected, yet most natural event, showed her again the one of all the Braithwaites whom she least cared to see.

Annie liked Gerald Gibson, as everybody in the theater did—a grave, quiet, thoughtful-looking man, whose reserved manners impressed those around him with respect, even though it was often merely the result of his having nothing in particular to say. He might have been the son of a cheesemonger, but he was as perfect a gentleman not only in look and manner, but in mind, as if he had been the son of a duke. Annie knew, though she had known him only a few weeks, that she could speak without reserve to him. On the evening after she had seen Lilian, therefore, she found an opportunity, when they were on the stage together, but not immediately concerned in the business of the scene, of alluding to the beauty who had made such a sensation among them the night before.

"I think I heard you say you were fortunate enough to know her, Mr. Gibson," said she, her interest peeping out from under the indifferent words.

"I don't know her well. I was introduced to her about ten days ago, and somebody got me a card for an 'At home' at her house."

"She is very beautiful, ain't she?"

"Yes, very, for those who admire massive beauty."

"Then don't you admire her?"

"Yes; but I have seen women I admire more."

"I don't like such frosty enthusiasm. Is she nice, pleasant, amiable?"

"I don't think 'amiable' is quite the word for that type of woman. But she is very brilliant, very charming."

"I used to know her once before she was married," said Annie in a low voice. "I am glad to hear she is happy."

"I am scarcely able to judge of that. Ladies act so well, even when they are not on the stage, and they are often charming when at heart they are very miserable; so the novelists say."

"You don't think she is miserable, do you?" asked Annie, anxiously.

"Indeed I have no reasons for thinking so. She seems to have everything she can want, beauty, wealth, position, a good husband."

"Then Mr. Falconer is nice?"

"He is generally popular, I believe; but I have scarcely seen him."

"Ah!" escaped suddenly from Annie's lips. She thought those last words significant.

She could not bring the conversation round to Colonel Richardson now without exciting his suspicions, so she merely asked him not to mention that she had ever known Mrs. Falconer.

"I wish to remain *perdu* to my old friends until I have got on—if I ever do get on," she added, sadly.

"You will get on, Miss Langton. How can you doubt it!"

"How can I do anything but doubt it? I have waited so long, and seem no nearer the end."

"But you must be nearer the end."

"Ah—but what end?"

She turned away with a little shrug of the shoulders, and his eyes followed her with interest. She was not massive and he found more attraction in her face than in those of all the professional beauties.

A few evenings later, as he was leaving the theater when his share of the performance was over, he saw Miss Langton in front of him walking down the quiet street where the stage-door was. A gentleman standing on the opposite pathway crossed over and raised his hat to her. Gerald Gibson saw her start, stop, hesitate, and finally put out her hand. Gerald passed them, but neither noticed him; and he recognized the gentleman as Colonel Richardson, whom he had met at Mrs. Falconer's.

"That was the reason of her interest in Mrs. Falconer then!" thought Gerald.

CHAPTER XII.

Gerald Gibson had not gone many yards further down the street, after seeing the meeting between Miss Langton and Colonel Richardson, when he was overtaken by a fellow-actor, Aubrey Cooke.

"Did you see who little Langton was talking to?"

"Some friend of hers, I suppose. I didn't notice."

"It was Frank Richardson, the man there was all that scandal about a few years ago—Lord Berwick's wife—don't you remember?"

"Well?"

"Well, I'm sorry he has got hold of little Langton, that is all."

"You are sorry without cause, then. Miss Langton is a long way above his level. She can't refuse to speak to him, for he knew her people well years ago."

With unerring certainty Gerald Gibson had jumped to this conclusion. The other looked surprised.

"Oh, you know all about it, then? You are the favorite one for whom Miss Prim opens her lips. Well, I really am glad to hear it, for she is the flag I always hold out when old ladies tell me there are no virtuous women on the stage; and, if she were to go I don't know where on earth I should look for another."

"You are too cynical, Cooke."

"Don't shy long words at me. If I deserve them it is because I was led away to a meeting of the Society for the Mutual Improvement of the Clerical and Dramatic Professions this afternoon. Capital institution—the parsons looked happy and the pro.'s looked good. But that can't last. Good-night."

Aubrey Cooke was not at his best with Gibson; the two men had too little in common. But he was a clever fellow. He had a plain, silly face, a bitter tongue, and a manner which found favor with most women. He adored women. Those, however, he worshiped the most deferentially would scarcely have approved of the manner in which he spoke of them among other men in their absence, for there was a strong dash of young Paris in his adoration. He was too shrewd to make many mistakes; and no man knew better the exact tone in which to address any particular woman of his large and varied acquaintance. He bore Miss Langton no ill-will for repeated unmerited snubs; the caprices of women are infinite, prettier and less prim women abounded, and he could revenge himself so easily by an epigram—not a slanderous one, but none the less cutting—in the dressing-room.

When Annie first recognized Colonel Richardson as he crossed the road toward her, her impulse was to walk on; but anxiety to hear something about the family at the Elms changed her intention, and she stopped, shook hands with him, and allowed him to walk down the street with her.

"I knew you the moment you came on," said he. "It was a happy thought to go on the stage; I admire your courage."

"I don't think it was courage that sent me on; and at present I have had no reason to congratulate myself on my attempt, I assure you. Did Mrs. Falconer know me?"

"No. She did not care for the piece, and was not paying much attention to it. She does not know you are on the stage, for she told me she thought you had become a governess somewhere. You have done better than that."

"Yes. And the rest of the Braithwaites? Have you seen any of them since your return?"

"No; but Mrs. Falconer gives a very bad account of some of them."

"What does she say? Tell me quickly, please."

"It seems there have been quarrels among the brothers lately, about money matters, I believe. Sir George and Harry are the chief disputants, and Mrs. Falconer never knows what the next news about them may be. But I am paining you——"

"No, no; I want to hear everything. Will you tell me all you know about my husband? Is he well? Is he no steadier?"

"I believe he is well now; but he was ill some months ago."

"Ill. What was the matter with him?"

Colonel Richardson hesitated.

"You know his habits are rather irregular, and he had ridden too much and excited himself too much, and I believe he was ill from the effects of overexcitement. But why do you wish to know these things? You are happily spared the wrangles and disturbances of that unlucky household now. You have the interest of your own career to occupy your mind; it is much better for you not to concern yourself any more with the doings of that barbaric crew."

"Don't say that. Every word you say makes me reproach myself more. I am not heartless, though I see now how selfish it was of me to sneak away as I did. You will hardly believe that I thought I was doing what was best for my husband as well as myself. I thought he was too young to be burdened with a wife. We did not suit each other; I seemed to irritate him to worse brutality; we were spoiling each other's lives and our own."

"You were quite right to come away. He would only have crushed your life out by his coarse cruelty before now, if you had stayed with him. How could you, with your sensitive feelings and cultivated tastes, bear with that uncouth boor? I used to wonder at your patience with him when I first knew you in town with him."

"I was wrong, though," said Annie, gravely. "If I thought I could do him any good I would go back now."

"I beg you not to do anything so rash," said Colonel Richardson, hastily. "Your husband is worse than an uncouth lad now; he is a coarse, savage-tempered man. Lilian—Mrs. Falconer—his own sister, is afraid of him; and you know she is not meek-spirited."

"What does he say of me? Does he never speak about me? Do you know?"

"The last time his sister saw him he told her that, if he ever met his wife again—and he used language which neither she nor I could repeat to you—he would 'crush the beauty out of the face that made a fool of him.' Forgive my repeating his words to you; I think they will be the best warning I can give you to keep out of his reach."

Annie sighed.

"You don't make me afraid of him; you only make me pity him as I would a fierce hound who had been unwisely treated. If Harry were to crush my face, as he said, in a fit of passion, it would be the one thing which would make him treat me tenderly ever afterward."

Colonel Richardson looked surprised.

"You almost make me bold enough to wonder——"

"Why I left him? I suppose my strongest reason really was that he was unbearable to me. His tenderness was odious as his anger, and worse than his neglect. I should dislike him more than ever now; but I should know how to treat him more wisely."

Colonel Richardson understood women too well to say more on that subject. He turned the conversation.

"Mrs. Falconer expects her brother William next week," he said. "Shall I bring him to the theater and see if he knows you?"

Annie caught eagerly at the idea of seeing her favorite William again. She had nothing to fear from his knowing where she was, and she was anxious to find out whether he was growing into a less worthless man than his brothers. He was now eighteen. She was anxious, too, to learn whether he still retained the affectionate remembrance of her. So her last words to Colonel Richardson were a repetition of her injunction to bring him to the theater without any warning that he would see her. She did not doubt that he would know her, especially as he was the one member of the family who knew she was on the stage.

The season was nearly over now, and night after night she scanned the audience anxiously in the hope of seeing those two faces she knew; but it was not until the very last night of all that, as she came on to the stage, she saw a tall young man in the stalls half rise from his seat, with the exclamation, just loud enough for her to hear—"Annie!"

At the end of the street William met her, and could hardly be restrained from embracing her, regardless of appearances. He was broader, manlier in figure; but in his manner to her he was exactly the same as before. She was thankful to see that he did not look dissipated, and he hastened to assure her that he had observed all her commands, that he read a great deal and "quite liked it." He had not lived much at Elms, having passed most of his time with his uncle, his mother's brother, in Ireland.

"And, Annie, I'm not going to lead an idle life. I'm going to be a soldier."

"Well, that is the next thing to it."

"No disrespect to the army, I beg, madam. It is very hard work to get in at all nowadays. No Braithwaite ever had to study so much before as I shall have to do to pass the exams. I'm sure to be 'plucked' the first time, of course, and very likely the second. I must get through the third time, you know, or else it will be all up with me."

"You must get through the first time," said Annie indignantly. "If you don't, I will never speak to you again."

"Oh, yes, you will. If I don't pass, you will have to console me, and, if I do pass, you will congratulate me. Oh, Annie, I wish I had been old enough to marry you, or that you had married George, so that you might come back to the Elms again." No suggestion that she should go back to Harry, however. Annie looked up at him quickly.

"How is Harry? He is not anxious for my return, I suppose?"

"Oh, to think of your being his wife is intolerable! He is not worthy to look at you. Sometimes he is sorry, in a maudlin sort of way, that he can't see you, and complains that you have deserted him, and that you are the only woman he ever cared about. But that is all nonsense, and he says it only when he is drunk. He drinks worse than Wilfred. And a few months ago——Well, never mind that! You mustn't trouble your head any more about him."

Annie listened in silence, her heart aching with remorse. She knew well enough now that she had done irretrievable wrong in leaving her husband, whom at least she could, at the entire sacrifice of herself, have kept from this. But it was too late now, she told herself. If she returned to him now unbidden, with the feeling of repulsion toward him a thousand-fold stronger than ever, she could not expect a welcome, she could not even repress the disgust she felt.

She told William that she was going to leave town and travel with a theatrical company, to gain experience in better parts than she could hope to play in London yet. He walked all the way home with her, and, looking at her gravely as he stood saying the last words to her, he complained that she was thin and pale.

"Do you know, Annie, you are so much altered I should hardly have known you. You have lost all your pretty color, and your eyes are not half so bright as they used to be. It is all that beast Harry, making you have to work for your living!" he broke out, passionately. "He deserves to be kicked!"

"Come, be reasonable, William; that is not Harry's fault. Women must expect to 'go off' in looks, you know, as they grow older."

"But you are not old. That is nonsense."

"I am two-and-twenty. When you last saw me, I was not nineteen."

"Well, you ought not to have changed so much in less than three years. Never mind," added he affectionately, seeing that his words seemed to depress his sister-in-law—"I love you just as much as ever; and you will soon get back your color when you get out of London and forget all about Harry again."

And he kissed her and bade her good-bye most unwillingly; for the following morning he had to go back to the Elms, to see George about the expenses of a "coach" to cram him for the examination he would have to go through.

Annie went up-stairs to her rooms—she could afford to have a sitting-room now—feeling ashamed of the pain his remarks upon her looks had given her. It was a fact she had known for a long time now, that her beauty had fallen off, so that there were barely traces of it left. A thin, brown face, without a tinge of pink in the cheeks, and with scarcely more than a tinge in the lips, eyes from which the brightness of hope and joy had gone, and a weary, worn expression, were what less than three years of lonely work and disappointment had left of her youthful prettiness. No woman, and especially an actress, can suffer the sense of lost beauty to be suddenly brought home to her without a pang, and Annie's vanity was strong enough to make her cry at William's evident regret.

"Perhaps Harry himself would not know me," she thought to herself, "and would be disgusted if I were pointed out to him as his wife."

So she cried herself to sleep.

When William arrived at the Elms next day, he was even less inclined than usual to meet his brother Harry on friendly terms. For he looked upon the latter as being the cause of Annie's exile—so he chose to consider her voluntary flight—and therefore as the cause also of all her struggles and the terrible alteration in her looks. So the lad avoided his brother as much as he could until dinnertime, when there was no help for their coming in contact with each other, as their places were set side by side. An unlucky accident brought the name of the half-forgotten wife into the conversation. Wilfred rallied his youngest brother, who had not been at the Elms for some time, upon being "so confoundedly abstemious."

"One would think little Annie were still here reading you sermons across the table with her pretty eyes," said he.

The blood rushed to the lad's face, for Harry uttered an oath at the mention of his wife.

"I wish we had never frightened the dear little thing away," Wilfred went on, in a maudlin manner. "She was our little bit of righteousness. It made me take to bad courses, her going away did."

This was not a happy speech, and it was followed by a minute's silence on the part of all three of his brothers; Stephen was not there.

"Why don't you hunt her up, Harry?" went on Wilfred, who either wished to irritate his brother or had less tact than usual. "I wouldn't let my wife leave me in the lurch, if I had one, and go tramping about all over the world, amusing herself without me."

"She may go to the deuce for what I care, if she isn't gone already!" burst out Harry.

William clinched his fists and tried to keep still. The injured husband went on:

"A little, sly, vagabond governess, glad enough to entrap a gentleman into marrying her, and then cutting away and bringing disgrace upon his name!"

"Disgrace!" cried William, turning with flashing eyes upon his brother. "As if any wife could disgrace you! As if Annie, who was a thousand times too good for you to black her shoes, could have any worse disgrace than to be your wife!"

"You hold your tongue, you young cub!" said his brother, doggedly. "I say she didn't deserve a decent husband."

"Well, she didn't get one"—this from Wilfred.

"She didn't deserve a decent husband, and she couldn't be expected to stay in a respectable house."

"What respectable house?"—Wilfred again.

Harry went on without noticing the interruptions.

"It was natural that her vagrant instincts should get the better of her again, and she should take the first chance of going off on the tramp."

"You infernal liar!" shouted William, too much excited to be careful. "She is no more a tramp than you are. And, as for her 'vagrant instincts,' you stupid ass, they have led her into much better society than she would ever have got into with you at her heels!"

All the others were startled, and William checked himself as he was going to say more. Harry brought a rough hand down on his shoulder.

"So you are in the secret, are you? Come now, out with it; where is she?"

"Out of your reach, luckily for her."

"Yes, but you are not, unluckily for you!" said Harry, thickly, rising to his feet and standing threateningly over his brother, not heeding Sir George's voice crying, "Sit down!"

"Now, then, where is she?"

William thrust away his chair and faced his tipsy brother steadily.

"I would not help to put her in your power again by telling you where to find her, even if I knew, if you were to tear me to pieces!"

He stepped aside quickly to avoid the lunge Harry made at him, and left the room.

"Bravo, young un!" said Wilfred.

The baronet afterward tried gentler and subtler means to find out Annie's hiding-place from the lad; but William kept the secret safely.

Meanwhile, the fugitive wife was preparing for a new experience. She had, as she had told William, resolved upon leaving London for awhile, hoping that practice in the country might mature her talent and enable her at the end of a few months to take a higher position than she could aspire to at present. She knew very well that, once out of London, it would be by no means easy to get back; but the feeling that she was advancing no further, and could not hope to advance further without more experience, prevailed over every other; and she thought herself fortunate in getting an engagement, in a traveling company, just about to start on tour, to play second parts in old comedy. It was not going to what are considered the best towns in a theatrical sense; but it was a good company, and Annie had heard that one of the actors of the theater she had just left would be in it too.

She had heard Gerald Gibson speak of going into the country, and had come at once to the conclusion that he must be the actor alluded to; she was very glad of this, for he was one of her favorites.

When, however, she got on to the stage of the theater which had been engaged for their rehearsals, which was as dark as most stages are in the day-time, she saw no face she knew among the people assembled there, except that of the manager who had engaged her.

"I thought you said I should meet one of my late companions," she remarked to him when he shook hands with her.

"Yes, Mr. Cooke is here somewhere," he answered.

"Oh, Mr. Cooke!" she echoed, in a tone of evident disappointment.

Now Aubrey was standing in the shadow only a few feet away from her. He was always particularly quiet when he was not remarkably noisy, and, having nobody to talk to at the moment, he had been still as a statue, and had heard every word of this short colloquy, and noticed the tone of Miss Langton's exclamation: and he was nettled by it. For he had made up his mind that she was decidedly the most attractive of the ladies of the company, and had resolved to pay her the compliment of devoting his attention to her during the tour.

But, after this unconsciously administered rebuff, he had to resort to the other alternative—of basking in the more easily won smiles of the leading lady, Miss Muriel West. All that Annie could see of this lady in the dim light on the stage was that she was very handsome, with great, winning, velvety brown eyes shaded by long, black lashes, and that she was very badly dressed, apparently in odds and ends from her stage wardrobe.

They were rehearsing "She Stoops to Conquer," and Miss West played Miss Hardcastle, while Annie herself was Miss Neville. Annie discovered in the course of the morning that Miss West had a sweet, rich voice and a kindly manner, an unrefined accent, and a rather heavy touch in comedy. During the succeeding rehearsals she further discovered that Miss West was good-humored and amusing, and that she already exerted a strong fascination over most of the men of the company; Aubrey Cooke, foremost as usual where a charming woman was concerned, being absent from her side only when he was wanted on the stage for his part of Tony Lumpkin.

The rest of the women were uninteresting. There was a common but clever girl of about her own age who played old women; she called herself "Lola Montrose," but did not look like it, and was dressed in clothes which would have been neat and appropriate if she had not tried to "smarten herself up a bit" with large bunches of cheap but brilliant artificial flowers. And there was a well-born and well-educated girl who had gone on the stage against the wishes of her friends, and who stayed on it against the wishes of the audience; she played chamber-maids; but, though she could make witty speeches of her own off the stage, she always failed to extract the wit from any speech she had to make on it. And there was also a curiously incapable girl who was the manager's niece.

On the day of the last rehearsal, before the tour began, Aubrey Cooke followed Annie to a corner of the stage, where she was standing quietly, as usual, rather apart from the rest.

"I beg your pardon," said he shyly—Aubrey was very shy sometimes—"I hope you won't think what I am going to say impertinent; but I couldn't help overhearing part of your conversation with Miss West this morning about—about your living together."

"Oh, yes! She was suggesting that we should lodge together, as it is so much cheaper than living apart. And she knows all about touring, and I know nothing at all about it. I thought it was very kind of her."

"She meant to be kind, I have no doubt," mumbled Aubrey. "But I don't think arrangements of that sort ever answer, unless people know all about one another; and, if you have not settled anything, I would strongly advise you to try lodging for a week by yourself first; and then, of course, after that you would know all about everybody, and be able to make arrangements with any lady you liked. I hope you will forgive my interference; I could not help seeing that, as you say, you know nothing at all about touring yet."

Annie had scarcely time to thank him for his advice before he had raised his hat and left her. Aubrey Cooke was a gentleman, and, in spite of her apparent prejudice against him, he felt sympathy with the forlorn little lady. When Annie left the theater that morning, Miss West was coming out at the same time, and for the first time Annie saw her complexion by daylight; and the force of Aubrey Cooke's advice struck Miss Langton at once, for the pink and white and black of the leading lady's beauty showed a difference of tastes between them which was more than skin-deep.

CHAPTER XIII.

Before the company Annie had joined started on a tour, she had heard more tidings to distress her about the Braithwaite family. It was Aubrey Cooke who brought them this time. He was telling her that he had met their late companion, Gerald Gibson, at Mrs. Falconer's the day before.

"Oh! Do you know her too?"

"Yes; I have known her much longer than Gibson has. He and I have long arguments about her."

"I can guess which side you take."

"I always take the part of a beautiful woman. And Gibson really does her cruel injustice. She might sit for the portrait of the favorite handsome panther-woman of the lady novelists."

"I expected something more complimentary than that. I don't call that high praise."

"Don't you? Well, I don't know any pretty woman who would not feel flattered at being called a panther; most of them only get as far as to be like cats."

"Now you are absolutely libelous! I know you will go on to say that panthers are as cruel as they are graceful, that they delight in human victims, and you might add, if you dared, that the pursuit of them was an exciting sport. And then you will ask if the parallel does not hold good."

"Indeed, I shall say nothing so commonplace, Miss Langton. I always maintain, to begin with, that beautiful women are not cruel. It is not their fault if we crowd round them in such numbers that they mix us up a little, and hurt our feelings by forgetting us. I have a great advantage over most of my rivals in one respect—my appearance. I heard a lady call me the other day the nice, quiet young man who looks so stupid. She was asking a man named Colonel Richardson who I was."

"Colonel Richardson?"

"Yes. He is a gentleman whom I always meet at Mrs. Falconer's, a very old friend of the family, I believe."

Now Aubrey Cooke had noted well, without appearing to remark it, the expression of pain and anxiety which passed over Annie's face as he mentioned that Colonel Richardson was always at Mrs. Falconer's. But not having the least suspicion that she herself knew the popular beauty, he misunderstood the cause of her distress, and connected it with the fact of the meeting he and Gibson had seen a little way from the stage-door some nights before; and he wondered whether she knew that Colonel Richardson was married, and whether she had heard certain old scandals connected with his name.

For the first few weeks of the tour Aubrey saw very little of Miss Langton. She had taken his advice and drawn back, as civilly as she could, from the proposal of living with Miss West, whom she soon found out to be a coarse woman of not too reputable life, whose beauty and a certain rough good-humor made her dangerous to many men. She saw through the motive of Annie's shyness at once, and said, with a laugh:

"I suppose I am not good enough for you, little Puritan?"

But she showed neither anger nor bitterness about it, and was consistently kind, after her fashion, all the time the tour lasted, to the quiet little girl to whom she had taken a capricious liking. So that Annie could not help a sneaking liking for her, especially as Miss West showed, in parts requiring dramatic power, a rough force which in some scenes kept Annie spell-bound in the wings watching her, and asking herself if this were not genius. And then Miss West would destroy the illusion by coming off at the side, scolding the prompter for not being at his post, and calling for stout or for brandy and water.

Annie, therefore, chose to live alone, the only girl of her own standing in the company being the amateur chambermaid, who was so ostentatiously poor and aggressively economical that Miss Langton felt that life with her would be a sort of voluntary martyrdom.

She had some trials with lazy landladies, extortionate landladies, maids-of-all-work who did not give her enough attention, and others who gave her too much. They had been traveling some weeks, when, in a certain town which is one of the oldest in England, she got into some lodgings where the landlady was always out, and, being a lone widow who kept no servant, sometimes left her lodgers to wait upon themselves more than was meet.

Aubrey Cooke had rooms above Annie's in this house, and, on reaching the door, tired, hot, and hungry after a long rehearsal of a piece which had just been added to their repertory, Annie found her fellow-lodger kicking the paint viciously off the inhospitable portal.

"It is of no use, Mr. Cooke," said Annie, resignedly. "The stupid old woman has gone to market, and we shall have to wait till she comes back, unless we go and hunt her up where she is making her bargains in stale cabbages."

"But it is abominable to make her lodgers stand kicking their heels in the blazing sun, while she is haggling over a penn'orth of onions!" said he, with another lunge at the door.

Annie meanwhile had been prowling about.

"Do you think you could open the kitchen window, Mr. Cooke?" she asked, dubiously. "We might get in there. It isn't far from the ground."

It was a small window, just low enough for him to reach the fastening easily with his pocket-knife. In a few minutes he had pushed the fastening aside, scrambled up on to the sill, opened the window, and got in amid the crash of timber.

"What have you done?" asked Annie, anxiously, as he appeared again, disguised in flour and paste.

"I've fallen into a lot of things, it seems," said he, "and I believe I've sprained my ankle."

"Oh, my roly-poly pudding!" cried Annie, not heeding his ailments in the unhappy discovery.

"I'm afraid it is done for now," answered Mr. Cooke, as he removed the body of the uncooked pudding from his sleeve. "It will do for a poultice for me, however," he said, cheerfully; "and Mrs. Briggs will put it down in both our bills, so it won't be wasted. Wait, I'll give you a chair to help you up."

She got in; and they both began to look about for something to make dinner of. Annie went to the cupboard, while Mr. Cooke opened a door and fell down two steps into the back kitchen with a cry of joy. He had knocked his head against a skinny-looking bird, already plucked, which was hanging down from the ceiling. But Annie shook her head contemptuously when she saw it.

"It is one of Mrs. Briggs' prehistoric chickens, and it would want a lot of preparation before we could cook it. Besides, I don't know how, and the fire is out."

So they hunted again, and, not finding anything but bones and Mr. Cooke's cheese, Aubrey went out to buy chops, having said doubtfully that he thought he could cook a chop, but wasn't sure, while Miss Langton set to work to make a fire. When she came back, after a rather long absence, they were both radiant; for Annie, as she let him in, told him in great delight that she had made a lovely fire, and found where the plates, and knives, and forks were kept, and he pulled out of his pockets a number of small parcels and a gridiron, and produced from under his arm a huge cookery book, which he laid triumphantly down upon a bag containing cheese-cakes.

"The baker's wife lent me this; so now we can have fifteen courses if we like. This will tell us how to make a *vol-au-vent à la financière*, or a *fricandeau de veau* with *sauce piquante*, or——"

"But it won't tell us how to cook a chop without burning it to a cinder, or how to boil a potato when I can't find where they are kept," said Annie, taking up the gridiron and turned it over thoughtfully.

"Why, I can show you what to do with that!" said he, with superiority.

And at last, after a great deal of unnecessary trouble and excitement, and after having burned their hands and scorched their faces and gone through a sort of purgatory on a hot early September afternoon, they did succeed in cooking the chops; and then Aubrey danced round them in affectionate pride, while Annie suggested that they should dine in her sitting-room, which was only on the other side of the passage.

"Oh, no," said Aubrey; "let us have it in here, and then we can do some more cooking!"

So they pulled the kitchen-table out of range of the fire, and put bits of firewood and paper under the rickety legs, and laid the cloth and arranged the knives and forks with elaborate carefulness, and Aubrey rushed to the tap and filled a jug which they then discovered to have contained milk; and, the mania of cooking being still strong upon him, he insisted on putting the battered cheese-cakes into the oven "to revive them," and then made buttered toast "for dessert," to work off his culinary energy. And Annie laughed at him, and enjoyed herself very much. And then she suggested boiling some water for coffee, which she knew how to make, she said.

"Yes, because it doesn't require any making. Everything that demands a little science falls to me," said Aubrey, decisively, putting the kettle on the fire so that it immediately fell over on its side with a loud hiss.

However, the coffee was made at last, and of course Aubrey said it was the only time he had tasted good coffee out of Paris; and, the landlady not having yet returned, though the afternoon was drawing to a close, Annie was rising to put away some of the things, when Aubrey stopped her.

"Don't be so wrong-headed as to save that unprincipled old lady trouble," said he. "Besides, I dare say she will stay away till about nine o'clock, and we shall want the things again for tea."

Annie made a grimace.

"Then we shall have to wash them up."

"That is very simple. Put them all in the sink and turn the tap on."

He was suiting the action to the word when Annie stopped him.

"Well, don't let us go away then, because the fire might go out, and then poor Mrs. Briggs might find it cold when she comes back," said he, with unexpected solicitude.

He did not want to break up this *tête-à-tête*, in which Annie, for the first time, had been in her most charming, happiest mood with him.

"Do stay," he said coaxingly. "Let us tell each other stories by the firelight. I'll begin; I'll tell you a beauty that I made up myself, all about ogres and a good little girl and a bad little girl."

He was patting Mrs. Briggs' rocking-chair persuasively, and at last Annie allowed herself to fall into it, while Aubrey went on in a chirping tone:

"There was once a very dreadful ogre as bad as he was ugly—he had a mouth as big as mine—and he had for his play-fellows and companions all the bad little boys and girls in the neighborhood; but of course the good boys and girls ran away as soon as they saw him, especially one little girl who felt quite sure that he would eat her up if she spoke civilly to him. So she was always as distant as she could be, and sometimes made the poor ogre quite uncomfortable, which of course was quite right and proper; until one day she met the poor ogre when somebody had stolen his dinner—and hers too, by the way—and instead of eating her up as she expected, he did his best to make himself as agreeable as circumstances would permit; and——What are you laughing at, Miss Langton?"

"I was laughing at something I was thinking about, Mr. Cooke. You can't expect me to keep my attention fixed on your idiotic nursery stories."

"Oh! And so at last the good little girl got quite saucy; and—I really must beg you to restrain your mirth at your own private thoughts, Miss Langton. It is not courteous when a gentleman is doing his best to be entertaining— and instructive as well. To resume. And so the ogre wondered to himself whether the good little girl would feel quite sure for the future that he didn't want to eat her up, and whether she would think he was not such a bad fellow after all and not half a bad cook at a pinch. That is all, Miss Langton, unless you would like the moral."

"Let us have the moral, by all means, if you can find one in all that tissue of nonsense."

"I pass over your impertinent comments in silence. The moral is——What have I done to make you dislike me so much, Miss Langton?"

"I don't understand you, Mr. Cooke. If I disliked you, should I have devoted all my energies, as I have done this afternoon, to preparing your dinner and being to you all that Mrs. Briggs ever was and more—for she never gives you coffee after dinner?"

"Your civility to me to-day has been dictated by the purest selfishness. If it had not been for me you would have had to go out and buy your own dinner, and you would not have known which side of the gridiron to hold. I repeat, without me you would have been a forlorn, dinner-less woman. Look here—there is no making a bargain with a lady, because she can always cry off when she likes. But if you would only believe that nothing would give me so much pleasure as to be able to render you any service at any time, and that your reserve really does hurt sometimes, I should be so glad of having had this chance of telling you so."

He got shy against the end of this speech; and Annie turned toward him a face which looked very sweet as well as pretty in the fire light.

"I do believe it," she said, simply. "And I promise you that for the future you shall not only not have to complain of my reserve, but you may think yourself lucky if you do not have to check my forwardness."

"Madam, my innate dignity will awe you sufficiently," said Aubrey haughtily.

But he looked as much pleased as his inexpressive face ever allowed him to look. And when Mrs. Briggs came in just in time to get tea ready, affecting great surprise at their being home before her, and protesting that she had understood both of them to say they would dine out, they were both still chatting amicably by the kitchen fire. Aubrey was in such high spirits that he seized the occasion to thunder forth a long harangue at the frightened and apologetic old woman.

"Is this the way to treat two members of a profession which numbers in its ranks the fairest of England's women and the noblest of her men? Woman, do you take us for amateurs? Your four hours of trifling and foolish chattering in the market-place—a thing which Bunyan condemns as most reprehensible—have been gained at the expense of an afternoon of unspeakable suffering and wretchedness to two of the most pecuniarily desirable inmates who have ever condescended to take up a temporary residence under your inhospitable roof!"

Mrs. Briggs was overwhelmed.

"I am sure, sir, I am very sorry. But you looked pretty comfortable sitting there by the fire together."

"Comfortable! This woman says we looked comfortable," said Aubrey, turning in amazement to Annie, who hastened to say:

"And so we were, Mrs. Briggs—at least, I was. As for Mr. Cooke, some people are never contented, you know."

And she ran away laughing to her sitting-room, while Aubrey went up-stairs to his, singing Siebel's song in "Faust" in a very loud but very melancholy voice.

After that afternoon in Mrs. Briggs' kitchen, Miss Langton and Mr. Cooke were very good friends. Annie found in him just the same boyish high spirits which had made William such a delightful companion, while the fact of his being well-educated and witty gave him a charm in which the Braithwaites were one and all sadly deficient. So that it gradually came to be a matter of course that he should find out what was worth seeing about each town which the company visited, and that he should then take her to see it, and that, if they were in sentimental mood, they should unite in conjuring up pictures of the olden time in the ruined abbeys and crumbling walls they inspected; while, if they felt inclined to scoff at antiquity, they laughed together. The half-tender tone of deference which gradually grew up in his manner to her did not cause Annie the least uneasiness. She looked upon him as a universal lover, who could not keep sentiment quite out of his intercourse with any woman, and, if any one had told her that Aubrey Cooke was growing seriously in love with her, and that her friendly manner was encouragement, she would have been very much amused at the suggestion.

But Aubrey had in truth grown quite conscious of the fact that this capricious little woman, with her alternate fits of cold shyness and madly high spirits, who could parry his nonsense with nonsense just as wild one moment, and the next hold her own in a serious discussion, had a charm for him which made all other women seem insipid in his eyes. She was lovely to him; even when her little brown face looked colorless and unattractive to others, it was full of pathetic interest to him; when she was looking her best, when the wind had brought the bright hue of health to her cheeks and her eyes were sparkling with fun or easily roused excitement, he could not take his own vacuous light-blue eyes off her face. If his face had been more expressive, she could not have failed to discover that his interest in her was deeper than was safe for his own peace of mind; but unluckily Aubrey's features were the most perfect mask ever worn by a man whose feelings were in reality as keen as his intellect.

Time after time he had made up his mind that he would propose to her at such a time, at such a place. For it had come to this, that he felt he must make her promise to be his wife, if she would, before this tour was over. But, whenever the moment came which he had looked upon as propitious for the plunge, his heart failed him, or she would be in the wrong mood, too friendly or too satirical, and the question had to be put off. After all, there was no need to hurry matters; there were some weeks of the tour to run yet, and in the meantime their intercourse was delightful, and in the awful possibility of her saying "No" there would be an end of even that.

And there was a burden on his mind which he was anxious to find an opportunity of removing. It concerned Colonel Richardson and the interest Miss Langton took in that handsome Lovelace. He made himself an opportunity rather clumsily. They were reading an epitaph of the usual order on some man who seemed to have had all the virtues, to have been beloved and respected by everybody, and to have made a blank in the universe by his death.

"He was too perfect," said Aubrey. "I suppose his widow put up this as a salve to her conscience after worrying her husband to death."

"Well, perhaps she really thought it."

"Perhaps. In that case he must have been a handsome scamp, a sort of Colonel Richardson," he hazarded, watching her.

"You should not take it for granted that all women like scamps."

"All women seem to like Colonel Richardson."

"Well, he is nice! He knows just how to treat them, to be interesting and amusing without making love to them."

"Oh, I beg your pardon! I should not have been so rash as to sneer at him if I had known he was so lucky as to have such a strong advocate in you," said Aubrey, out of temper.

"Advocate? What nonsense! He has plenty without me."

"That is why I am surprised to find you worshiping at such a general shrine."

"Worshiping! Really, Mr. Cooke, you are quite rude."

"I did not mean to be, I assure you. I only envy him his luck."

And Aubrey stalked off over the old tombstones and began digging out bits of moss from a wall with the end of his cane, too angry to trust himself to say any more.

"Good-bye, Mr. Cooke; I am going home!" sung out Annie; and, before he had made up his mind whether his dignity would allow him to follow her, she had left the churchyard and disappeared from his sight behind the wall.

That decided him, and in a few strides he was out of the gate and crying humbly from behind her.

"Miss Langton, aren't you coming to have another of those tarts you liked so much, as we arranged?"

"Not if you are going to stalk off to the other side of the road if I happen to say something you don't agree with."

"I beg your pardon. I am in a bad temper this morning, I suppose. I will agree with everything you say. I think Colonel Richardson is the nicest man I know."

"Then there we sha'n't agree," said Annie, smiling; "for, although I think his manner is good, I don't much care about him."

"Don't you?" interrogated Aubrey, delightedly! "I'm so glad! Do you know, I didn't think he was the kind of man you would like much. Then you said what you did only to tease me?"

"Did I?" said Annie, surprised that he should make such a fuss about a trifle. "I don't think I did. I say, shall we stay here next week, as we are not going to York?"

"No; we are going out of our route a little. The governor has got us a week at Beckham."

"Beckham!" cried Annie, while all the color fled from her face.

"Yes. Why, what is the matter?"

"Nothing," said she, in her usual voice, but the color did not come back to her cheeks.

Now, Aubrey knew very well that "nothing" would not affect Miss Langton as that mere mention of a place had done; but he saw, too, that she did not intend to give him a truer answer. It was not difficult to come to the conclusion that there were unpleasant associations connected in her mind with the place to which they were going; and, after long deliberation, he made up his mind definitely that Beckham should be the place where he would at last screw up his courage to the point of asking her to be his wife.

"If she likes me—and I think—I almost think she does"—he reflected that night—"why, my proposal will be the very best thing to drive any unhappy recollections of the place out of her head. If she won't have me—well, there is a river at Beckham!"

With which dark suggestion Aubrey blew out his candle and went to sleep.

———————————

CHAPTER XIV.

Annie felt half inclined at first to request the manager, on the plea of illness, to let his niece, who was her "understudy," play her parts for the week the company were to spend at Beckham, and take her chance of his allowing her to rejoin them at the next town they visited. The incompetent little niece was eager, as Annie knew, for such a chance, and there would probably be little difficulty as far as that part of the matter was concerned.

But, besides the fact that she could ill afford to lose even one week's salary and risk the canceling of the rest of her engagement, she felt sure that there was one person whom the plea of illness would in no way deceive. Aubrey Cooke's attention had already been awakened to her reluctance to visit Beckham, and he was far too sharp a young man not to be dangerous if she were to give him involuntarily a clew to a secret she did not want to trust him with.

And the secret of her marriage she wished to keep from all her present associates. The miserable tie seemed to be less binding when all around her were ignorant of it. For a long time she had almost forgotten it in the unfettered life she had led since she left Garstone; but the remembrance of it had begun lately to irritate her strangely. There was now nothing on earth she dreaded so much as the possibility of her husband's finding her out, and in a fit of capricious obstinacy or tyranny insisting on her return to him. The thought of being again at the mercy of that ignorant, drunken boy filled her with a disgust which was now not even mingled with pity. And she was to be brought against her will to the very town which he and his brothers visited almost daily.

But, after long reflection, she decided that the risk of her being recognized in Beckham was not so great as she had pictured it to be in her first terror at the thought of going thither. The families living round about Beckham, as is usually the case with country towns, very seldom visited the theater—the Braithwaites never. Upon William's authority, she was so much altered that, with the help of a veil and other such simple disguises, she might pass unrecognized even by people among whom she had lived. When the young men from the Grange came into Beckham, they were almost always on horseback or driving, so that it would be easy for any one on foot to avoid them; and, above all, she was on the alert to escape them, while they had not the least suspicion of her coming. In the town itself there was very little fear of her being recognized by the inhabitants. She had not been in it much at any time, and was very little known there. The mere change of name would be enough to prevent their identification of "Miss Lane" or "Mrs. Harold Braithwaite" with "Miss Langton."

So, when the company arrived at Beckham, Annie was still with them. No one noticed any difference in her manner from her usual rather stolid composure, when she stepped with the rest on to the platform at the station which had more than one moving memory for her, except Aubrey Cooke, who watched her narrowly, and at once decided that she had been there before. She was too wise to deny it when he asked her carelessly whether she knew the place, and then she set herself to the task of finding lodgings as near as possible to the theater. She succeeded in engaging suitable rooms in a back street within a few minutes' walk of it; and she was growing secure in her *incognito* when they had played for two nights and she had seen no signs of the Mainwarings or the Braithwaites, when an incident happened which brought her into contact with the one she most dreaded to meet, with quite unforeseen consequences.

Aubrey had not yet found the golden opportunity he sought, for Annie declared that there was nothing in the least interesting to be seen in Beckham or round about it; and, the weather being wet and cold, she seized upon this excuse to decline walks with him. The third day of their stay was the fifth of November, and a friend of the manager had invited some of the members of the company to some simple festivities, which included a bonfire and fireworks, after the performance. On the same night, Miss West, the leading lady, had invited Aubrey to supper, and, on his pleading a previous engagement, she said to him with some pique and in no very subdued tones that she knew whose charms outweighed those of any society she could offer him, and warned him emphatically that the pleasures he preferred were far more dangerous than those he rejected.

"Your little prude will throw you over some fine morning when you least expect it. I know what those quiet little women do. And you won't be able to console yourself so quickly for her defection as I can myself for yours."

And Miss West marched away to bestow the charms of her racy speech and artistic complexion where they were better appreciated. For indeed Aubrey Cooke's indifference to her rather overpowering fascinations had become very marked since he had found metal more attractive in Miss Langton, whose promised presence at the house he was going to visit that night had more charm for him than fireworks.

The lady and gentleman who gave this entertainment were delighted with the good nature of Mr. Cooke and the two brother-actors of his who were present, when they took the rockets and catherine-wheels out of the clumsy hands of the coachman and superintended the exhibition themselves, to the great delight of the children, who had been put to bed and then pulled out again, a few hours later to enjoy these midnight festivities. But the young men certainly condescended to enjoy themselves at least as much as the children, and Aubrey in particular fired squibs and burned his fingers and his clothes with great spirit. When at last the bonfire was lighted and the whole party jumped and whooped round it, and even the most timid were excited to stir the burning twigs with a pitchfork and then run screaming away, Aubrey had time to sneak round to Miss Langton's side and pay her the grateful attention of putting into her hands an old garden-rake which he had hunted out on purpose for her; and they tossed the blazing boughs together; and, as the lurid light shone on her face, and she hopped about over smoldering branches and expiring squibs with the help of his friendly hand, he felt that the moment was come. In the excitement and hurly-burly which were going on around them, nobody noticed the tenderness with which he drew her back a few yards from the bonfire, on the darker side of it, when her foot turned over on a glowing twig.

"Take care; you are getting tired. You must not play any more now," said he gently.

"Let me go back and give it just one more toss," pleaded she earnestly but meekly. Annie had the charm of always yielding to any assumption of authority in small things very submissively.

"No, I cannot allow it. This jumping through the fire is a heathenish custom highly unbecoming in an enlightened young lady of the nineteenth century."

"Oh, yes, it meant something, didn't it?" cried she, interested. "The Canaanitish children were passed through the fire to propitiate Moloch. And I have heard of a lot of Irish and German superstitions about bonfires."

"Yes, they are all about luck and love. If you want to see whether your love will be fortunate, you set a blazing hoop rolling down a hill, and, if it reaches the bottom still alight and is not caught by any obstacle, then you know she loves you back."

"Where did you find out that? Have you ever tried it?" she asked lightly.

"No," said he, in a whisper; "I should not dare."

They were both silent for a moment; the fire had fallen into mere smoke and blackness on the side near where they stood, and they could not see each other's faces. But Annie heard the quick, loud breathing of the man beside her, she could see him bending down over her with one hand seeking hers, and a terrible fear leaped up suddenly in her heart, as she moved quickly away from him with a low sound that was almost a cry of pain.

Aubrey stood still, without attempting to follow or detain her. She could not have misunderstood him, and she shrunk away; that was enough for him. It was a very hard and very unexpected blow; he had by no means felt over confident of his success with her, but at the worst he had counted upon her giving him a hearing, and this abrupt repulse stung him to the quick.

He did not stand there long watching the flickering light and shadow cast by the burning pile in front of him. He sprung through the fire into the middle of the group of howling, delighted children; and took his place as the moving spirit of the throng with greater zeal than ever.

And, when they had all grown weary, and had burned their clothes and scorched themselves as much as they would, and the dying bonfire was at last left to the men-servants to rake out, and, the children having been sent to bed, the rest sat down to supper, Aubrey Cooke was the wittiest there as he had been the most active outside, and he gave to Annie's watching eyes only this one sign that she had wounded him—he did not look at her.

When they broke up, between two and three o'clock in the morning, the two other actors and the other actress who had come left Miss Langton as a matter of course to the care of Aubrey. But she slipped past him and went on by herself. He did not attempt to overtake her, but followed at a short distance, in case she should be frightened by a stray drunken rough in going through the narrow streets which led to her lodging.

She was just in front of the house where Miss West lodged, when the door opened and two or three gentlemen came down the steps. The foremost, who was walking very unsteadily, staggered against her as he was turning round to speak to his companions. She gave a frightened cry, and rushed past him in terror. As she heard first a laugh and then a man's footsteps behind her, she broke into a run, but stumbled against the curbstone of the pavement as she went over a crossing, with the man close upon her. He caught her when her foot slipped; and then, as she turned round sharply, she suddenly gave a startled cry and clung to his arms, sobbing out:

"You, Aubrey! Thank Heaven!"

"My dear child, who did you think it was?"

"I thought it was that tipsy man!" she whispered, shuddering.

"The clumsy brute didn't hurt you, my darling, did he, when he ran up against you? I would have punched his head——"

"No, no, no!" she cried, clinging to him again, in fear of his returning. "He didn't hurt me at all; he scarcely touched me. But I thought it was he who was running after me, and I was frightened."

"That is all because you were a silly girl and were too proud to let me see you home. It is a 'judgment.' Why, you are shaking all over still! I didn't think you were such a little coward!"

He soothed her tenderly, with a very happy remembrance of her delight in recognizing him, and of the impulsive closing of the little hands on his arm. He began to think that repulse of a few hours before might be differently construed; she could not have smiled up more than gratefully into his face as she was doing now if he had been repugnant to her. Other women might, but not Annie Langton.

And Aubrey was right. She had felt just what her face expressed, that the one person in the world whose presence inspired her with perfect confidence had suddenly appeared at the very moment when she dreaded the approach of the person she most feared to meet.

For, in the half tipsy man who had staggered down from Miss West's door and reeled against her, Annie had instantly recognized her husband. He had not known her, he had scarcely seen her, for the little figure had flown past almost before he had recovered his balance; but in the first moment of terror, Annie imagined that he had seen, known, and was pursuing her.

She walked on with Aubrey very quietly, very silently, her hand on his arm and his hand on hers, listening to his gentle, playful scolding with a little laugh now and then, but without speaking much, satisfied that she was safe with him, and that she need not talk to show him that she felt so. When they came to her door, she disengaged her hand and held it out while bidding him "Good-night" with a smile that made Aubrey bold. He took her hand in his, passed his other arm round her, saying, in a quick, jerky whisper:

"Annie, you do—you will trust yourself to me, won't you?"

There was no eloquence in his speech; but for once his light eyes spoke very plainly, his voice broke into tenderness. Annie trembled. Her eyes, as they met his, shone with a light he had never seen in them before. But before he could speak again, before he could draw her into his arms, the light had faded. She gave him one look so wildly, unutterably sad that he never forgot it; then, with bent head, she slipped gently out of the grasp of his arm and turned to the door. She could not see the lock, for the tears were gathering in her eyes. After a few moments, Aubrey, who had stood behind her without speaking, took the key from her shaking hand and opened the door for her.

"Thank you, Aubrey. Good-night," said she, in a quavering voice, without looking up.

"Good-night, darling!" he whispered back, managing to give one last despairing squeeze to the little fingers before she shut the door.

He went home to his lodgings utterly bewildered, but resolved to get from her the next day some explanation of her extraordinary treatment of his advances. She had certainly understood him. She had at first repelled, then encouraged him. He had seen in her eyes the very look he had wished to call up in them, and the next minute it had changed to an expression of plaintive misery and regret which had chilled his hopes even as they rose.

But the next day, when he called upon her, he was told Miss Langton was not well, and could not see any one. He knew very well that she was only putting him off, and he made up his mind that at night she should not escape him. She took care however not to be caught alone, and her share in the performance was nearly over before Aubrey, always on the watch, saw Miss Montrose, who had been standing at the side with her, go upon the scene at her cue and leave Annie by herself at last. Then she heard his voice behind her; she could not escape now, for before long she would hear her own cue, and must be on the watch for it.

"Good-evening, Miss Langton."

"Oh, good-evening, Mr. Cooke!" She gave him her hand; it was trembling a little, and she did not look up into his face.

"I have not had an opportunity of speaking to you before. You will let me see you home?"

"Not to-night; I have promised to go to supper with Miss Norris."

"You are putting me off, I see. Is it fair, Annie? Is it right? Am I not worth an answer?"

"An answer to what?"

"To what I said to you last night. You can't have forgotten so soon. If I were a stranger, if I were the most contemptible wretch living, if you had always treated me with open dislike, you could not have misunderstood or forgotten what I said to you last night."

Annie turned and looked up at him, pale under her *rouge*.

"I have not forgotten, nor understood—at least, I think not. I thought you too would have understood—that I tried to avoid you, because I feared, I knew my answer, if I must answer, would give you pain."

"Then you don't like me?"

A ray of vehement passion flashed from her dark eyes.

"Don't torture me! You know I like you; but I can't—I can't do more! I don't know whether I have done wrong—I never meant to lead you to feel like this. How could I go on avoiding you when I was lonely and you were kind?"

"Why should you avoid me? Why should you not love me?"

She did not answer; but there was no mistaking the misery on her face for coquetry or caprice.

"Are you bound by some other engagement, Annie?"

She shuddered. Before he could speak again, she turned quickly to him.

"Don't ask me any more; believe what I say, that I am suffering more than you can, and it is my own fault. I am bound by an engagement in which love is out of the question, and always must be. What love is to most women ambition is to me."

"Do you mean that you will marry for ambition? You, Annie? Wait, wait a little for me; I will get on—I can—I'm not a fool——"

"Hush!" said Annie sharply. "It is impossible; I can never marry you! You are only torturing me, and all to no end. I cannot marry you; I cannot love you!"

"You could if you would, Annie. I could make you love me; you are always happy when you are with me."

His words moved her, and she stopped him abruptly.

"Happy? Yes, for the time. We have been good friends, that is all. But there is something more in life than you can give me."

"What is there?"

"Fame, position, the means of getting on."

"Is that what you care for most?"

"What if it is?"

"It is not; but, if it were, I would get those for you easily enough."

She laughed, but not merrily.

"I think you overestimate your powers."

Aubrey's face looked in that moment as if carved in wood, save for the steady shining of his light eyes. He said, quietly:

"Oh, I do, do I? Well, you shall see."

They were both silent for a few moments, and then Annie heard her cue and went on.

This conversation took place on a Thursday evening, and during the next two days Annie avoided Aubrey still, and he did not again seek an interview with her, but contented himself with simple greetings, and with watching her quite unobtrusively. She missed his companionship keenly, far too keenly.

She did not dare to leave the house all day, fearing as much to meet him as to meet any of the Braithwaites, yet holding her breath when there was a knock at the front door, in the hope that he at least had come to ask after her. But he did not come. On Saturday night, as she was leaving the theater, Aubrey came out, followed by a boy carrying his portmanteau. For the first time for three days, he ran after her.

"Good-bye, Miss Langton; I am going to town."

Annie started.

"What! You are going away?"

"Only till Monday. I am going on business. You will wish me good luck?"

"With all my heart!"

He wrung her hand and ran on without a word. They could not trust themselves to speak again. The next day Annie left Beckham with the rest of the company.

On Monday night they met once more at the theater. Aubrey was looking paler and plainer than usual, and gave as a reason for his altered appearance that he had not been to bed for the last two nights.

"May I see you home to-night, Miss Langton?" asked he, as soon as he found a chance of speaking to Annie. "I will not say a word that could offend you. I will not touch upon the—the forbidden topic," he whispered, earnestly.

Annie could not refuse; but it was hard work for her to hide her agitation—and her pleasure—when she once more found him waiting for her that night at the stage-door, and slipped her hand falteringly within his proffered arm. She had no need to be afraid; his manner was as cool and composed as if she had been his grandmother, and piqued her into similar calmness.

"I thought you would like to know how I got on in town," said he at once, in the most matter-of-fact tone. "I went up about a London engagement—at the Regent's Theater—and I've got it!"

"I'm so glad," said Annie, coolly.

"Well, that is not all. I've got an offer of an engagement there for you too."

"Not really?"

"I have, though. I knew there was a part in the piece they are going to play which would suit you down to the ground, so I mentioned that there was a lady of remarkable promise in the company I was in, and said just what I knew would attract attention about you; and it happens that the manager wants some one for the part I have in my eye, and I think you are pretty sure to get it if you write."

"Oh, Mr. Cooke, I don't know how to thank you!" said Annie, in wild delight, for more than one reason.

"Don't mention it, Miss Langton," said Aubrey, in his old, deferential manner; then he turned the conversation. "I met an old favorite of yours last night—Gibson—at Mrs. Falconer's."

"Oh! How is the beauty?"

"Well, she affects great distress about one of her brothers, who is ill, and not expected to live. It appears he fell down as he was getting into a dog-cart, awfully tight, last Wednesday night. But I don't think she is as much afflicted as she would be if mourning didn't suit her complexion. And, though she mentioned that he was quite alone, she did not suggest going to nurse him."

"Did she mention the name of the brother?" asked Annie, quite quietly.

"Yes; she called him 'poor Harry.'"

Annie heard without giving one sign that the news moved her. For the rest of the walk she spoke little, and with an effort. At her door he was struck by the marked constraint of her manner as she bade him good-bye. When she had unlocked the door and he had turned away, she said:

"Whatever you hear of me, remember I am not ungrateful."

When Aubrey got to the theater on the following evening, he found that the manager's niece was to play Miss Langton's part, and learned that the latter had thrown up her engagement and had already left town.

CHAPTER XV.

The news of her husband's illness had fallen like a knell on Annie's ears; for in a moment she saw that the bright vision of pleasure and satisfied ambition which Aubrey's words about a London engagement in the same theater with him had called up could not be indulged in, except at the sacrifice of an unmistakable duty. It was her husband who lay ill, neglected and solitary. For one moment she tried to stifle conscience by saying to herself that she did not know where he was; but then she felt ashamed of the flimsy excuse, for she could not doubt that he was at Garstone Grange. Aubrey had said that it was on Wednesday night that the accident had happened to him, and it was on Wednesday night that she herself had seen and even touched him in the streets of Beckham. She must go to him, and at once, before Aubrey could guess her secret, before she herself, in an unguarded moment, should let him know how much this separation would cost her. She dared not trust herself to think what a great part of the fact of his being engaged at the same theater had had in her joy at the prospect of playing again in London; it was a dangerous subject, and she shunned it instinctively. She tried to keep her thoughts fixed on this one simple idea—she must go to Garstone, nurse her husband through his illness, bear his brutal temper and thankless snubs as best she might, and then slip back quietly into her free stage life once more, taking her chance of getting a town engagement.

So, on the morning after her talk with Aubrey, she got the manager to cancel the rest of her engagement, and, having packed her trunk the night before, she left for Beckham within an hour of his releasing her. She looked restlessly and eagerly from the windows of the cab as she drove to the station "to see if any of the company were about." At last she caught sight of Aubrey Cooke going down a street, with his back to the cab, therefore so that he could not see her; and after that she looked out no more, but sat with burning cheeks and her eyes fixed on the front seat of the cab, all curiosity and interest gone out of her.

She got to Beckham at three o'clock in the afternoon, and drove straight to the Grange, which she reached before the dark November day had closed. To her surprise, the man-servant who opened the door recognized her at once.

To her questions he replied that Mr. Harold was being nursed by the housekeeper, that Lady Braithwaite and Mr. Stephen were abroad, Sir George was in town, Mr. Wilfred in Leicestershire, and Mr. William somewhere—he did not know where—"studying."

Annie then asked to see the housekeeper, and learned from her that Harry's accident was indeed as serious as Aubrey Cooke's words had implied. He had slipped as he was getting into the dog-cart, one night after supping with some friends in Beckham—Annie happened to know something about those friends—and the wheel had passed over him and broken his left arm, besides inflicting other less serious injuries; he had not yet quite recovered from another illness, and had been disregarding his doctor's orders. After being taken to a surgeon by the gentleman who was with him, to have his arm set, he had insisted on being driven back home to the Grange at five o'clock in the morning. The housekeeper continued that he had then, contrary to the advice she had ventured to give him, insisted upon drinking brandy in the billiard-room; that she had waited about, not daring to go in and speak to him again, until she heard a fall and a groan, and, running in, had found that he had fallen and again displaced his broken arm. She had got him to bed with the help of the men-servants and sent for the doctor; but no skill could prevent inflammation of the wounded limb, and he was now lying in a high fever and could recognize no one.

"I would strongly advise you not to see him, ma'am, until he is quieter. He is very violent, and he uses dreadful language."

"I don't suppose he says anything worse than what I have heard him say when he was in full possession of his senses, Mrs. Stanley," said Annie, quietly. "It is not fair that all the care of nursing my husband should fall upon you; so, if you please, I will go to him now."

Mrs. Stanley led the way to the room to which they had carried him—not his own, but a larger and more convenient one. She drew the arm of the young wife through her own as they entered, for Annie had grown very white and was shaking from head to foot when her husband's voice, speaking disjointedly to an imaginary listener, met her ear. She recovered her self-command before venturing to look at him; but, however strong her emotion might have been, it would not have affected him. He took no notice of her presence; his wide-open eyes did not even see her.

Annie did not give way again; but from that hour she took her place by his bedside alternately with Mrs. Stanley, listening to idle babblings of his useless vicious life, to invectives against the carelessness of grooms, the meanness of his brother George, the "airs Sue gave herself." But there was never one word of herself; she had passed out of his life; been forgotten, as if those few months of their married life had never been. Only once did he refer to her, and that was not to Annie, his wife, but to Miss Lane of Garstone Grange.

"Saw the pretty little governess going to church; felt half inclined to go too, just to look at her," he murmured once while she sat by his bedside listening. But then he rambled off into talk which concerned a dog he had bought, and Susan Green, the blacksmith's daughter, and let fall some epithets which, it occurred to Annie, would apply particularly well to Miss West, at whose house he and his companions had been supping on the Wednesday night, or rather Thursday morning, when she had run against him in Beckham Street, and when he had met with his accident.

It was a hard punishment for the weakness of marrying him and the fault of leaving him that she was suffering now, as she listened to his wandering talk about other women, which showed his contempt for a sex he did not understand, or think worth the trouble of trying to understand. And all the while she had to try to overcome the disgust with which he inspired her and the longing to be again in the society of one man, one brilliant, interesting companion, for whom every word she uttered had a charm, every action of hers was right.

When Mrs. Stanley took her place in the sickroom, she would fly like an escaped bird out of doors, and wander through the fields and the now leafless copses by herself, rejoicing in her temporary freedom, trying to forget the horrible fact that she was married, and the very existence of that unconscious, senseless clog upon her life that she had left in the darkened room up-stairs. These rambles brought almost as much pain as pleasure to her; they recalled to her so vividly the long marauding expeditions she had had with William, when they used to return home laden with birds' eggs and ducks' feathers, and moss-covered twigs, all of which William had to carry as soon as they got near the house, for fear any of the household should think that Mrs. Harold Braithwaite was so childish as to care for such rubbish. Harry had been merely an every-day trial then, to be shirked as much as conscience permitted; now he had become, and by her own fault, an obstacle to her happiness which there was no possibility of removing.

She had returned to the sickroom one afternoon to relieve the housekeeper, and, finding that Harry was sleeping quietly—a fact which made her a little nervous, as it proved he was getting better—she opened a book and settled herself in an arm-chair by the fire, whence she could see any movement of the invalid's by merely raising her eyes. The book was George Sands' "Consuelo." Opening it at first carelessly, the earliest pages fixed her attention, and before long she bent over it, completely absorbed in the fascinating story.

She did not see the sick man's eyes open, fall upon her, and remain fixed, at first vacantly, then intently, upon her bent head. She did not even notice the slight sound he made as he struggled to raise himself on his elbow, nor the faint gasp of astonishment he gave when, having succeeded, he had satisfied himself that it was his long-forgotten wife.

"Annie!" he exclaimed, in a voice hoarse with weakness and with no warmer emotion than amazement.

She looked up and said "Harry!" with just the same amount of tenderness.

"Why are you here?" he asked curiously, as he fell weakly back upon his pillow.

"Why, to nurse you, of course!" said she in a soft voice, rising at once without any noise or bustle, but in a quietly matter-of-fact manner.

She came to the bed, arranged his pillow more comfortably, raised his head, and gave him something to drink, while he stared at her silently and received her attentions without any remark, until she quietly went back again to her arm-chair and "Consuelo." Still he gazed at her fixedly, and, as she opened the book at the right place, which she had been careful not to lose on hearing her husband address her for the first time after nearly four years' separation, he said:

"You've gone off shockingly!"

"Yes, I know I have," said Annie, quite calmly, putting her finger on the line she had come to as she looked up. "But you had better not talk now," she added, coaxingly; "it is very bad when you are still so weak."

Down went her head again; but, with characteristic tact, he insisted on continuing:

"I don't think I ever saw anybody so much altered. I suppose that is why you have come back. You found nobody else would admire you any longer, so it was time to come and saddle yourself on your husband."

Instead of being stung to the quick by this reproach, which was meant to be very severe, Annie had some difficulty in repressing an impulse to laugh; but she only said, soothingly:

"It is all right, Harry; I am going away again as soon as ever you are well. I'll turn away so"—and she moved the chair round to face the fire—"and then you won't be annoyed by the sight of my ugly face."

She went on reading, or pretending to read, for some minutes, until her husband's voice once more interrupted her.

"A fine lot of affection you seem to have for me now you have come back! I dare say you wish I was dead all the time. Never even asking me how I feel! What did you come at all for?"

Annie put down her book again, and came toward the bed.

"I didn't think it was good for you to talk just at first. I thought, if I sat quite quietly, you would go to sleep again."

"No, you didn't; you wanted to read your book. What is it?"

"It is a French book called 'Consuelo.'"

"French! Oh, of course—something too learned for me!"

"It is not learned at all. I'll translate it to you if you like; but I don't think you would care much about it."

"Oh, no; it would be over my head, of course!"

His voice was growing very feeble and husky. Annie poured some medicine into a glass and brought it to him.

"Now," said she, coaxingly, as she slipped her hand under his pillow to raise his head, "you had better drink this, and then lie still for a little while. You are not very strong yet, you know."

"I sha'n't drink it—I won't have that vile stuff poured down my throat!" said he, in a weak, dogged whisper.

"You had better take it. Can't you feel how weak your voice is getting?" said Annie, persuasively.

"I won't take that, I tell you! That won't do—do me—any good! Fetch me some brandy-and-soda."

"No, I can't do that; it wouldn't be good for you."

"Do you hear what I say? Fetch me some brandy-and-soda!"

He made a feeble, spasmodic effort to knock the glass out of her hand; but she held it out of his reach, and, laying his obstinate head, which she was still supporting, gently down on the pillow again, she put the medicine down on the table.

"Don't you mean to obey me? I won't drink your filthy poisons! If you want to get rid of me you had better doctor some brandy for me, and then perhaps I'll take it."

"The brandy by itself would be poison to you now, without my doctoring," said Annie, quietly. "As soon as you are well again you can drink what you like, you know; and the more faithfully you follow the doctor's orders now, the sooner you will be able to drink as much brandy as you please."

She said it in a very soft, gentle voice; but she could not quite keep the scorn she felt for him out of the last words. Weak tears of impotent anger gathered in Harry's eyes.

"You treat me like a dog! A fine make-believe your wifely duty is. When I'm well again I'll turn you out of the house at an hour's notice—that I will!"

She saw that he was exciting himself dangerously; and fearing the effects of this emotion upon him in his weak state, she took the hand he was convulsively clinching on the bedclothes in one of hers, and putting her lips to it, said, in the most winning tone the actress could assume:

"My poor dear Harry, I would give you what you want if I dared; and when the doctor comes, I will ask if you may have it. And I will go away when you like; but you will let me stay until you are well, won't you?"

Harry was touched by this unexpected appeal.

"All right; you may stay," he murmured magnanimously.

"And won't you let me give you your medicine? I'll drink some of it first, if you like, to show you it isn't poison."

"No, that is only nonsense. I'll take it," whispered the grumpy invalid, conquered; and when he had drank it, and she laid his head gently down again, he said, "Thank you. You may kiss me if you like, old girl."

Annie availed herself of this permission—not enthusiastically, but still not without a touch of tenderness; and she sat in the chair by the bedside until he went quietly off to sleep again.

The next few conversations she had with her husband, who got better rapidly with the careful nursing he received, were after the same pattern—a little wrangle, with taunts and sneers on his side, and careless submission on hers, followed by a sort of tame reconciliation. Before long she had managed, by a firm refusal to do anything which she did not think good for him and a very gentle manner, to get the upper hand of the obstinate invalid; and, when Mrs. Stanley had a tussle with him on account of his unwillingness to have his wounds dressed or to take his medicine at the proper hours, she always went to Annie to get over the difficulty. Sometimes during a battle with the housekeeper he would say:

"Well, send Annie, then, and perhaps I'll have it done."

This flattering preference was received by its object with anything but gratitude. To be called up from her sleep in the middle of the night, or to be sent for in the course of a meal, because "Mr. Harold says he won't take any slops, ma'am, unless you come and see that his beef-tea isn't hot enough to scald his throat," did not fill her with any pride in this rise in her husband's esteem. At last, one night, when he was fairly on the road to convalescence, she flatly refused to go when Mrs. Stanley came to say Mr. Harold would not let her dress the wound on his shoulder, but wanted his wife to do it.

"Tell him I say you can do it much better than I, Mrs. Stanley; and, if he won't let you do it, he must wait till to-morrow morning," said the undutiful wife sleepily, as she turned over and shut her eyes again.

The next morning Harry, who was to go down-stairs for the first time that day, bounced over on his side away from her as soon as she entered his room and came up to the bedside. Annie walked softly toward the door; then the invalid, who had recovered much of the power of his lungs, roared:

"Stop! Where are you going?"

"I am going to breakfast," said she, calmly.

"Without even wishing me good-morning! After refusing point-blank just to step along the corridor in the night when I might have been dying! You're a nice wife!"

"Now, look here, Harry; I don't pretend to do more than just my simple duty to you, and don't for a moment set myself up for a model wife."

"I should think not indeed! Everybody would laugh if you did."

"Everybody would laugh, as you say, if I pretended to show any affection for a husband so selfish that he will break a night's rest of a very good nurse—I have been that, remember—on the most trifling pretexts. I dare say you think it an honor to choose me instead of Mrs. Stanley to put on a poultice or arrange a bandage; but I assure you it is one I don't appreciate. You are nearly well now, and the task I set myself of seeing you through your illness is over. My presence can only irritate you now, and I think of taking the hint you have often given me, and going to-day."

"Go? What—leave me here all alone when I've shown you I like to have you near me? All right—go along then, you hard, heartless vixen! No, no," he called, as she turned again toward the door—"Annie, Annie, I didn't mean it—I'm not ungrateful—I have been selfish! Don't go till I'm quite well; don't leave me all alone, Annie, till I can get about again! I like to hear your voice; and you move so quietly, and you talk so prettily—I'm always dull when you're out of the room—I'm sorry I've been so cross. Don't go, Annie, till I'm quite well. Wait till next week. Won't you wait just till next week, Annie?"

She came back to his side again, looking very grave.

"Look here, Harry," she said; "you are well enough now for me to speak to you seriously, as I could not speak when you were lying there likely to die. You have been very rude to me and ungracious, considering that I came simply to do my best to get you well quickly. Now the duty I set myself is over, and I assure you, strange as it may seem to you, I feel no irresistible wish to stay here a moment longer than is necessary. If you wish me to stay here still and do my best to amuse you until you are strong enough to amuse yourself again, I will do so, on one condition. It is that now you will drop the tone of childish insolence to me which I have excused on account of your illness, and speak to me as other men speak to their wives—no better than that," she added, with a slight shade of irony.

"So you want to preach and domineer over me," protested Harry, rather sulkily, "just because I said I didn't mind your being in the room. Yes, yes, I will be civil," he added hastily, as Annie's head moved away; "I didn't mean to be rude to you: I really am grateful for the way you have taken care of me. Only don't speak to me in that hard voice: just say something in your soft, pretty way, and I shall come round directly. You always get over me when you speak in your soft voice, you know."

"Well, then, may I go to breakfast, Harry?" said she, smiling, and taking the hand he involuntarily stretched toward her.

"Yes, yes; I won't be selfish again. Kiss me first," said the invalid, in a more contented tone.

And Annie put her lips lightly to his forehead and left the room. It was very tiresome that she should have to delay her departure from the Grange for this whim of her capricious husband. She hoped that she might be able to leave in a day or two, especially as George was expected at the Grange; and, if she were to remain until his arrival, she knew well that she would find it difficult to get away. For she could not fail to see that, while she had lost the first freshness of her beauty, she had acquired, by her early encounters with the world and by contact with the wits of the green-room, other charms of even greater power, which a man of Sir George's type would be likely to rate highly—especially in the country, where women who can talk are rare. She had no longer the least fear of him, and she only dreaded, in worldly-wise feminine vanity, not his attraction for her, but hers for him.

For the longing to be again at work in her profession was strong upon her, and an unacknowledged wish to see that member of it whom she liked best was stronger still. She knew, too, that these few days of delay in returning to London might make the difference between her obtaining or losing all chance of the engagement Aubrey Cooke had spoken of to her. Her excitement and impatience grew so high as she thought the matter over during her solitary breakfast, that she felt obliged to throw a shawl round her and rush into the open air to calm the fever rising within her before returning to her peevish lord and master up-stairs. How could she induce him to let her go at once, without exciting the spirit of contradiction in him which would make him tease her to stay because he saw she wished to go? She had turned reluctantly toward the house again, and was going indoors to Harry, who would probably be dressed and up for the first time since his illness now, when a wild but delighted shout from the gate frightened her. She saw a tall figure racing over the lawn toward her, and in another minute she was in William's frantic embrace.

He lifted her off her feet, he made little rushes at her, he danced round her with savage cries, he showed ecstasy in every uncivilized and unheard-of way, asking her when she had come and why she had not written to tell him.

"I didn't know where you were, William, my dear boy," said Annie. "Did you know I was here?"

"Rather! What do you think I've come for except to see you? And I saw George in town yesterday, and I've told him, and he is coming, and Wilfred and everybody; and we'll have the whole place lit up, and—Hooray! I must give you another hug!"

He was suiting the action to the word when the window of Harry's room, which was on that side of the house, was thrown sharply up by the invalid, who was sitting by it, and his angry and no longer weak voice called out:

"Be off! Leave her alone, you impudent young scamp! Annie, come here; I want you. Why have you been so long gone? You don't care what happens to me!"

"I'm coming," said Annie, resignedly.

CHAPTER XVI.

Annie soon found herself in a difficult position between the brother-in-law she liked and the husband she disliked. William was always wanting her to be out of doors with him, Harry teased her with sulky reproaches if she was away from him for more than half an hour at a time. The invalid came down to the drawing-room, which was well warmed and cheerful, on the second day after William's arrival, leaning on his brother's arm. The ascendency over him which Annie had gained in the sickroom she managed to maintain still; and the artless William would make gestures of admiration and astonishment at Harry's docility to her from behind her husband's back, and there was much unpleasantness on one or two occasions when his brother caught him. William also made himself obnoxious by calling Harry "the Ogre," sometimes out of hearing of his elder brother and sometimes within, and by assuming an intimate knowledge of Annie's movements during the four years of her absence from the Grange, which Harry of course did not possess.

In these early days of her return Annie put off questions about the way in which she had occupied those four years, and left Harry to imagine that she had supported herself by teaching. Her skill in conversational fence being much greater than that of either of her companions, she could always lead the talk into what channel she would; but it was growing a delicate matter to avoid collision between Harry and William, each of whom considered himself to have an exclusive right to her attention, when the situation was changed by the arrival on the same day, though not by the same train, of Wilfred and Sir George.

William was dispatched by Annie to Beckham in the dog-cart to meet his eldest brother, and, when he was gone, Harry, who, under his wife's care, was getting rapidly through his convalescence, fidgeted about the room, and at last knocked over a gypsy-table covered with trifles.

"All right, Harry; I'll pick them up," said Annie, hearing a muttered oath from her husband.

"What are you in such a hurry for? I do hate a woman to be in a hurry," said he, testily, noticing unusual haste in his wife's movements as she knelt on the floor gathering up the things his clumsiness had scattered.

"It is getting very late, and I must dress for dinner now George is coming back."

Harry flung himself into a chair and scowled at her.

"Oh, all this fuss for George! Your appearance didn't matter for me, I suppose? I'm only your husband!"

"My dear Harry, if you will take the trouble to think you will see that, as, since you have been ill, you have not had late dinner, I have not insulted you by changing my gown to see you eat toast and mutton-broth in your dressing-gown. Besides, I should like to hide the falling off in my looks which you were kind enough to tell me of from George, who will not hurt my vanity by mentioning it, if he does notice any great change."

"Look here, Annie! I didn't want to hurt your feelings; I didn't think you were vain; and—and—do you know—I really—I think sometimes, when you tell us anything to make us laugh, for instance, you look prettier than you ever did. You—you look so mischievous, and your eyes sparkle so, you make one want to kiss you—only then—then, somehow, you never seem to want to be kissed—at least not by me!" he added, testily.

Annie burst out laughing, a little constrainedly perhaps.

"Why, whom should I want to kiss me except my husband?" said she, carelessly, as she bent over her occupation of fitting together two pieces of broken Dresden china.

"I don't know, I am sure," said Harry, rather sulkily, feeling that his conciliatory speech had not met with the response it deserved—"George, perhaps."

"Why, surely you are not jealous of George, Harry!" she cried, laughing more naturally.

"I don't know that I'm not; but it wouldn't make much difference to you if I was, would it?" he asked; and, as, for one moment, she did not answer, he walked, with the aid of the intervening chairs, from the one on which he was sitting to one beside her, and laid his sound arm, the right, on her shoulder. "It wouldn't make any difference, would it?" he repeated.

Annie looked up rather mischievously.

"I don't think it would, Harry."

This was a disconcerting answer to a husband.

"Oh, very well!" said he, gruffly, after a minute's pause. "Then I see what I am to expect;" and he got up to walk away with offended dignity; but, not having recovered his strength yet, and having tired and excited himself already that afternoon, he staggered before he had gone many steps, and immediately he found his wife's arm in his. "Thank you," said he, haughtily; then he added, with the air of a martyr, "I'm not well yet, not nearly well; I'm not strong enough to walk steadily."

"Oh, well, Harry, I've seen you walk just as unsteadily when you were quite well!" said Annie, dryly.

Harry snatched his arm from her, and fell into the nearest chair, flushing violently.

"Very well, ma'am; you call me a drunkard now! I shouldn't have thought any woman would have the heart to make fun of a sick husband; but you don't care for anything as long as you can laugh and scamper about the garden like a great tomboy with that infernal long-legged idiot William! You are enough to make any husband drink, just to forget you, you unfeeling little creature, you!"

"Come now, Harry, I don't think you can say it was I drove you to drink; and I think you would have forgotten me pretty quickly even without that assistance," said she, passing her hand soothingly down his arm and speaking in a caressing voice, the charm of which always told on him when she chose to use it. "You know very well that it will not require any more crimes on the part of your wicked wife, for instance, to induce you to undo all the progress you have made toward getting well during the last few days by sitting up to-night drinking with George and Wilfred."

"And what do you care if I do?"

"It is no affair of mine, of course, and I shall not annoy you and bring down a storm upon my own head by interfering. To borrow your own words, it would make no difference if I did."

"How do you know it wouldn't? Don't I always do what you wish?"

"I think the temptation to do what I don't wish will be stronger now you will have pleasanter company than a faded wife."

"Whoever called you 'faded'? I never did—you know I never did! And you know I like your company. I never knew you so pleasant before."

"Oh, you don't think me pleasant always!"

"No; because you say such nasty things—things you never used to dare to say when I was well. Now I'm ill, you think you can say anything, because I'm not strong enough yet to think of anything just as cutting to say back. But I'll pay you out when I get well again, clever as you are." He spoke in a rather irritated tone, but not ill-humoredly; she was so smiling, so careless, that he was as much amused as annoyed by her.

"I sha'n't give you a chance, because I have some very important business in London, and my duty as your nurse is over, and to-morrow I shall go to town."

"And when are you coming back?"—excitedly.

She did not answer.

"When do you mean to come back, I say?" he repeated, in a louder voice.

Still no answer. Harry clutched his wife's arm.

"Then I shall not let you go! You are not my nurse; you are my wife, and I forbid you to leave me again—do you hear? What is this business you speak of? What is it? I have a right to know—and I will know!"

Annie did not attempt to remove her arm from his grasp, but looked slowly up at him with a steady, cold, firm expression in her dark eyes, which silenced him even before she spoke:

"You have a right to know, and you shall know. I can't tell you all now, but just this. For four years, during which you never took the trouble to find out whether I was starving—and I was not so very far off that sometimes—I have been working to lay the foundation of a career for myself—an honorable career, I need not say, even to you. I have been put back a little, just as I was going to make a great stride forward, by coming to nurse you. I have fulfilled that duty now, and, now you are well, I am only wasting my time here. You must let me go. I will come back when you please, if I can, and I will let you know everything you wish. But my presence, now you are all going to be together again, would only irritate you—already it seems to be the cause of your quarreling with William. You will be disgusted again with my 'learned airs,' and with my preaching—for I shall not be able to keep myself from uttering useless remonstrances when I see you going on in your old way, as I know you will, and bringing back the fever, and making yourself ill again——"

"But, if I make myself ill again, you will have to nurse me."

"Indeed, you are mistaken!" answered Annie, raising her eyes to his with spirit. "If now, after being warned, you choose, rashly, to put your life in danger, and to undo all the good our constant watching and nursing have done you, I shall not consider myself bound to sacrifice myself any longer to a man who could be guilty of such foolish and selfish conduct, whether he is my husband or not."

"Then you would leave me to die while you went on enjoying your 'career,' as you call it?"

"I would leave you to take your chance."

Harry began to tremble all over, and the tears rose to his eyes. His hand relaxed its hold on Annie's arm, and fell down by his side.

Softened, frightened by the effect of her words, Annie clasped her little hands on his shoulder, and told him not to take her words so seriously, that she had spoken them only because she wanted him to take care of himself and get well fast.

"No, you don't—no, you don't! You want me to die, so that you may be free!" said he, in a hoarse, tremulous voice, keeping his head turned away from her.

Happily, his own emotion prevented his noticing the effect of his words on Annie, whose cheeks flushed suddenly, and whose tongue faltered as she was about to interrupt him. He continued:

"I see, I see! You want me to drink and kill myself, or ruin myself, so that you may go away and get praised for being a martyr! Go away—go away from me! I don't want your little soft hands about me, when all the while I know your heart is hard and you hate me!" said he, shaking her off, vehemently.

Annie rose slowly, and walked with downcast head toward the door. But she had not shut it behind her before her husband's voice called her back.

"Annie, Annie—come here—only one minute! I want to speak to you!"

She returned, and stood, with her eyes still down, very meekly before him.

"Annie," said he, stretching forward to take her hand and draw her toward him, "I didn't mean what I said just now. I was only in fun—at least I didn't think what I was saying. I—I wanted to see if you would believe me. I know you don't want me to die; and look here—if you will promise not to go away yet I won't sit up with George, and I will drink only just what you let me, and I'll do just what you tell me—till I get well."

Annie shook her head.

"I will—I swear it! Now you will stay, won't you? Here—give me your other hand. There! I swear to do just what you tell me—till I get well. Now promise not to go to London. No—you swear, too," said he, eagerly.

"I promise——"

"No, swear."

"I swear not to go to London till you are quite well, if you don't do anything rash. There—I hear the dog-cart. Harry, I must go to the door to meet him."

"Meet who?"

"George, of course."

"Confound George!"

But Annie was already out of the room.

She was flushed with the excitement of the successful battle she had just had with her husband, and with the other excitement of meeting her eldest brother-in-law, and George showed nothing but pleasure at sight of her. They came into the drawing-room talking brightly, and the baronet scarcely exchanged more than a couple of sentences and a hand-shake with his surly brother, so pleased was he to find a pleasant woman again in his house.

When Wilfred arrived, just before dinner, he in his turn engrossed her completely; and at dinner these two new-comers took up so much of her attention that the convalescent Harry, who was at dinner with the rest for the first time since his illness, began to look very black, and to find fault with everything which was put before him.

"I can't eat that. How am I to hack at it with only one hand?" he growled, when the servant offered him some mutton.

"Shall I cut it up for you, sir?"

"No, I won't have it; I don't want anything at all!" said he, looking with a frown at his wife, who turned from George to tell the servant to bring the plate to her, and dutifully cut up the mutton, which her sulky husband, without thanks, then condescended to eat.

Annie had put on a very pretty pale gray silk gown with elbow-sleeves and square-cut bodice edged with dainty lace, and a long spray of pink azalea fastened carelessly on one side of the neck. She was delighted at the pleasure they all—except her morose husband, who tried hard not to laugh when his brothers did at any speech of hers that amused them—evidently took in her society; and she smiled and laughed and chattered and looked so charming that not one of the men could keep his eyes off her for more than a few moments at a time.

"Have you seen anything of the Mainwarings, Annie?" asked George, when dinner was nearly over.

"Oh, yes! I met Mrs. Mainwaring the other day with a volume of 'The Band of Hope Review'—I don't know whether you have heard of it—under one arm. She said she thought of coming to read to Harry, if he would like it, to cheer him up."

Something in Annie's demure tone set them all laughing.

"I said he would be delighted; but we didn't think too much excitement was good for him just at first. And she asked if Sir George had any good books in his library, and I said, 'Oh, yes!' and she said I ought to read some to him. I said I thought I ought, and I came back and read him the *Sporting Dramatic News* all through."

"Oh, Annie, she wouldn't have you back in her schoolroom now!"

"No, indeed she would not!" answered Annie promptly.

When she rose to leave the gentlemen, there was a little anxiety in her manner as she glanced toward her husband. He was sitting with his eyes fixed doggedly upon his plate, his face was already rather flushed, and his hand was round the stem of a glass of Burgundy. She knew how little weight a word from her was likely to have now; but it was her duty to try, and she did try. As she passed him, she put out her left hand, with its one ring—her wedding-ring, which decorum now forced her to wear—lightly on his shoulder, and, as he gave no sign, she bent down and slipped the slim white fingers gently up to his neck. He smelled the faint perfume of the azalea on her breast, heard her quickened breathing as he still hesitated.

"Do you remember?" she whispered softly.

He raised his eyes, sullenly still, to the little, pleading face. She was irresistible at that moment, with her smiling lips and her sparkling eyes, her head a little on one side in entreaty. There came a flash from his eyes; her womanly fascination had won from him what his promise would have failed to get. He got up, and, leaning on her slight shoulder, let her lead him out of the room.

Annie was so much pleased with this unexpected little triumph that her bright humor infected him now that he was alone with her; and, as she dragged the easiest chair before the drawing-room fire for him, she chattered on so that he had no time or inclination for the complaints he was going to make against his brother George's brutal indifference to his illness. He was much annoyed when, in a very short time, they heard the dining-room door open and the voices of the other three in the hall.

"Hang them all! They make so much noise. Annie, I think I'll go to bed; and I want you to come and read to me."

But George had heard the last words as he came in.

"No, no, Harry! Go to bed by all means, if you will; but you mustn't make a victim of Annie. You have had my Lady Sunbeam all to yourself for weeks; you must let her shed a few rays on the rest of us now."

Before Harry could make an angry reply, Annie broke in:

"Harry has no wish to deprive you of such a very simple pleasure; I will shed my rays upon you, as you poetically term it, by playing you the very few new pieces I have learned since you last heard me, George. And, Harry, you are feverish—you had better not stay up; I have nothing to play that you have not heard, and I will come up and read you to sleep by the time you are ready for me."

She rang the bell without giving him time to answer; and Harry, who was really too worn out to make much resistance, grumblingly went off with the servant, who lent a stout arm to his tottering master.

Annie went to the piano, and played one thing after another, and sung a French song which they only half understood, but which sent them into fits of laughter, until George, who was leaning on the instrument, grew more interested in the talk he was having with her than in the music; and, as her fingers, from idly playing, at last ceased altogether and lay on the keys, he said:

"Come into the conservatory. You love flowers, and there you will let me smoke, I know."

Annie shook her head reluctantly.

"I mustn't. I've promised Harry to read to him. He will be past being read to and do nothing but growl if I delay any longer," said she, with resignation, as she rose slowly and shut the piano.

"How you have managed to tame the bear, though!" said George, admiringly. "Of course gratitude or courtesy is out of the question with him; but I thought even submission was, until I saw him follow you out of the dining-room to-night. But then an archangel couldn't have resisted you as you looked at that moment," continued he, in a low voice, bending down to look into her eyes. "It was hard to see a look like that wasted upon such a clod."

"Do you think so?" said Annie, laughing lightly, as she went up-stairs and he followed her. "Why, that is only the old story! It is the 'clods' of the earth who get the benefit of all the beauty and grace and pleasant things in the world."

"You have grown cynical, Annie. Come in here for a few minutes and explain yourself."

He led the way into the dimly-lighted picture-gallery, where Annie and William had had their first game of battledoor and shuttlecock four and a half years before. She sunk down upon the cushioned ottoman to which George led her, and looked gravely at him as he seated himself beside her.

"It is very easy to explain," said she. "Do not all the people who spend their lives in the practice of any art, clever people generally, and capable of hard thinking as well as hard living, waste their efforts for the careless enjoyment of others who have not half their brains, or their courage, or their capacity? The rich *parvenu* who doesn't know a Rubens from a Rembrandt, patronizes the rising painter and delights afterward in the boast that he 'made that man, sir.' The wise man writes for fools to read. And the actress gives days of study to her share in a piece which the dressmaker in the pit condemns as 'very poor stuff.' It is always the same."

"You speak very bitterly."

"Yes. For you see I range myself on the side of the hard-working, capable ones. Don't you know how I have spent these last four years?"

"No, no; do tell me," said George, with a shrewd guess at her answer, bending lower over her in his interest.

"I have spent them on the stage."

"The stage!" echoed another voice.

They both started and looked round. Behind them, leaning against the wall, not far from the door, was Harry, in his dressing-gown, pale, heavy-eyed, sullen. He looked at his wife with fierce eyes and frowning brows.

"So you are an actress! I don't wonder you were ashamed to tell me how you passed your time."

"I was not ashamed, Harry," said Annie, calmly, rising and going toward him. "If you think I ought to be, you have only to say a word and you shall never be troubled with me again."

"You are in a great hurry for me to say that word, and, by Jove, for once I feel inclined to please you! An actress! No wonder I find you ready to listen to soft words from any man! No wonder the words from me which used to set you blushing for pleasure can't touch you now! You are just a thing for everybody to look at—not a wife for me! Go away; I would rather fall than that you should touch me!"

He was tottering, and his forehead was wet with weakness and passion. He would not take George's help, but staggered along by the wall to the door. There the housekeeper met him, and Annie, standing still in the middle of the picture-gallery, heard him say:

"Brandy, for Heaven's sake, brandy, whether it is poison to me or not!"

CHAPTER XVII.

Annie turned with a piteous expression of face to George when her angry husband had left them.

"What can one do with a man like that?" she said. "It is impossible to reason with him, impossible to understand him. He is like an overgrown child."

"I don't know about that," answered George, quietly. "I think I can understand this last outbreak pretty well."

"What do you mean?"

"Why, when you left him, you were a little timid lily, whose charm was quite lost upon a great senseless brute like that," said George, with sentiment; "now you have come back a———"

"A great flaunting dahlia, whose charm must be apparent to the meanest observation, and particularly to a person of my husband's tastes!" finished Annie, looking up at him very gravely.

His sentiment was dispelled; he was obliged to burst out laughing.

"You are too sharp for me. You know very well I did not mean that. You are a charming woman who can hold your own in any society; you have caused quite a flutter among us poor rustics; and Harry, finding himself the possessor of something everybody else admires, with dog-in-the-manger instincts, wishes to keep all to himself the treasure whose value he himself would never have discovered and is quite unable to appreciate."

"You are too severe upon poor Harry. He has a lot of good qualities—you know I always said so; only—unfortunately they are qualities which don't harmonize very well with mine."

"Nor with anybody else's. It is unfortunate, certainly. He would be charming on a desert island."

"I really think he would be happier there," said Annie, with a sigh, "if he had a horse and some dogs. He is kind to animals, and they seem to understand him. Good-night, George; I must go to him now. And the chances are even whether he will try to hit me if I go near him, or insist on my remaining in the room till he goes to sleep."

She shook hands, and left the baronet gazing admiringly at her little figure, as she disappeared swiftly and silently down the corridor toward the room her husband occupied. She tapped at the door; but, getting no answer and hearing no sound, she opened it and went in. Harry was lying on the bed in his dressing-gown, and her first thought was that he was not sober. But when she opened the door to Mrs. Stanley a minute after, and saw that that dignified lady held a spirit-decanter in her hand, she whispered:

"Take that away, please. He has gone to sleep, I think."

"That is all right. I was as long as I could be, and I brought it myself, in hopes that you would be here when I came back."

The housekeeper went away, and Annie, fearful he might take cold, drew a rug softly over her sleeping husband. The touch roused him; he turned over toward her, and, just half opening his eyes, threw his right arm round her neck as she was bending down, and instantly dozed off again, tired out. The action moved Annie, and she knelt down beside the bed, careful not to disturb him by displacing the arm that held her in an unconscious caress until his next movement, when she woke him up, told him to go to bed, and left him before he had time to remember his anger against her and spoil the effect of that half-unconscious embrace.

But the next morning he was in a gentle mood, and did not allude to her distasteful career when she brought him his breakfast. This good-humor lasted until he went down-stairs, and, after looking in the various rooms, found his wife in the library with William, having tracked them by their voices and laughter.

William, with great tact, instantly assumed an appearance of preternatural solemnity on his brother's entrance.

"What is all this mystery? What are you doing in here?" asked Harry, crossly.

"I am helping William with his studies," said Annie.

Upon this her promising pupil grew blue with suppressed laughter, and Harry's manner got more and more unpleasant.

"Oh, I should have thought you had had enough of schoolroom work! However, since you haven't, and I'm not too proud to take a lesson, you shall give me one, too," and he flung himself into a chair with an uncompromising surliness which was not encouraging to a teacher.

Taking no further notice of him, Annie proceeded with her dictation.

"Lorsque Telemaque et ses compagnons—virgule——"

"Oh, confound your French!" growled Harry.

And William burst into a roar of laughter; while Annie, seeing that her amiable husband had started up with evil intentions toward her pupil, made signs to the latter to leave the room, which he did, exploding again as soon as he got outside the door.

"Why do you encourage that donkey to take up your time?" asked Harry, when he had exhausted all the offensive epithets at his command on his youngest brother.

"I am very fond of William," said Annie, quietly. "It was I who first encouraged him to study; and now it is a great pleasure to me to help him."

"A fine lot of study you get through, I have no doubt! You were studying very hard when I came in, weren't you?"

"Now look here, Harry; you are absurdly unreasonable," said Annie, wearily. "Of course William and I don't sulk through a long morning's work, as if I were a snuffy old professor of fifty who didn't care a straw about his pupil except as a mere learning-machine. I couldn't care for William more if he were really my brother. You never used to complain when he and I were out in the fields and woods together all day long. He was my constant companion when I was very miserable and lonely; and am I to snub and sit upon him, now that he has taken to reading so that he may be more of a companion to me than ever?"

"What do you want with his companionship? I can't think what you can see in a great, clumsy gawk like that. He isn't even clever."

"He is good-tempered, and—he is fond of me."

"Much you care about anybody's being fond of you! You are the coldest woman I ever saw, and all your pretty—I mean all your affected little ways are just acting. Yes, that is what they are—just acting!" repeated Harry, as if struck by a happy idea.

"Very well, Harry. Then why don't you let me go and act on the stage, where I shall get applauded instead of worried about it?"

"Because I don't choose to let you go," said he doggedly. "And I don't choose to see myself slighted and treated as if I were nobody at all, just for that great ignorant, ill-mannered boy. And I won't allow any more of these humbugging lessons—do you hear?"

"I hear you certainly," answered Annie softly.

"That means that you won't obey me, I suppose?" She did not reply.

"Very well then; I sha'n't say any more," said Harry, shaking with passion; "but, when I find him again grinning at you over his copy-book and swaggering about with his French, I shall just pitch his books and his tomfoolery into the fire and punch his head for him."

"That will be very wise," remarked Annie gravely. "And, if you were only to treat in the same way every other person who can talk to me on subjects that interest me and who does not grumble at me from morning till night, I am sure I should become a much better wife and a much more entertaining companion for yourself." She had risen and walked toward the door.

"Where are you going?" asked Harry sharply.

"To meet Lilian at the station. You know she is coming to-day, and Stephen with her."

He let her go without further comment; but, when she came down-stairs again, ready to start, she found him in the hall playing with a hunting-crop.

"I say, Annie, are you going to the library at Beckham?"

"Yes."

"Will you get some books for me?"

"For you!" said his wife, in amazement.

"Yes, for me"—very irritably.

"Oh, yes, certainly! What books shall I get?"

"Oh, anything you like!"—and, without looking at her, he marched off into the billiard-room.

"I hope there is nothing the matter with his head," thought Annie, anxiously, as she got into the carriage.

Annie went to the station to meet her sister-in-law, without any of the nervousness she had once felt before an interview with that imperious beauty. If Lilian should resent the change in her position at the Grange, Annie was quite ready to go, and was rather hoping that Mrs. Falconer's arrival might pave the way for her own departure. She bought the *Era* on her entrance into the station, and, having some minutes to wait before the train from London was due, went into the waiting-room, cut the leaves of the paper roughly with a pencil she happened to have in her pocket, and glanced through the pages eagerly. She found what she wanted—a notice of a morning performance in which she knew that Aubrey Cooke was to play a part; and, with flushed cheeks and beating heart, she read that he had made the chief success in the piece, in a character so well played that the critic pronounced him "the coming comedian." Annie knew that this sentence was one she had heard before of other young actors who never came to anything in particular. But her pleasure in reading this testimony to his talent was none the less great, and with trembling fingers, she almost involuntarily drew a shaky line with her pencil down that part of the notice which referred to him.

She was looking brilliant when she met Lilian, who complimented her on her appearance, and said she had heard from her brothers that she would now have to subside meekly into the second place, since Annie had grown into such a charming woman.

"But you might have let me know you were on the stage," said Lilian, with good-humored reproach. "I find now that I know several of the actors who were with you at the Regency. And only think! I went there one night when you were playing in the piece, and never recognized you."

"I recognized you, though."

"Did you? Can you see people you know among the audience when you are acting?"

"Oh, yes! And I saw Colonel Richardson."

"Most people can see him when you are about," broke in Stephen, who had come from town with his cousin, but had sat silent in the carriage until now.

This was a bolder speech than he would have ventured to make in the old times to Lilian, Annie thought. She noted that the cripple had grown much older-looking; his face, which had once been handsome, was thin and wasted, and he looked sullen and discontented.

Lilian took no notice of his remark, and asked Annie if she had seen many of the people of the neighborhood since she had been at the Grange.

"Yes, most of them have called, to my surprise, since William let out to old Mrs. Knowles that I had been on the stage. She and her niece made a tentative call, and I suppose the rumor spread that I did not bite, so everybody came and praised my wifely devotion, which I certainly did not deserve."

Lilian laughed.

"Harry ill must be a great trial, though."

"He is rather; he has such strange freaks."

"Husbands always have, dear. Only fancy—my husband wanted to prevent my coming to the Grange!"

"Really? For what reason?"

"Oh, he disapproves of my brothers, or some such nonsense!" said Lilian lightly.

But Stephen raised his eyes to his cousin's face with a penetrating look which Annie noted and remembered.

Dinner that night was a banquet of rejoicing. The two ladies were both, in different ways, among the most charming women of the day. Lilian was very handsomely dressed in dark red velvet, which showed off her fair, queenly beauty well; Annie, in maize-colored silk, with soft folds of Indian muslin about the throat, looked like a little fairy. The style of each was so different from that of the other that their attractions did not clash, and Annie's quiet, simple manner of saying amusing things was the best contrast possible to Lilian's laughing impertinences.

Lilian was very anxious to know at once all about her sister-in-law's stage-experiences, and was seized with a strong desire to become an actress herself.

"Don't you find people off the stage very dull after the nice, amusing people you meet in the theater?" she asked at dinner.

"Oh, no! Some stage-people are dreadful bores, and many are coarse and many commonplace. They are not all alike, you know, any more than people off the stage."

"But all the actors I have ever met have been so bright and amusing. I know two who were at the Regency, where you acted—Mr. Gibson and Mr. Cooke."

"Oh, yes; I heard them say they knew you!"

"Don't you like them? Are they nice in the theater? They are two of the best-bred men I have ever known."

"They are very nice men, indeed, and very clever actors; I like them both immensely."

"And Mr. Gibson is so handsome, and does not seem to know it. But he must, for I should think all the women in the theater must be in love with him. Were you not a little in love with him?"

"In love with a beggarly cad of an actor?" shouted Harry, scandalized.

"You don't know what you are talking about!" said his sister, coolly. "Of course your manners are not those of Mr. Gibson; they are those of his valet. Didn't you think him very handsome, Annie?"

"Yes, very. And he has such a sweet voice."

Her husband's voice, for the moment not at all sweet, uttered a growling protest.

"And Mr. Cooke? He is not handsome, but he is charming. Don't you like him? Oh, I know you must, for I saw that you had marked his name in a critique in your paper!"

Annie blushed as she answered that he was very nice, too, and very clever; she had an uneasy feeling that her husband was glaring at her across the table and noting her change of color.

During the few minutes which remained of the ladies' stay in the dining-room, Harry never took his eyes off his wife's face; and she was conscious of this, though she did not once look at him.

In the drawing-room Lilian was quite affectionate.

"You were always a good little girl; but I had no idea you would bloom into such a clever woman," said she, with her white hands on the shoulders of the smaller woman.

"How—clever?" asked Annie, laughing.

"Why, at keeping your own counsel! But you may trust me. There is always some one nicer than one's husband, and when one's husband is Harry! I think your discretion does you great credit. As soon as I heard you were on the stage, I tried to find out who it was that had induced you to go on, or to remain on; and you had been so very discreet that nobody could link your name with any other. And it was not until I mentioned those two names at dinner that I found you out. And nobody could have seen you wince but me. I am very clear-sighted in these matters."

"Indeed!" said Annie, calmly. "And may I know which of my fellow-actors I am dying for love of?"

"I did not say that. I know your conduct is circumspection itself. But I know which of these two gentlemen is—nicer than Harry."

"Oh, you might put them both together and bracket a good many more with them under that heading!" said Annie.

"I dare say. But you need not look so ostentatiously indifferent. I should think it must be impossible to know Mr. Gibson well without admiring him."

"Well, that is true, certainly," assented Annie, not giving the least sign of the relief she felt at hearing Lilian utter the wrong name.

She did not in the least mind that her sister-in-law should imagine her to have a preference for Mr. Gibson; but she would not for worlds have it suspected that she could have the faintest warmth of feeling for—Mr. Cooke.

When the gentlemen came into the drawing-room, Harry was not among them, and William said he had gone up-stairs to his room. A few minutes later a servant came in to Annie, asking if she would go to Mr. Harold, who had sent word to say that he was ill and wanted her particularly. She went at once, and judged, as soon as she entered his room, that his ailment concerned his temper more than his health.

"You sent for me, Harry? What is the matter? Don't you feel well?" she asked kindly.

In answer, he suddenly produced the *Era* from the side of his chair, and brought his fist down with a thump upon the unfortunate pencil-mark by Aubrey Cooke's name.

"Who is this man Cooke?" he asked savagely.

Annie glanced carelessly down at the paper, and said:

"Mr. Aubrey Cooke? Oh, he is one of the actors whom I knew at the Regency—one of the very actors Lilian was speaking of at dinner!"

"Yes, I know that very well; and you need not pretend to be so mightily indifferent, because I know more than that," he said, with an affectation of penetration through which Annie easily read anxiety and curiosity.

"Do you?" said she, smiling. "Then, if you know so much you must know that this curious jealousy you have been cultivating lately was never more out of place than in the case of the men I have acted with. And, if you don't know as much as you pretend, ask Lilian."

Harry looked at her searchingly for a few minutes, and then dropped the paper, disarmed.

She was looking so pretty in the light evening dress, with her graceful head crowned with the coils and curls of her shining brown hair, that he would have liked to drop his offended dignity and draw her into his arms and kiss her. But the unconscious Annie had another blow to inflict. She held in her arms a pile of books, and, when his face relaxed a little after her reassuring answer, she took one up in her hand.

"I have brought you some books from Beckham, as you asked me to do," she said. "And you don't know what trouble I had in finding anything I thought you would like. I turned over half the books on the shelves, I think. Here is 'Sponge's Sporting Tour,' and 'How I Became an M. F. H.,' and a book about horses, and——"

She handed him a volume with her eyes still bent upon the others as she read their titles. But she looked up startled, as he snatched it from her and flung it with all his force against the opposite wall.

"Harry!" she exclaimed, amazed at the fury in his face. "What have I done now? It is impossible to please you!"

"Yes, because you don't care—you don't try. I am just an ignorant boor, to be fed and clothed, and smoothed into good temper when I am growing dangerous, and to be slighted and told lies to when I protest against such treatment. You see I know all about it, though I am such a clod!"

She had walked to the other end of the room, picked up the book without any show of annoyance, and was trying to restore an unruffled appearance to the crumpled leaves. This action exasperated him still more.

"There now—it doesn't matter what I do, because it's only Harry! Very well then! There—and there—and there—and there!"

At each repetition of the word he flung another of the volumes she had incautiously placed within his reach, not at his wife, but at the wall by which she was standing.

"Really, Harry, you ought to be in a lunatic asylum!" said Annie, out of patience at last.

"So I shall be very soon, if you go on treating me like a child, when I love you like a man!" burst out Harry, passionately.

His wife looked up at him, from where she was standing at the other side of the room, in astonishment.

"Yes, yes—stare at me as much as you like; I do love you, and I'm not the fool you think me, except in caring for you! Do you think I don't know that you look down upon me, and that everybody thinks you thrown away upon me? Why, I knew that in the old days when I first married you; but then you just avoided me, and I didn't care. But now you come back, pretty and bright and charming, not cold and shy as you used to do, you flutter about me and nurse me and coax me into good-humor, and make me laugh and get me to do everything you wish; and then, when I want to show you I love you for it, you shut me off with a little laugh, just to show me that I am only Harry, and whatever I say and whatever I do doesn't matter. I say it is cruel, wicked, and, however good and clever you may be, you are treating me badly!" he ended, his voice breaking down.

"Harry!" was all his astonished wife could utter.

"I know I'm not a companion for you," he went on, "but you don't want me to be, you won't understand that I want to be. I asked you to get me some books; but I wanted books that you liked, so that I might read them and talk to you about them, like William and George. And then you bring me a lot of sporting trash, as if I wasn't fit for anything but the stable!"

"Harry!" whispered his wife again, making a step toward him.

He looked up at her eagerly, waiting for her to come to him. But she stopped.

"Well, are you afraid of me?" said he.

His tone was not inviting; but Annie understood him this time, knelt down by his chair, and let him put his arm round her.

"Annie, will you try to love me?" he asked, huskily.

"Yes, Harry, I will try."

CHAPTER XVIII.

Annie left her husband's room that night, after his most unexpected declaration of love and her own promise to try to return it, in a state of bewilderment in which thought was for a long time impossible. That his affection for her was anything more than a passing caprice, the result partly of jealousy of his brothers, and partly of pique at her own indifference, she did not for a moment believe. If her heart had been quite free, she might have been less skeptical, or more clearly touched by this acknowledgment of the strength of the influence she had gained over her rough and hitherto careless young husband. But she knew how deep lay the difference between his nature and her own, and since the first weeks of her marriage she had given up all hope of their ever harmonizing with each other except in the most superficial manner. Through his passionate words she had seemed, in spite of herself, to hear the ring of another voice, and she felt, with a thrill of shame, that no words of the man she had sworn to love could wake in her an emotion so strong as that she had felt at the few faltering words in which Aubrey Cooke had confessed that he loved her.

And Aubrey Cooke was out in the world working hard, as she felt, to win position and money, to make himself a name, to rise to the heights of the ambition she had encouraged; and perhaps even yet, in spite of her discouraging words to him, he was nursing the vain belief that she would some day be his, and longing for the time when they should wander out together again, and have more long talks, in which the words of each seemed but to express the unuttered thought of the other; while Harry, her husband, would remain an ignorant idler to the end of his life, ill-tempered, arrogant, unsympathetic to her, as if he had been an inhabitant of another world. And this man she had promised to try to love, with the honest, solemn intention of keeping her word to the best of her power! But she confessed to herself, with a shudder at the thought of the self-sacrifice she would have to make if his caprice were to last and she were to have to put off indefinitely her return to the stage, that she had an uphill task before her.

The next morning she met her husband in the expectation of finding him as ungracious as usual. But Harry had apparently been thinking out the position, and come to the conclusion that the effort must not be all on his wife's side. At any rate, he was gentle and considerate, and asked her if she would drive him out, in a courteous tone which seemed to admit the possibility of a refusal.

It was the first day that he had been out of doors since his illness, and he was very good-tempered and happy, sitting wrapped up in rugs by his wife's side in Lady Braithwaite's pony-carriage; and, after that trial of it, the daily drive became an institution. Annie found that the explanation they had at the time of that little episode of the sporting-books had had the satisfactory result of making Harry more docile than ever; and when, in the country lanes through which they drove for miles each day over the frost-bound earth, she started him on some favorite topic of his, such as the training of race-horses or the advantages of a straight saddle, she found that she could continue her own train of thought almost undisturbed, by the help of a nod of approval every now and then; and she found him quite an endurable companion.

But unfortunately Harry was not so stupid as he was ignorant, and one day, when Annie had given a pleasant smile of approbation of what he was saying without having listened to it, he suddenly stopped short in the middle of a sentence, and, looking round at him in surprise, his wife found that he was sulking.

"Go on, Harry; that is very interesting," said she innocently.

"No, it isn't; you don't know what I was talking about," he returned sullenly.

"Yes, I do, Harry. You were talking about—horses," said she, with what she thought a safe guess.

But her husband looked blacker than ever.

"I wasn't talking about horses, as it happens. It shows how much you care what I say. I'm much obliged to you for letting me see that I bore you. Stop! I'll get out;" and he tossed off his rugs.

"No, no, don't, dear Harry! Let me drive you home. It is only a little way; but it is too far for you to walk yet. I'm very, very sorry I was so inattentive; but the fact is I—I have something on my mind that is troubling me; and so———"

"Have you, Annie?" he asked anxiously. "What is it?" Then, noticing the expression of his wife's face, his manner changed, and he cried roughly, "It is a lie! It is an infernal excuse! Stop, I tell you, or I'll jump out without your stopping! Now I'll be hanged if I let you drive me out any more! You are just a little hypocrite, pretending to listen and be so sweet, when all the time you don't care what I say if I talk myself hoarse. Go and talk your learned jargon with George, and William, and—the deuce, if you like! I'm going to Joe Green's, the blacksmith."

She had stopped, seeing it was of no use to try to argue with him in this mood, and that to disobey him would only be to see him break his neck before her eyes. And she drove home full of remorse, after watching him vault over a gate to take a short cut to the village, and making one more effort to stop him by a piteous cry of "Harry!" of which he took no notice.

To the blacksmith's—where Susan Green lived! This, then, was the end of his revived affection for herself, that the very first walk he took led him straight back to the vulgar charms of the blacksmith's daughter.

It was a bitter, unpleasant thought, even for a wife not sufficiently fond of her husband to be jealous. It was a humiliation which brought up in her mind the image of the one man who thought her charms superior to those of any other woman. She did not feel jealous, but insulted by the rude speech of her husband, who, after she had used every care, every charm at her command to fulfill her duty to him in sickness and in convalescence, rewarded her with a coarse taunt and an openly expressed intention of leaving her for the society of a girl of low birth and not unspotted name.

She drove home, and, as soon as she had taken off her hat and mantle, went into the library, where, in spite of Harry's rough prohibition, she still continued to give William lessons in French. Dusk was coming on; but it was light enough for her to see the figure bending over a book in a low chair near the window. She crossed the room and put her hand on his shoulder.

"William, how wrong of you to try your eyes like that."

He looked up. It was not William, but Harry.

"You, Harry?" murmured his wife, in astonishment.

"Yes, me—Harry. I may try my eyes as much as I like, mayn't I?"

She took the book gently from his hand. It was "Sartor Resartus."

"You have not been reading this?" she gasped.

"Yes, I have. I saw it lying on the table with your book-marker in it, so I took it up to see what it was like; and I've read six pages, but I'll be hanged if I can make head or tail of it!"

"Nor can I," said Annie.

"Well, what do you read it for then?"

She hesitated.

"It was written by a great man, a 'mighty thinker,' and I like to try to find out what he means."

"Well, I think it is a very dull amusement. Thomas Carlyle"—looking at the title page. "Mighty thinker, you say. I've heard of a mighty hunter——"

"Oh, you are thinking of Nimrod! It's not the same person," said Annie.

"You are laughing at me! Very well!"

"Yes, I am," said Annie, smiling, and putting her arms affectionately round his neck. "But I think, if I didn't laugh, I should cry—I feel very much touched by finding you—finding you here trying to read my dull books when I was feeling very angry with you for running away from me as you did."

Harry rubbed his curly head against her responsively without saying anything for a minute. Then he looked up searchingly into her face.

"Annie, I want to ask you something. Just now Ste—some one told me they had seen Colonel Richardson in Beckham several times during the last few days, and had seen you talking to him."

"Well?"

"Well!"—sharply. "And why didn't you say anything about it?"

"There was nothing to say. I met Colonel Richardson, I spoke to him, and that was all. What is there strange in that?"

"Oh, nothing, of course!" He paused for a moment and looked away from her. Then he burst out, but as if to himself: "It was Colonel Richardson who came dangling after you four years ago. You always liked him."

"Harry, don't be so absurd as to be jealous of Colonel Richardson! Indeed you have never had the slightest cause to be so."

"How can I be sure of that?" said he, turning upon her suddenly. "One thing I am certain of—that is, that, during these four years that you have been away from me, you have met somebody you liked better than me. I don't say it was unnatural—I don't say I'm surprised; but I say that I know I'm right, and I'll find out who it is, as sure as I'm your husband! You say I've no need to be jealous of any actor—and I don't myself think you would lower yourself as far as that——"

"You forget that I'm an actress," said Annie, composedly.

"Were an actress; but you're not one now," answered he, hastily. "Well, if you never cared for any actor, why not for Colonel Richardson? He is handsome, and knows how to talk to you about the things you like."

"But I have told you already that I never cared for Colonel Richardson: and your persistent jealousy is an insult to me when I tell you it has no foundation. He belongs to a type of man which has no attraction for me."

"What type's that?"

"He is an idler; and I have worked too long and too hard myself not to despise idleness in a man."

Harry gave a grunt of disapproval.

"I suppose you call me an idler."

"Well, I don't think you are much else," said she, smiling.

"It seems to me, Annie, you expect a precious deal too much of a man," he grumbled presently, in an injured tone. "To please you he must slave like a nigger, whether he has any need to work or not, and read himself blind over the dullest trash that ever was printed, and never talk about anything he himself likes, but chatter by the yard about things that haven't the least interest, and beam all over with smiles when he is annoyed."

Annie laughed.

"I don't think I ever expected all that of anybody, and certainly not of you, Harry."

And weary of this useless discussion, she left the room as Stephen entered it. The friendship between her and the cripple had never been great, and he was now rather jealous of her position in the household, which had become stronger than that of his adored Lilian, with whom, however, he had begun of late to have serious quarrels. Harry had let slip the fact that it was Stephen who had informed him of Colonel Richardson's presence in Beckham, which had so needlessly excited his jealousy. Annie wondered what his object could have been.

When she left them together, Harry jumped up from his chair and faced his cousin.

"What do you come tormenting me for with your humbugging stories about Annie and Richardson? She doesn't care a straw for the fellow!"

"Doesn't she? Oh, that's all right!" said Stephen, meaningly.

"No; she only spoke to him out of civility," said Harry, raising his voice, but looking anxiously at the other. "Here—what do you mean with your confounded shrugs and squirms? Look me straight in the face, and say out what you mean?"

The cripple was trembling and his face paling, but not with fear of his companion. He hesitated for one moment, then said, in a hurried low voice, as if the words were wrenched from him against his will:

"Very well; don't mind what I say. Of course I am warning you only for fun, for my own amusement. First go and tell her what nonsense I've been talking, and then—then let her meet Colonel Richardson at the lower gate at eleven to-night, and, take my word for it, you won't be troubled with your wife any more."

"Liar!" hissed out Harry.

"Oh, it is only my fun, of course," sneered the cripple.

Harry stood for a moment leaning heavily on the table. His first instinct was to seize his cousin by the collar and confront him with Annie; but the next moment a terrible fear that this was the truth that he was hearing seized him, and a sudden desperate resolve stopped his hand and restored him to an appearance of calmness.

The hideous story seemed to him in his excited state only too likely. This would explain her anxiety to get away, her comparative coldness toward himself, and would justify the suspicions he had, not of her purity, but of her faith.

"I hate her, I hate her," he said to himself, as he dashed away from Stephen, out of the library, and flung himself down upon a seat in the empty billiard-room, with his head in his hands. "I thought I did, and now I know it. The little, deceitful, heartless vixen! I'll just take a leaf out of her own book, and see if I can't be loving while I mean all the time to make her suffer. You despise me, do you, my lady? I'm a clod, am I? We'll see to-night if we can't turn the tables for once. You thought you could turn me round your little finger, I'll warrant, and laughed at me, and thought me a boor and a silly fool to be fond of you. But you are mistaken, my fine lady! I hate you, I loathe you, and I'll prove it to you to-night!"

But one thing in his programme it was beyond Harry's strength to carry out. He could not act; and, when he met his wife just before dinner, and would fain have concealed, under soft words and caressing manners, the passionate indignation which was raging in him, he was obliged to turn away from her brusquely after the very first words. She noticed his agitation; but it was as impossible as it was unnecessary to fathom all her husband's caprices, and her own manner then and at dinner was exactly the same as usual. Stephen watched him as he glared at his wife; and, when dinner was over, he fastened himself on to Annie to prevent a conversation between her husband and her. This was not difficult; for Harry, for the first time during his wife's stay at the Grange, had disregarded all her entreating looks, and excited himself so much with wine that she kept carefully out of his way when the gentlemen came into the drawing-room.

Except for that incident and Harry's consequent sullenness, the evening passed off as usual, until, at half-past ten, Annie and Lilian retired for the night. Then Harry, instead of joining his brothers in the billiard-room, sprung up from the corner where he had been sulking and watching for the last hour, snatched up a hat in the hall, and, without waiting to put on his overcoat, slipped out, without being seen by any one, into the garden. It was a snowy February night, and he shivered as, hot with wine and mad excitement, he first stepped into the keen air; but he strode down over the lawn toward the bottom of the garden, reckless as to the effects of the cold and wet on his not yet robust frame. He reached the lower gate; but, to his intense relief, there was no one there, no sound to be heard. He waited a few minutes, and a deep sense of joy, followed by the determination to transfer his revenge on to Stephen, who had played this trick upon him, had risen in his breast, when he heard the faint sound of wheels and hoofs over the soft snow, and saw through the falling flakes a close carriage coming slowly up from the direction of Beckham. It stopped at the gate. Harry held his breath; the carriage door opened, and a man in a thick great-coat stepped down into the snow. It was Colonel Richardson.

Harry, who, on the approach of the carriage, had crept in among the leafless snow-covered trees and the tall evergreens of the shrubbery, uttered no sound; but his right hand went swiftly to his coat-pocket and drew out a revolver, which he thrust into the breast of his coat without again relaxing his hold of it.

Colonel Richardson walked up and down in the snow in front of the gate, stopping after every few steps to listen, and to shake the thick flakes off his coat impatiently. He never came very near to the motionless figure among the trees, for there were a low wall and a thick growth of laurel and rhododendron bushes between them. And the spot Harry had chosen for his station was on the lower side of the gate, while any one coming from the house would come down to the upper side, so that Colonel Richardson, peering anxiously in impatient expectation through the branches, never once glanced in his direction.

When, in a low voice, he gave the coachman some direction, and the carriage went on a little way, and then turned slowly round, Harry recognized it as a hired carriage from a livery stable in Beckham. His hand still round his revolver, he was on the alert for the next movement; but the carriage, having turned so that the horses' heads were toward Beckham, stopped again before the gate.

Time went slowly by for both men, the watcher and the watched; while the latter stamped the snow from his boots, strode up and down, and showed ever-increasing impatience, the former remained as still as ever at his post among the laurels. He did not feel the keen wind, or the falling snow, or the cold of the damp, white mass beneath his feet, which was striking into his frame and chilling him to the bone.

For almost the first time in his life thought had got hold of him, and was torturing him with sharp pangs which deadened the sense of bodily discomfort within him. His hatred of the man who stood there, unconscious of his presence, and the deadly errand which brought him, blazed as fiercely as ever; but his anger against his wife was dying away, and giving place to pity for the beautiful little creature who had so rashly given her happiness into his keeping four years and a half ago, to be punished for her rashness by his brutal neglect and indifference.

"Yet I meant to be kind to her. I did not want to be cruel. Am I such a brute that I can't help it? I have tried to be gentle with her lately, and she likes me no better. She comes back to tantalize me into loving her as I never thought I could love any woman, and then runs away with this blackguard, who would just throw her over when——Good heavens! No! Even he couldn't desert her!"

His lip quivered, and there came a choking feeling in his throat.

"Thank Heaven I'm in time to stop her! She'll have to stay with me now; but she will find a way of making it more a punishment for me than for her, I expect. What an ass I am to care about her—I mean, to have cared about her! I'll just show her the difference now. She shall see if it wasn't better to have a churlish husband for a slave than for a master. She despised me, did she, and thought me a fool for letting her do what she liked with me? Yes, that is the way with women. Well, now it is her turn to do what I like; and I sha'n't be so soft about it either. I'll just——Confound her, I've a good mind to let her go off with him, and snap my fingers at her and be rid of her! Ay, and I would, too, only she is my wife, worse luck, and I must do for my honor what I wouldn't do for her. No, that I wouldn't! Oh, good Heaven, will she never love me? I'm not good enough for her; but I'm not such a cur as that fellow!"

As the minutes dragged on, a hope began to rise within him that she was not coming, after all, while he could see, to his joy, that the anxiety of the man he was watching had grown keener. Still they heard no sound, though they listened intently, the one in hope, the other in deadliest fear.

At last Harry saw Colonel Richardson turn his head quickly, as if his ear had caught some expected sound; then he laid his hand upon the latch of the gate. Still Harry heard nothing.

But a minute later, through the falling snow, he saw above him, swiftly approaching down the soft, white track of the pathway, a woman's figure; and with a silent curse and a heart heavy within him, his eyes turned quickly to the man who was stealing his treasure. Colonel Richardson had raised the latch of the gate, opened it, and stood inside, waiting. Harry's anger blazed up with fresh intensity.

"I'll shoot him like a dog!" thought he.

And he stepped out from the shrubbery on to the pathway, drew out his revolver, and covered the other man with it as steadily as he had ever aimed at a partridge. Then he stood still, waiting for the other to turn and see him. But Colonel Richardson's attention was fixed on the rapidly approaching figure. Harry would not look at her. It was not until the two had met that his eyes, in watching the man, fell upon the woman also.

"I could not get away before; the boys were all over the house," she was whispering, deprecatingly.

His hand with the revolver dropped to his side as he sprung forward and in a few strides reached them and dragged her away.

"Lilian!"

At twenty minutes to twelve that night Annie was roused from sleep by knocking at her door.

"What is it?" she cried, sleepily.

But the answer startled her into wakefulness.

"Annie, Annie, open the door, for Heaven's sake!"

It was her husband's voice, but hoarse, feeble, and broken.

For one instant she paused. But there came another faltering knock, and Harry's voice again, more feebly still, called:

"Annie, Annie, let me in; I am dying!"

She flew to the door, unlocked and opened it; and Harry, his coat wet with half-melted snow and covered with blood, staggered forward into her arms.

CHAPTER XIX.

"Let me stay here! Don't send me away!" were Harry's first words, as his wife led him to a chair and supported his head against her breast.

"Yes, yes, you shall stay. Oh, Harry, what have you done? You are drenched to the skin and cold as ice! Where are you hurt? Is it only here?"

She touched his forehead, from a cut in which the blood was still flowing.

"That is all—I think," said he, drowsily. "But I'm—cold."

He was shivering violently. She rang the bell for assistance; but it was too late to avert the consequences of that night's work, and before morning the fever was back upon him. It was impossible to learn from him how it had happened. When his mind wandered, he talked disconnectedly of herself, sometimes tenderly, sometimes angrily and jealously, but always of her. Annie sat up by him all night, and in the morning, with softened tread and pale, downcast, anxious face, Lilian crept in. He did not know her—he did not know any one.

"Go and get some rest now, Annie; I will watch by him," she whispered.

"Why, Lilian, you look as if you had sat up all night, too! What is the matter with you?"

Lilian did not answer for a minute, but stood watching the restless movements of her sick brother; and, when she turned again to Annie, her proud gray eyes were full of tears.

"I may as well tell you now, for you are sure to learn it as soon as poor Harry comes back to his senses—if he ever does."

She paused, and the other listened curiously for her confession, for a confession she felt sure it was that she had to hear.

She was right; for Lilian went on:

"Annie, you must not despise the poor fellow any more. He can act like a man if he can't speak like a professor. If it had not been for him, I should have run away last night with—Colonel Richardson."

"Oh, Lilian!"

"Don't interrupt me," went on the other hurriedly—"I may not feel inclined for confession again. I was to meet him—Colonel Richardson—at the lower gate. Well, Harry was there."

"But how was that?"

"He thought it was you who were going off."

"I!"

"Yes, yes, he did. I know whose doing that was. Stephen had guessed or found out something, and not having the pluck to stop me himself, and not wanting a general row, he got Harry to suppose it was you who were going off with——"

"But Harry would never have believed that I——"

"Why not?" said Lilian, in a hard tone. "Have you returned his affection for you so very warmly as to make it impossible for him to think that you cared for any one but him? However, it is not for me to reproach you, especially on the score of want of wifely devotion. When he found it was I, Harry tried to drag me away; but I struggled to escape from him, and told him not to interfere with me. He would not let me go, and I told him——You will be shocked, Annie, but I loved the man—I do now—and I was desperate. I asked Harry how he could be sure he was not too late. And he looked me straight in the face very steadily, so that I felt awfully ashamed of myself, and he said, 'I may not be in time to save your character, but at least I will save your reputation.' And for a moment I stood quite still, hesitating, while he still held my arm. He had a revolver in his other hand. Before I spoke again, Herbert—Colonel Richardson sprung forward, snatched the revolver from him, and struck him in the face with it, while he tried to pull me away. But Harry never let go, and that decided me. I told Herbert he was a coward to strike a man hardly recovered from illness, and that I would not go with him. Harry, poor fellow, could not have kept me back then; I had to support him; and I led him back here, and we slipped into the house; and he begged me to bring him to your door, and go to my room, and no one should know anything about it, if I would promise never to try to go off again. I didn't promise—I hadn't time; but I never will, all the same. And, Annie, he is worth loving. Do try to love him back! Oh, you would if you knew what it is to have a husband who is a monument of all the virtues, but a monument in stone!"

And the wayward woman, who, with all her faults, had generous impulses, laid her beautiful head on the bed and sobbed.

She insisted on sharing Annie's duties as nurse; and, when Harry, after being long in danger for his life, at last flickered back toward convalescence, the first person he recognized at his bedside was his sister. Her passionate nature, which in many respects resembled his, had been deeply moved by what he had done for her, and still more by the unexpectedly quiet and dignified way in which he had done it. She had had time to see the depth of the social abyss into which her proposed flight would have plunged her. Her long-standing preference for Herbert Richardson she had not subdued—she felt that she could not subdue it; but she had broken off even her correspondence with him at Harry's request.

Brother and sister drew near to each other, with far deeper mutual affection than they had ever felt before, during Harry's slow return to health. They felt that they had much in common, both ardent, passionate natures being tied to colder ones, who could not or would not respond to their warmth with the entire abandonment they craved. There the likeness in their positions ended, however, for Lilian had never even tried to sound the depths in the heart of her middle-aged husband, while every look, every touch that Harry bestowed on his wife told wistfully of the longing he had felt to be master of her love as he was already of her duty.

The gentleness and even the tenderness of her care of him now would have satisfied any one less exacting. But fondness had made the young fellow clear-sighted; and he knew, or thought he knew, that her heart could give more than that, if he could only reach it.

Annie herself, who seemed in this matter to have exchanged wits with her husband, growing duller of perception as he grew brighter, fancied that his fondness for his sister had grown stronger than his fondness for her, and, after a moment's pique, she felt glad of it, as it rendered an avowal she had to make all the easier.

It was on the first day after he had again joined the family circle that she found an opportunity of speaking to him alone, and of telling him, under a promise of secrecy, that George had told her he was in serious difficulties, and feared that he would not be able to keep up the establishment at the Grange much longer. Harry listened rather indifferently. He had been so accustomed to hear of these difficulties, not only since his brother had been the head of the family, but also in his father's lifetime, that, as it had never been his business to find a way out of them, they had altogether ceased to excite any emotion in him, beyond a faint wonder why people could not keep these matters to themselves, without worrying other people about them, and an injured feeling that the head of the family would want to cut down his allowance.

"George is always in difficulties," said he.

"Ah, but it is serious this time! We really must think about it."

"Well, what does he want us to do? Sell matches or enlist? There is nothing else for any of us."

"Yes, there is, for one," said Annie, cautiously, watching him. "Look here, Harry: I've had an engagement offered me which will bring me in so much money that, if I save, we might live upon it before long."

"Who's we?"

"You and I, of course."

"And do you think I would live upon your money?"

"I think you would be very unreasonable not to do so, if I could make enough to keep us. I don't believe George will have enough for us all much longer, and then——"

"Then it is I who should work, not you."

"I think it is the one who has been used to it who should work, and that, you know, is I," she said, smiling.

But Harry did not smile back. He moved restlessly on his sofa.

"It is not like you to taunt me, Annie; yet—yet your words sting somehow," he said at last.

"Oh, Harry, you know I did not mean that! Don't you see, Harry, dear, you have been very ill, and won't be strong for a long time after this second attack; while I have done nothing but enjoy myself for more than three months."

"Yes, you have. You have been nursing me," said he, tenderly.

"Ah, but that wasn't work; that was pleasure, except when—when you were so very ill this last time!" rejoined she gently. "And now I have had an offer to play a part in London which would just suit me, and might make me a name, and to have six guineas a week for it. And, if I don't take it, I may never have such a chance again!" she added, with ill-concealed eagerness.

"I see," said Harry, turning upon her sharply. "All this time that I have been ill you have been plotting to get away from me as fast as possible."

"I will tell you what I did. I saw that a piece was to be played at the Parthenon—a translation of a French piece—in which there was a part I longed to play; so I wrote for that part, mentioning all that I have done on the stage: and it so happened that they were in a difficulty for an actress for that very part, and I got the offer yesterday, and must send an answer to-day. I would not have gone for the world if you had not been safely through your illness, and if Lilian had not been with you; but, Harry, dear Harry, if you do really feel the least gratitude for my coming back to take care of you, if you really feel for me one spark of the fondness I seem to see in your looks, let me go! You are not ambitious as I am—you have not had to toil and fret at the impossibility of getting on, as I have; but, if you can even picture to yourself how terrible it is to forego success when at last it seems to be coming to you, you will let me go—you will let me go—you will let me go!"

Her violent excitement had brought the tears to her eyes. As she knelt beside the couch, her great, passionate dark eyes fixed upon his in entreaty, the tears welled up in his eyes too as he snatched her into his arms.

"I can refuse you nothing. Heaven forgive you—you will break my heart?"

A week later Annie's trunks were packed for London. On the last day before her departure from the Grange she took a long ramble by herself through some of her favorite fields and lanes, where a mild March was already bringing forth the signs of spring. She had promised to be at the old church at four, to undertake for the village organist a commission of getting him some music in London. She got there too soon, however; so, having fortunately provided herself with the key, she went in and up the winding-stair to the top of the old square tower. She had a letter to read which she had had unopened in her pocket since the morning; and, when she got at last on to the tower and had gazed for a few minutes upon the wide expanse of country commanded by the hill on which the church was built, had looked a little regretfully at the budding trees and the river and the town of Beckham beyond, an ugly, smoke-begrimed place indeed, but which bore a deceptive beauty when seen from a distance on a sunny afternoon in a haze of its own smoke, she drew out her letter, which was directed to "Miss Langton," and tore open the envelope.

She knew whom it was from—a young actress who had been with her at the last theater Annie had played at in London, who had then played silent "guests," and parts too small even for Annie, but who had since been promoted to the latter's place. Annie had written to this girl, who knew nothing of her marriage or of her private life, asking her to send her the address of some cheap lodgings which she had once recommended. The other had not only complied, but had, with the good nature so strikingly characteristic of members of the theatrical profession, undertaken to see the landlady and make terms with her about them. This matter was now settled— the rooms taken; so this letter could not be very important. So Annie thought. But she had not read the first two pages before the color in her face deepened, and she read on to the end with an intentness which only tidings of deepest interest could have called forth. The passage which had fixed her attention was the following:

"I met Cooke, who was here at the Piccadilly when you were, as I was walking along the Strand a day or two ago. He is at the Regency now, and the papers have cracked him up so in the part he is playing that I wonder he condescended to talk to poor little me. He asked how we were getting on at the Piccadilly, and I mentioned that you had been in the country, but were coming back to London. He seemed very much interested in you, which amused me, remembering as I did how much you always disliked him, and how you used to mimic him for my amusement in the dressing-room; however, I did not take him down by telling him that. Do you remember how I used to stick up for him when you said he was fast? Well, you were right, for they say the way he is carrying on with some woman who has been acting in the country with him—West, I think her name is—is something disgraceful, considering that he is engaged or half engaged to that little fair girl who made such a hit in 'Ophelia' last year. He is trying to get this West into the Regency, I believe."

This was the passage which had arrested Annie's attention, which she read through again and again with dry eyes, but with a bitter feeling of disappointment and shame. Then she let the letter drop from her fingers, and leaning against the flag-staff which rose from the top of the tower, she burst into heartfelt sobbing. She had cheated herself into believing that it was nothing but her ambition which impelled her in her eagerness to go to London; but now in the revulsion of feeling which suddenly made the thought of returning to town and her profession unutterably hateful to her, she saw with unmistakable clearness what the other and stronger motive had been which had made her enforced idleness at the Grange so hard to bear. She was still sobbing when she heard sounds behind her, and, looking round, saw her husband's head as he came slowly to the top of the stairs.

"What is the matter, Annie dear?" he asked anxiously.

"Harry, what made you come up all those steps? It is too tiring for you," said she, bending her head awkwardly to hide her tears.

"I saw you from the avenue, and I saw you were crying," he answered, as he mounted the last step and rested his hands on the low wall for support—he was not strong enough for much exertion yet. "What were you crying about, Annie? Not because you are going away, I know."

She had turned away to wipe the tears from her face, and, as she turned again toward him, she caught sight of her letter lying on the ground between them. He saw it at the same moment, and, although she had the presence of mind to pick it up very composedly, he at once came to the conclusion that in it lay the cause of her distress.

"Who is that letter from?"

"From Miss Taylor, who has been writing to me about the apartments I am going to have in town," she said, as she put it into the pocket of her mantle.

"Let me see it."

She considered a minute while pretending to feel for it, and made up her mind that it would be best to give it to him, as there was nothing in it which was likely to have any meaning for him. So she handed him the letter carelessly, and affected to be gazing admiringly on the landscape while he read it. But Harry got on to the right track at once.

"This Cooke—is he the Aubrey Cook Lilian talks about?"

"Yes; he was acting at the Piccadilly when I was there."

"He is a man in the habit of making love to every woman he meets?"

"I don't know, I am sure. I did not know him well, and you see, as Miss Taylor says, I never liked him."

There was a pause, but he was not satisfied.

"He must be a low, vicious, unprincipled fellow!" said he suddenly, keeping his eyes fixed steadily on his wife.

Annie winced.

"I suppose it is men like him who get the stage such a bad name?" he went on.

Still she said nothing, but leaned over the low battlemented wall of the tower, and kept her eyes steadily fixed on the smoke-hung town in the distance.

"I hope there will be no such hounds in the theater you are going to, Annie. If I thought you were going back to a place contaminated by the presence of such an infamous scoundrel, I would not let you go!"

Annie turned her head very quietly.

"What has he done?" said she.

"Done! Haven't you read that letter? Haven't you heard that he is engaged to one woman while he is hardly ever away from another—one of the vilest of her sex? Perhaps you think nothing of that?"

"Well, you see," said Annie very slowly, looking full into his angry face, "I have known so many men do worse things than that." After a minute's pause, which her husband did not attempt to fill, she went on, "I have known married men who neglected, insulted, and even struck their wives within the very first months of marriage, who gave what little attention they had to spare for anything so contemptible as a woman to the lowest of the sex—men who crushed the beauty out of their young wives by brutal carelessness and cruelty, and who thought that years of abandonment, and almost every wrong a man can do a woman, were amply atoned for by a burst of capricious affection—affection so selfish that it never lost an opportunity of wounding the object of it."

Harry listened to this outburst without an interruption. His head sunk and his chest heaved as she grew more excited; but when she had finished, he raised his blue eyes to her face, and asked very quietly:

"How have I wounded you?"

Annie was not quite prepared for this. She answered, after a little hesitation:

"By insulting the profession to which I belong—which has given me all the happiness I have known since my marriage with you."

"No," said Harry, sharply. "By speaking candidly about one of its members—that is how I have hurt you; and it was just to turn me off from abusing him that you broke out with a catalogue of my faults, which Heaven knows I don't deny. I tell you again, I may be a brute and a boor and anything else you like to make me out, but I'm not a fool; and, when you tell me you dislike this Aubrey Cooke, I tell you you are lying to me."

Annie faced him again very quietly.

"I have not lied. I told you I disliked Aubrey Cooke when I was at the Piccadilly. I tell you now that I have loved him since then, and that now I hate him. Are you satisfied?"

The passion in her words was convincing, but Harry was not content. He kept his gaze fixed on the frank eyes of his wife for a few moments, then looked away with a heavy sigh, murmuring:

"Hate him! That's no good. I'd rather you did not care one way or the other."

Annie was touched. She had fully expected a violent outbreak on her husband's part when he should hear her confession. She put her hand softly on his sleeve.

"Harry, you need not be frightened indeed; I shall never care for him again."

But Harry, without even trying to detain her hand, shook his head.

"It is a very bad sign to hate a person," said he. "I never hated any person but you, and just see where it has landed me. What does it matter if you don't care for him, if you don't care for me and won't stay with me! And as for the way you pitched in to me just now, do you think I should let you go off if I didn't feel I'd done you wrong in the old time and wanted to make it up to you? And if you won't let me make it up to you by letting me love you, I must do it by letting you go. It is true I have run after—after other people, but, Annie, I was very young—wasn't I?—and I didn't know, I didn't understand the charm of a woman like you then. How could I? I wasn't even a man myself, and you were afraid of me. But, Annie, I do love you and appreciate you now more than any actor who ever lived, and the thought of your going to be stared at by every one who cares to pay to look at you is awful—awful! And my darling, you are my wife, you know, and if you won't love me ever, I may as well go and cut my throat, for I—I—I——"

He broke off, fairly sobbing. Annie's heart was moved, and she hung her arms round him with one touch of the deeper tenderness of the woman he had longed to rouse.

"Harry, Harry, I'll come back, I'll come back—at Christmas; that is only nine months, and if you love me still then, I will never go away from you again!"

He pressed her to his breast, and kissed her and blessed her; and as the March afternoon began to wane they descended the ruinous stone stairs of the old tower slowly together, she with her hands to his shoulders following him step by step silently, but not unhappily. There was hope in her husband's heart, and it had affected her a little. The mellow sounds of the organ were pealing through the church where the organist was practicing as, at the bottom stair, Harry gave his wife a last passionate kiss before they left the shadowy building for the outer air.

And the next day Annie started for London.

CHAPTER XX.

The journey back to London was a very strange one to Annie; she never saw the landscape through which the train passed, she did not even remember the faces of her fellow-passengers afterward. Her mind was filled with fears for the future—for her own, for her husband's, for Lilian's, for George's, for that of all the family at the Grange, and for Aubrey's. She did hate him deeply, this man who had cheated her into making her look upon him as the most gentle, most courteous, brightest of companions and the most devoted of friends, when he was really nothing but a volatile, unprincipled flirt, who made love indifferently to her, or to a coarse woman like Miss West, or to a little giddy creature like the girl to whom Miss Taylor had said he was engaged. Perhaps Annie hardly dwelt enough, in her blame of Aubrey, on the question whether she herself had done right in concealing from him the fact that she was married, and whether, even supposing she had been free, as he imagined her to be, he would not have been justified in thinking no more of a lady who had dismissed him and disappeared without a word, and in transferring his attentions to women who would appreciate them more highly. But with all her blame was mingled sincere anxiety for him, and unselfish sorrow that he should have fallen into bad hands.

As for her own husband, she felt more kindly toward him now that she was away from the daily irritation of his presence, from the fear of his trivial jealousy, of his impossible demands. Their impossibility she could not question. She felt that she could never return, with the ardor which alone would content him, the passionate love she had inspired in a nature so different from her own, and, as it seemed to her, so antagonistic to it. The most that she could hope for was that, if his affection should indeed remain warm until next Christmas, when she had promised to return to him, the nine months of hard work upon the stage which she was about to commence would have wearied her into the semblance of contentment with a life so distasteful to her active mind as permanent idleness at the Grange with her uncongenial husband would be.

She had caught an earlier and faster train from Beckham than the one by which she had intended to travel, so that she arrived in London and drove to the house where Miss Taylor had taken apartments for her, two hours before the time at which the landlady expected her. The consequence was that the dirty servant who opened the door led her up to a dingy and cheerless sitting-room on the second floor, the grate of which was empty; and Annie's heart sunk with a feeling of unutterable wretchedness and desolation as she sat shivering, with her mantle still round her, on the dusty little sofa, watching the dirty servant as she knelt on the hearth-rug and tried, for a long time in vain, to coax some spluttering, damp little sticks and a handful of slaty coals into a fire. When it was sufficiently ignited to smoke violently, she retired, satisfied, leaving Annie to cough and choke and shiver, and wish herself back again at the Grange.

It was all her own fault that she was catching cold in an uncomfortable lodging, instead of being well cared for in the midst of her husband's family. The gratification of her ambition, which had brought her to this cheerless welcome, seemed an unsatisfactory sort of reward at this moment for the sacrifice she had made alike of comfort and duty—for self-reproach for her own hardness had been busy at Annie's heart since she received her husband's farewell kiss that morning.

At last, after emitting gusts of black blinding smoke, each one of which grew feebler than the last, the fire went out altogether; and Annie was reduced by this time to too spiritless a state to ring the bell and go through another ordeal of smoke and servant.

"I suppose they will come up at tea-time," she thought, as she went listlessly into the bedroom and began to unpack.

Dusk was coming on when she heard a knock at the sitting-room door.

"Come in!" she called out from where she knelt by her trunks. Then she heard no more, and began to think she must have been mistaken, when the knock was repeated. "Come in!" she cried a second time; and then she heard the door open, and a man's tread in the next room.

She rose from her knees, went in to the sitting-room, and found herself face to face with Aubrey Cooke, who was standing in his usual stooping attitude, looking paler and plainer than ever, with some parcels in his hands.

He was shy, nervous, and stood there without a word to say for himself. But the sight of a familiar face in this desolate, cheerless place had restored Annie in a moment to life and animation.

"Mr. Cooke!" she cried, as she went forward and shook hands with him. "How kind of you! How did you know I was coming? I am so very glad to see you!"

Her face had recovered its light, her eyes were sparkling with their old brightness. Aubrey got back his self-possession as he looked at her, and began slowly laying down his parcels upon the table and taking more from his pockets.

"Miss Taylor told me you were coming, and my unfailing instinct told me that, being a lady, you would have forgotten to have all the arrangements necessary for your comfort made before your arrival. Now you shall see whether I have forgotten how to do marketing. There is the twopenny cottage, there is the superior souchong, and there is the oleomargarine—the very best. And that is for you."

He gave her a little box, which she opened and found to contain ferns and gardenias. She sat down and handled them lovingly, with the simple pleasure of a child, and, when she looked up, she found Aubrey raking out the coals of the extinct fire with a poker.

"Never mind; leave it alone. It is out; and, if I ring and make the girl light it again, she will only fill the room with smoke. I am not very cold."

Indeed for the moment she had forgotten that she was cold; but she shivered now and then.

"But I am. Now you shall see what it is to have a universal genius about you. In ten minutes my art will produce from this gloomy heap of cinders——"

"A cloud of thick black smoke which will suffocate us both. Don't be silly, Aubrey; do leave it alone!" said Annie, petulantly, condescending to struggle for the poker.

But he would not let it go; so she resigned herself to watching while he broke up the little fragile box which had held the flowers, took the paper off his other parcels, and set to work earnestly to make a fire.

"You will look just like a sweep when you have finished," said Annie, with resignation.

"A little soap and water will remove all traces of the deed."

"Oh, of course, if you like to play at maid-of-all-work!" said she, contemptuously. Her spirits were rising again to the level of the old days when she and he were on tour with the Comedy Company.

He rose superior to her scorn, for, after a little trouble and one or two more gusts of smoke, the fire began to burn up brightly.

"Now ring for a kettle, and let us make tea ourselves," said he.

She rang, the tea-things were brought up, and in a few minutes Annie, refreshed and comforted, was listening to his account of his movements since they last met.

"I have created two characters, invented a new soup, written a book, cut it up myself in two papers, discovered my ideal woman two or three times, had two bad colds and one attack of neuralgia, lost fifteen pounds at cards, and narrowly escaped being married."

"To one of the ideals?"

"Of course not. One never marries one's ideal. No; this was to be the loveliest of her sex. Happily a man turned up at the last moment who had a prior claim to her hand, and I was saved."

"Happy woman!"

"I see you don't look at the case from my point of view, Miss Langton."

"No; I take up the cause of my sex against you."

"That is unkind. She treated me very cruelly, I assure you."

"For which and for your consequent deliverance from the trammels of constancy you are very grateful."

"Do you think I am inconstant, Miss Langton?" he asked, with sudden gravity.

"I am inclined to think so, certainly; but I look upon it as a very fortunate provision of nature," said she, half laughing nervously.

"Then you are wrong. If I am inconstant it is by philosophy, and not by disposition. You know, when people have toothache very badly they sometimes hold things that burn in their mouths, so that the small, sharp new pain may make them forget for the moment the old dull one."

"What a romantic simile!"

"So a man, when he has been badly treated by one woman whom he did care for, tries to find consolation—and does so find it very often—in flirtations with a dozen other women who have no power to make his heart throb faster, but who can make the time pass pleasantly enough."

"I have heard that sort of excuse from inconstant people before, and I think it a very clever one."

"And what excuse have you heard from the woman who was the cause of the inconstancy?"

Annie's cheeks flushed as she still looked steadily at the fire. He was taking her to account for her treatment of himself. After a few moments' hesitation she answered, in a light tone:

"You are talking too vaguely; put before me a clear case of a woman having done wrong to a man, which forced him to seek relief in inconstancy, and I will plead her cause and confound you."

"Very well. Suppose that a man had admired and shown his admiration of a woman who had rather reserved manners to most people. Suppose that her reserve with him had gradually given way, until she allowed him to be her constant companion, treated him with at least the show of complete confidence, exchanged opinions freely with him on every subject, and allowed her apparent preference for his society to be taken for granted."

"Did she allow him to make love to her?"

"No, she did something more dangerous; she allowed him to make love to every woman but her. He was too much in earnest to flirt with her, and she must have known it."

"I think that is an absurd conclusion to come to, that the woman must have known he loved her because he didn't tell her so. If women were to go by such a rule in all cases——"

"But listen. At last one day—or rather one November night—he did let her know in words that he loved her, and she—she made him think that his words agitated her."

"Perhaps they did—perhaps they agitated her disagreeably. They must have done so, if she was unprepared for them as you have made out."

"But later on she gave him an unmistakable proof that her liking and trust were as strong as ever. And then again she avoided him; and, when he insisted on an interview and an explanation, she put him off by telling him there was an obstacle between them, but still without telling what that obstacle was."

"What did it matter what it was, as long as it was insurmountable? That was all that could concern him."

"He ought to have been told what it was, so that at least he might not be left to think that it was merely an excuse to get rid of a man of whom she had grown tired. But she had another surprise in store for him; she disappeared without letting him know what had become of her."

"And he has spent his time ever since in a vain and romantic pursuit of her?"

"Oh, dear, no! He went back to town, furnished a new set of chambers, and has grown more particular about his cooking."

"And you hold him up as an object of sympathy? He is a man to whom an offer of sympathy would be an impertinence."

"He does not want sympathy, but justice; and, if he cannot get that, he will have revenge—and melodramatic revenge, of course, but small, spiteful, mean, and modern!"

"I don't think such a threat would frighten her from you."

"You are trying to pique me."

"I! Oh, no! What interest can I have in the matter?"

"Can you give me your assurance that you have none?"

The sudden intensity of his manner would have forced some show of emotion from Annie if she had not been on her guard.

"I take an interest in the affairs of any friend who has shown me as much kindness as you have, Mr. Cooke," said she, gravely, and with a little stiffness.

Aubrey was silent for a few minutes.

"Thank you!" he said, dryly, after clearing his throat two or three times.

Annie felt that the conversation had got to a difficult point, and, to avoid the awkwardness of the pause which followed, she rose. He rose too.

"I have intruded upon you too long, Miss Langton; you must want rest and quiet after your long journey," said he, in a casual-visitor's tone, which deceived Annie until she saw by the fading daylight that he was as pale as death, and that his lips were quivering.

"I cannot thank you enough for coming. I should have been so very dull here all alone on the first evening of my return, if it had not been for your charity," said she, with as much vivacity as she could put into her tone and manner.

"It was my duty, you are in my 'district.' May I come again?" She hesitated.

"Don't be unkind. I've been very good, haven't I?" said he, softly.

"I think you had better not come again, Mr. Cooke. It is different in the country, you know; but here, in town, the least thing is noticed and talked about."

"When do you play in 'Nathalie'?"

"I think in a fortnight or three weeks."

"It will be longer than that. In the meantime, you won't be rehearsing every day, and on the off-days you will be frightfully dull—or won't you?"

She turned away irresolutely.

"Let me come sometimes, and I won't abuse the permission;" and she let him go without a definite answer.

It was quite true that she would be dull and miserable by herself; she felt that as soon as she heard his footsteps going down-stairs. She wanted to go to the door, call him back, and tell him to come again soon; she even crossed the room to do so, but she turned back and sunk into a chair, ashamed of the impulse, for she knew that there was danger in his society. She felt that her indignation against him had faded away, that his presence had soothed her weary, excited mind as the presence of no other person in the world could have done, and that, if she saw much more of him, she would inevitably come to depend upon his companionship as she had done when they were on tour together. It had been harmless, pleasant intercourse then; but Aubrey's words on that November night had changed all that; and Annie knew she ought to have summoned courage to tell him that very afternoon what the nature of the obstacle between them was. But it was so much pleasanter and even easier to skate over the difficult matter of her sudden disappearance, and to avoid the "scene" which the tragedy-manner Aubrey had assumed when they approached this subject had threatened.

"I certainly did not encourage him to come," said she to herself, with a twinge of conscience. "Of course it does not really matter whether he comes or not, except that Harry would make a silly fuss if he knew that anybody who was at all young or nice came to see me. But there is nothing really for him to be jealous about; and, after all, I cannot shut myself up quite like a nun just because my husband is ill-tempered."

So, when Aubrey called two days afterward, and had the sense not to make any allusion to his love-grievances, she was very glad to see him, and flattered herself with the thought that he understood that there was no further question of a warmer sentiment than friendship between them. In this belief she was justified, for Aubrey had decided upon his line of conduct, and fell into the position of brotherly old friend in the most natural manner in the world.

After a few visits, during none of which did Aubrey recall, by word or look, his old love or its disappointment, she fell into her former perfectly open and unreserved manner with him, and felt unspeakably grateful to him for the good sense which had restored the old frank companionship between them. She grew happy again, attributed the change in her spirits to the prospect of her speedy reappearance on the stage, and wondered how she could have remained so long away from it. Under the influence of these brighter feelings she wrote an affectionate letter to her husband, with a little compunction at not having responded more warmly to his kindness when she was at the Grange.

Two days later, as Aubrey was leaving her sitting-room, where he had spent the greater part of the afternoon, after bringing her some books from Mudie's, he met the servant coming up the stairs, followed by a tall, fair young man. Annie's voice had just called out, "I shall expect you then!" and Aubrey had scarcely closed the door behind him, when the servant reached the top stair.

He stood on one side to let them pass, but the fair young man sent the servant down-stairs by a few words spoken in a low voice, and stood face to face with Aubrey just outside Miss Langton's door.

"These are Miss Langton's apartments, I believe?" said the stranger.

"Yes," answered Aubrey, deciding, as he looked at the angry face and impatient movements of the man in front of him, that this was some bumpkin admirer of the clever young actress, who looked upon him as a rival.

"And you are one of Miss Langton's friends, I suppose?"

"I have the honor of being one of her oldest friends," said Aubrey, coolly.

A deep flush spread over the face of the other man, who was evidently keeping himself in check by a strong effort of self-control.

"May I ask what your name is?" he asked, curtly.

"By what right do you ask such a question which cannot concern you?"

"That is my affair; and you need not make such a mystery about it, because I know who you are. Your name is Cooke—Aubrey Cooke!"

"Well, what then?"

"What then? Why, my name is Harold Braithwaite!"

But this announcement produced none of the effect he evidently expected. The pale, ugly young man still returned his look quite steadily, without expressing any sort of emotion.

"I dare say it is," said he, simply—"why not?"

"Look here," said the stranger, dropping his voice till it became a growl of passion. "I don't want a scene here. You had better go."

But Aubrey stood his ground very calmly.

"I am no more anxious for a scene than you are, I assure you. But, as you are a complete stranger to me, and can produce no authority for dismissing me, I must decline to move until I have given you a little piece of advice. Don't venture to dismiss a lady's friends without her authority——"

"I don't use her authority; I use my own."

"And you think that will be enough for me?"

"I think it ought to be."

"Do you know who the lady is you are speaking about so confidently?"

"Yes. You know her as Miss Langton, the actress."

"And you?"

"As Annie Braithwaite—my wife!"

Aubrey stood the shock well, but not too well for the other man to see that his announcement was a terrible surprise. This conversation had been carried on in low tones; but, as Harry raised his voice on his last words, Annie, in the sitting-room, had recognized it; and she opened the door and faced the two men, white and trembling.

"Harry!" said she, in a low voice.

"Is it true, then, that this man is your—husband?" asked Aubrey.

"Yes," answered she, hanging her head, and without looking at him.

"I must apologize for my discourtesy," said Aubrey, still white and shaking, turning, without another look at her, to Harry. "I had always understood that Mr. Braithwaite—was a short man;" and, raising his hat, he went down-stairs.

CHAPTER XXI.

Annie stood with her husband at the top of the stairs until she heard the street door shut upon Aubrey Cooke; then, recovering her self-command, she turned and said, "Won't you come in?" and led the way into her sitting-room.

Harry followed, and stood at first speechless with anger in the middle of the small room, while his wife moved restlessly toward the fireplace. Then, beginning to perceive that, for once, her self-possession was no greater than his own, he found words.

"So this is what your 'ambition,' your 'love of work' means!"

"What do you mean?"

"What do I mean? You know very well what I mean! Do you think I couldn't see through the farce your 'oldest friend' played to shield you? Do you think I don't know that this was the first time he had ever heard of me? When I told him my name, it was easy enough to see that it meant nothing to him. Answer me this: did he or did he not know you were married?"

He was working himself up to a white heat of passion, and Annie feared for the consequences of any admission she might make while he was in this mood. She tried to delay explanation by going to him, taking his hand, and attempting to draw him to a seat by the fire.

Dusk was coming on, and he could not clearly see her face as she approached him with bent head, but he felt that the hands into which she was trying to draw his were cold and trembling. He would not move from where he stood; but, with a sudden, almost rough motion, he raised her head and peered down into her averted eyes. She shrunk from the unexpected ordeal, and tried to edge away from him with an involuntary eagerness which incensed him still more against her.

"Is this all the answer you have to give me? You can't meet my eyes, you shrink away from my touch! Is this the welcome a good wife gives to her husband? Annie, answer me! Did that man know you were married?"

"Harry, let me go! You are hurting me! I cannot answer you anything until you let me go. See the mark you have left upon my wrist! How can you be so brutal?"

"You are not going to put me off like that," said Harry, firmly. "I know how you women will wriggle out of a subject you don't like, if you can. I am sorry if I have hurt you: you know very well I did not mean to do that; but I will be answered. Now sit down and get quite quiet and calm. I won't hurt you, whatever you say; but you must tell me the whole truth, because, if you tell me any lies, I shall find them out and be very angry about it."

His manner had grown calmer the moment he saw the red mark his strong hand had made on his wife's wrist, and felt how utterly powerless in his grasp the little creature was. He placed her gently in the very chair she had tried to induce him to take, and then stood before her, towering above her, and without turning his eyes again toward the chair in which she sat, gravely and doggedly waiting.

Annie felt cowed. For the first time in their lives, the husband stood in the position of the superior, and, as she sat guiltily there, understanding clearly for the first time that her husband had just right of complaint against her, and that, moreover, he was using that right with consideration and manliness, she gave a shy look upward, as if to see what change this inversion of their old attitudes toward each other had wrought in Harry's handsome, careless, boyish face.

It was too dark for her to see very clearly what little of his profile was shown in that position; she could only see that he stood very still, that, if he felt impatience, he was keeping it under strong control, and she began to feel dimly that in the argument which was coming he would meet her for the first time upon equal terms. As she still sat, with her head raised, looking up anxiously at him, he turned and his eyes met hers.

"Are you ready now?" he asked, simply.

"Ready for what?" said she, impatiently.

"Ready to answer some questions I have to ask you."

"Of course I can answer any questions you please; but I don't see the necessity of all this fuss about the matter. Whatever you have to ask I could have answered a long time ago," said Annie, indifferently. "But if you like to play inquisitor and give yourself the airs of a judge, why—it's nothing to me!"

"Can we have the gas lighted?" asked Harry. "I can't see your face."

She rose and lighted it herself, rather reluctantly. She would have preferred that the interrogation she would have to submit to should have been made in the twilight. However, he was not in a mood to be argued with, so she sat down again in the gas-light, with some work in her hand.

"You don't want that for a few minutes," said her husband, taking from her hands the stage-cap she was making. "I want you to look at me."

So she submitted again, with a shrug of the shoulders and a little, contemptuous laugh, which was rather forced, and raised her restless, dark eyes to his steady, blue ones, with an affectation of indifference which did not even irritate him.

"Won't you sit down? I can't look at you without cricking my neck while you stand towering above me like that!" said she.

"Thank you. I don't think I could sit down here quietly with you until I was a little more sure than I am of the footing on which I am here," returned Harry; and, for the first time, she noticed a nervous movement of his left hand.

He stepped back from her a little, however, so that she could see his face without inconvenience, and she noticed that he looked thin, that he had lost his bright color, and that the steady, set expression of his face made him look much older than when she had left the Grange.

"I don't understand you! Please let me know clearly what cause of complaint you have against me that makes you behave in such a strange manner to me," said Annie haughtily.

But she was not quite at ease; this character of culprit was new to her, and it did not sit so well upon her as the equally unaccustomed character of judge seemed to sit upon her husband.

"Who was that man I met outside your door just now?"

"Mr. Aubrey Cooke, a man who was acting at the Regency Theater when I was there. You must have heard me speak of him as one of my oldest friends upon the stage."

"One of your oldest friends? That is what he called himself. But the servant told me he was a relative of yours, who came to see you nearly every day."

"I am not answerable for the creations of a housemaid's fancy. Certainly neither Mr. Cooke nor I ever told her he was a relative of mine."

"But he comes to see you nearly every day?"

"Not so often as that; but he comes very frequently. Why should he not? I am at liberty to choose my own friends, and he is one of the best I have."

"Then why did you not introduce him to me just now when you came out of your room and found us both there?"

"I was too much taken by surprise——"

"And terror—that is what your face showed."

"I thought you had had some quarrel, you looked so angry; I did not know what to think; and the next minute Mr. Cooke was gone."

"It was the first time he had heard you were married, was it not?"

Annie hesitated for one moment; then she said:

"He always knew me as Miss Langton, like the rest of my theatrical friends. I don't know whether he had heard I was married———"

"That is a lie, Annie!" he burst out, with a suddenness which made her start. "You silly woman, why don't you tell me the truth? For the truth I will have; and, if I have to get it from anybody but you, it will be the worse for you and for him too."

Annie's gaze sunk under the fierceness which blazed in his eyes and recalled to her mind his old savagery at the Grange. He lowered his voice again as he saw her shrink.

"Annie, don't let me fancy you have anything to tell me worse than I have thought," said he, with a tremor in his voice. "You need not be afraid of me; I will listen calmly to whatever you have to say. I haven't always been a good husband to you, and I feel it quite as much as you do. But I have been fond of you, and good to you lately, and you might trust me a little, if only for the sake of that. Now tell me! You do like this Mr. Cooke, don't you?"

"Yes, of course I like him, or I should not let him come and see me."

"And he likes you?"

"If he did not, he would not take the trouble to come."

"And if it had not been for my existence, I suppose———"

"You have no right to suppose anything," said Annie, impatiently; "there is nothing to suppose. You are the only person who has ever found the slightest fault with my conduct. There is no cause whatever for your trifling jealousy, any more than there was at the Grange, where you teased me to death with your absurd suspicions."

"But you treated my jealousy differently then. It was trifling and tiresome, I dare say. But you just laughed it off lightly then, while now you grow impatient and restless under it."

"You see I have been left in peace lately, and am not consequently in such a high state of discipline as when I was at the Grange. I should have been better prepared if I had guessed that your jealousy would bring you up to town."

"It was not my jealousy which brought me, Annie, but something which I believe you care about just as little—my love. I got a letter from you yesterday—you seem to have forgotten all about it, or perhaps you wrote it just as a blind—I don't know—and you said in it you often thought of the

- 183 -

Grange, and you supposed by this time I could ride again as well as ever, and had nearly forgotten all about such a trifling thing as a wife. I got the letter at breakfast, and I said to myself, 'The little jade is trying to pique me! Then she does care about whether I forget her or not!' And I made up my mind directly I'd come and see you all unexpectedly, and see what you would say. And I didn't make too sure you would be glad; but, by Jove, I didn't expect quite such a cool welcome as I got!" And Harry's voice gave way just as he reached the last words, and he leaned his elbow on the mantel-piece and dropped his head into his hand, with his back to her.

Annie was touched, and she rose, with tears in her eyes, and crept up to him, and took his other hand. But he shook her off, and remained quite unsoftened by her tearful eyes.

"Don't come and hang about me now, Annie, and speak to me in your cooing voice, when I know you wish me a hundred miles away, or I shall think your caresses were never worth having," said he, passionately. "And I thought I could trust you; I thought you were so good, so pure! Even when I was jealous, I never thought you would pass yourself off as an unmarried girl, just that you might be made love to by other men—and when you knew all the time how fond I was of you, Annie!"

"Harry, Harry, do listen to me! I am not fond of anybody else—I have not been made love to. Why won't you believe me? Look at yourself in the glass, and see if you are not more likely to please a woman's fancy than—than Mr. Cooke—or anybody."

He had turned to look wistfully and reproachfully down at her, and she had seized the opportunity to fasten herself coaxingly on his arm, and to raise her other hand to his face to try to turn it toward the glass over the mantel-piece.

Harry was not vain, and his own face had no particular attraction for him; he gave a glance at the reflection of the little white fingers which were holding his chin, and then he took her hand gently from his face and looked at her.

"I don't set up for a beauty-man, and lots of the actors you meet are handsomer than me, I dare say. But it is more than I can understand how you could like an ugly, washed-out, long-nosed, lank-haired hunchback like that fellow I met outside! It is rather hard to be shunted for a man who isn't even straight!"

Annie winced under the speech; but she said:

"Then how can you be so absurd as to be jealous of a man who stoops—you, who are as straight as an arrow?"

"Ah, my limbs are all right; it is my head you complain of!" answered poor Harry, pitifully. "I believe my heart is all right, too, only that doesn't seem to matter to you clever women. I suppose that stooping fellow can talk by the yard."

"Mr. Cooke can ride and drive, too," said Annie, quietly. "Men who talk well can do other things, too, very often."

"He can stick on a Park hack, or drive a dog-cart a couple of miles without coming to grief, I dare say," returned Harry, in a louder voice. "But do you think he could break in an animal that had thrown every groom in the stable, or ride as straight as I can across country, or train a racer?"

"I don't suppose he is as much at home in a stable as you are, certainly," said Annie, coldly, "or that any of the actors I know are so well able to beat a groom at his own work. I must do you so much justice."

"Thank you. It is very clever of you to snub me like that; and I dare say you think, if I had any proper pride, I ought to go away after you have so plainly let me know how my vulgar stable-talk bores you. But I sha'n't," continued Harry, doggedly. "I was foolish to let you go away from me, and I was foolish to come after you; but, now I am here, I mean to stop." And he flung himself down into a chair.

"You mean to stay here!"

"Yes; and, when I go away, I mean to take you with me."

"Oh, indeed! Against my will?"

"I hope not—not if what you said to me a little while ago is true, Annie;" and he leaned forward on his elbows, with such wistful earnestness in his face and voice that his wife was forced to listen. "You say you are not fond of anybody else, you say nobody else has been making love to you, and you tell me I'm so handsome that I need not be afraid of anybody else. Well, if all that is true, and I'm such a nice, good-looking fellow, and you are so anxious to cling to my arms and caress me and introduce me to your friends, why on earth, as soon as I turn up, do you want to be rid of me again?"

"I don't want to be rid of you. But I am not going to be treated like a child, as if I could not be trusted alone."

"Well, I don't think any woman can, when she has a husband whose duty it is to look after her."

"Oh, your opinion of a husband's duty was not always so high, I think!"

"No, it wasn't. But I am all the more bound to fulfill it well now, when I have neglected it so long. Annie, don't be hard. Why did you come to me when I had got used to being without you, if you only meant to show me what a brute I was, and then repulse me when I tried, for your sake, to be something better? You don't know how you have hurt me this afternoon by showing me how sorry you were to see me again; I don't think I ever felt so knocked over as when, after I had met that fellow and knew who he was—for I'm not such a booby as you suppose, and I knew you liked that ugly Maypole better than me—you just said 'Harry!' without a smile or the least sign of pleasure when you saw me. I felt as if you had stuck a knife into me."

He stopped for a few moments, his voice all husky.

"And then see how good I've been to you! I've never even said a harsh word to you, though I know many husbands who would have said horrid things to their wives if they had caught them like that. But I swore to William that I would be very gentle to you, even if you were not glad to see me. I don't know what made him guess you wouldn't be; but I'll just punch his head for being so clever when I get back. And haven't I kept my word? If I had been so clever as these men you know, who can do everything, I should have been sarcastic; and, instead of that, I have let you be sarcastic, and I haven't even sworn at you;" and Harry looked up at his wife pleadingly, yet proudly, as if the force of conjugal affection and manly self-restraint could no further go.

"Harry, indeed I am glad to see you, and sorry you are still so thin. I should have told you so long ago if you had let me. But you made such a furious onslaught upon me at once."

"Very well then; we'll let by-gones be by-gones, and you shall come back with me, and we'll be as happy as crickets," said he, affectionately, as he jumped up from his chair and was on his knees beside her, with his arm round her, in a minute.

"But, Harry, I can't do that. I am under an engagement now which I am bound to fulfill. And, remember, we were not at all like happy crickets when we were at the Grange together."

"No, the Grange is a beastly old place, and nobody could be happy there; I don't wonder you got moped," he answered, hastily. "Now in town it is different. There is so much to be done in London, such a lot to be seen, so—so many books and—and picture-galleries and pretty dresses and clever people."

"But you don't care for those things, Harry."

"Yes, I do—at least, I shall when I've been with you a little while. And I've quite taken to reading, and——Oh, I shall get on capitally!"

"But what would you do without your dogs and your horses, Harry?"

"Do you think I can't get on without dogs and horses," said he impatiently. "I suppose you think I can't be happy unless I am loafing about a stable with my inferiors—only you wouldn't call them my inferiors!"

"How silly you are, Harry! When have I said anything like that to you?"

"You did only a few minutes ago."

"I did not mean it. I think it is a pity for you, who are devoted to the life of a country gentleman, to give up all your pleasures just to settle down to a life which would not suit you."

"But it isn't just for that, Annie; that is where you're wrong. If I cared for nothing but the country, I should stay there. I can get on without horses, though I am fond of riding and driving, as you know; and I can get on without dogs, though I miss old Ponto every other minute; but I can't get on without you, Annie. I have tried, but it is no good; so, as you won't come into the country with me, I must come to town to you."

Annie was silent, more puzzled by, than grateful for, this devotion. Then she said, in a low voice:

"I can't accept such a sacrifice, Harry."

"Then will you come back to the Grange with me?"

"I can't do that. I have accepted an engagement, and I must go through with it."

"What makes you so much more particular about the engagement which binds you to act so many times a week for a certain manager than about the one you are under to me, your husband?"

"That is not fair. You allowed me to make this engagement."

"Well, I don't ask you to break it. All I ask is to let me stay with you and take care of you."

"But, Harry dear, you would be very uncomfortable here. The rooms are so small and so shabby——"

"Well, come with me to the Bingham Hotel; they have nice big rooms there, and we shall be very comfortable."

"But they are frightfully expensive!"

"Never mind that. George forked out this morning; he had kept me very short for a long time, so he gave me a check, and told me it was the last I should see of his money—with a black look, to prevent the pleasure from being too much for me. That is just like George, you know."

"But perhaps he meant it; and, if so, you ought to be careful."

"So I will be careful, and you shall help me. I'll give it all to you to take care of as soon as I get it cashed. Fifty pounds will last a long time."

"And before that is gone I shall be earning a better salary than I ever had in my life!" said Annie.

"But I sha'n't live upon your money. Do you think I would sponge upon my wife? I am not going to give you a chance of despising me again."

"Then what will you do when the fifty pounds are gone?"

"Write to George for some more, of course."

"But supposing he could not or would not send you any more?"

"Supposing the skies were to fall? Go and pack up your trunks, my darling, and we'll go off and have a new honeymoon—only this time you shall have a kind husband instead of a cross one!"

There was no resisting him in his imperiously loving mood; and Annie, scarcely yet understanding this new situation of affairs, went, with the husband's hands gently pushing her, into the next room; and while she was busily filling her trunks, she heard him ring the bell, order the week's bill and pay it; then he burst into the room, threw his arms round her, and gave her a huge hug as she was closing the last box, and whispered:

"This is tremendous fun—running away with one's own wife!"

CHAPTER XXII.

Annie felt a curious and altogether new sensation as she submitted to be carried off to the hotel by her husband, whom success in this small enterprise had restored to the happiest and most affectionate of humors. It was the first time since the early days of their marriage, when the privilege had soon palled, that she had gone about with him as a protector, and the pride and pleasure in the position which he ingenuously showed, surprised and amused her.

They were, as he had predicted, very comfortable at the hotel. With astonishing tact, Harry forebore to press his grievances against his wife, and devoted himself to banishing the remembrance of the "clever man who could do everything" by taking her to theaters and picture galleries, and to the park, and to expensive dinners at the best restaurants, with an assiduity which could not fail to touch her. Indeed Annie did not quite know what a happy passage in her life this was until after it was over. She wished to be, and she thought she was, tormented a little by self- reproach caused by her bad treatment of Aubrey Cooke; but the feeling was not strong enough to outweigh the delightful sense of repose she began to feel in the consciousness that she was surrounded by a great love. Her husband was so watchful, so affectionate, refrained so consistently from exacting demands of demonstrative fondness from her, that she had no time, no excuse for such a sentiment as real regret. He insisted, against her will, upon taking her to and from the theater to rehearsal, and asked her, when she objected, whether she was ashamed of him.

"If you are, say I am an old servant of the family," said he, proudly.

But Annie silenced him imperiously; and the confession she made in the theater that she was married, and that the handsome young fellow who brought her backward and forward was her husband, while it brought down upon her some accusations of coquetry, sent her up in popular opinion as the possessor of such a tall, well-bred-looking lord and master.

Life had gone on very smoothly in this way for nearly a week, and it was the day before the opening night of "Nathalie," when Harry, finding himself at the end of his ready money, thought of changing his check.

In the evening Annie noticed that he was rather preoccupied during dinner, and when she asked whether he had got some gloves he had promised her, he said he had not been able to get them yet, but she should have them on the morrow.

"Did you change the check, Harry? You said you would give the money to me to take care of," she suggested, laughing.

"No, I haven't changed it. The fact is," he continued, seeing a look of perplexity on his wife's face. "George has overdrawn his account a good deal, and they won't cash such a big check until they have heard from him."

"But fifty pounds is not such a very large sum; and your family has banked there for years and years, I know. Doesn't it seem rather strange, Harry, that they should refuse when they know you so well?"

This was a rather unfortunate suggestion, as the character of the Braithwaite boys had not always stood high in money matters; but Harry only said:

"Oh, it will be all right, of course! I wrote to George this afternoon, and I shall get an answer to-morrow or Monday. Don't you feel awfully nervous about to-morrow night?"

"Indeed I do. If it were not for the way you take me about and divert my thoughts, I believe I should make myself ill by the way I worry myself about it. I must go now; rehearsal begins at seven, so I shall be wanted at half-past."

This was the night rehearsal, on the eve of the production of the new piece. For a week the manager had not slept, weighted with doubts about the success of a performance which had cost him months of thought, care and actual labor of body and mind. He was a popular man, and the members of the company sympathized with him, though their own lesser responsibility sat far more lightly upon them, and the green-room during the last rehearsals, when doubts far outweighed hopes regarding the piece they were all at work upon, rang with laughter as the foremost wits of the company made cruel jokes upon the "governor" and his troubles.

The next morning, just as Annie was starting for the last rehearsal of all, a telegram came for her husband. He read it and thrust it into his pocket without any remark and without any offer to show it to her. She was getting used to quiet self-reliance on her husband's part: but this action surprised her.

"From George?" she asked rather diffidently.

"Yes. Stephen is coming up this morning to see me, with statements from George—not very cheerful ones, I fancy. But don't trouble your head about that, darling, or you will be unfit for to-night. We shall pull through right enough, never fear!"

"Why, I am not nearly so anxious as you are, Harry! I shall get my salary next week—six guineas—and then, if we only live a little more economically, we shall get on splendidly."

"Yes, yes; it will be all right. There is the hansom outside. I must send you alone this morning, my darling, for I must stay at home to see Stephen when he comes. Good-bye—good luck to you, Annie."

He put her carefully into the hansom, giving her hand a tender lover-like little squeeze as he helped her in, and went back into the hotel for his cigar-case, to pass away the time with a cigar as he walked up and down outside, waiting for his cousin.

When she returned from rehearsal, in a hansom by Harry's orders, she found Stephen waiting outside the hotel to receive her. He was looking pale and anxious, and she asked him hurriedly what was the matter.

"Come in and I'll tell you," said he.

He led her into the coffee-room, which was empty.

"You have bad news, Stephen, I am sure! What is it? Where is Harry?"

"He told me to break it to you. He has quite given way under it. You will try not to be very much shocked, won't you? It is about George. He——"

"Not dead?" whispered she, white to the lips.

"Oh, no; he is quite well! But he has smashed up."

"Poor fellow!" said she sympathizingly, but much relieved. "Is he really quite ruined?"

"Yes, I am afraid so; he has been in difficulties for a long time now, you know. The Grange will have to be sold, of course; but it and the land are so heavily mortgaged that that won't relieve him much. He has expected the crash for a long time, and Wilfred and I had some notion of it too; but Harry never dreamed of such a thing, and it has knocked him over altogether."

"But why does he take it so much to heart? He will be better off than anybody now I've got such a good engagement."

"It seems he wanted to persuade you to give up acting and go and live with him at the Grange; he told William and me so just now."

"William!"

"Yes: I brought him up with me, and he is with Harry now, unless Harry has turned him out of the room; for, when your husband said you were growing fond of him, William said that was nonsense, and I had a lot of trouble in getting them to leave each other alone."

"But it is true, and it was very wrong of William to contradict him. He has been very kind to me, and I am quite glad that at last I can do something for him."

"Frankly, Annie, I don't think he'll let you. He is very obstinate, you know, when once he gets an idea into his head; and he has taken to thinking that it would be beneath his dignity to live on your earnings. And really, you know, I think he is right."

"But how is he to live any other way?"

"I don't know, I am sure; I think that is what is bothering him, and the thought that he will have to leave you."

"But he mustn't do that."

"Then you had better go and tell him so; he has been crying about that. He says, just as you were beginning to like him, all his work is undone again, and you will call him a loafer."

"I will go to him," said Annie; and she left Stephen, and went up-stairs to her sitting-room, where William rushed at her directly she opened the door.

She saw that Harry was lying on the sofa, with his face in the cushions; but she could not get at him at once, for "the child" was dancing round her, glancing at Harry and crossing his fingers with an expressive grimace, to intimate that his brother was in a bad temper and had better be left to the solitary enjoyment of it.

"He will only snap at you," whispered he, as Annie pushed past him gently and went toward the sofa; and William, with his soft whistle, went out of the room.

She passed her fingers through her husband's rough hair, and turned his face gently toward her. She could see that he had been crying, and, with a sudden great tenderness, she drew his head on to her breast and kissed him without a word.

It was only by a great effort that he kept back the tears which came to his eyes again at this demonstration; and Annie wondered how it was that he was so much overcome.

"Don't give way like this, Harry, I can't understand you," said she reprovingly, as he sat by her side and drew her toward him.

"It is very hard for poor old George, especially as he has known so long that it was coming; but William is provided for, as your uncle in Ireland is looking after him, and Stephen has a little money of his own and Lilian is all right, and you and I will have plenty of money next week."

But Harry bounced up from the sofa at this point saying that it was luncheon-time, and she must be starving after her long rehearsal; and ten minutes later they, with William and Stephen, were sitting together at table, trying to divert their thoughts from their gloomy prospects by talking of the piece Annie was to play in for the first time that night.

As soon as luncheon was over, Harry insisted upon making his wife lie down to get some rest before the exciting duties of a "first night" began. Sleep was out of the question for her; she lay repeating the words of her part, which she had known for weeks, in a fever of unnecessary anxiety, lest the words should slip from her memory at the last, or lest, in the excitement of the all-important first performance, she should hurry her speeches unduly—a fault to which she was prone.

Harry softly opened the door from time to time and crept in, sometimes without her even hearing him. He always found her engaged in the same way, softly going over her lines to herself, and each time he retreated, looking harassed, and rather disappointed.

They had dinner early, for she had to be at the theater at half past seven. Harry went with her, and, as they drove along together in a hansom, he was very quiet and silent, holding her hand in his, and speaking only in answer to her. If she had not been so greatly preoccupied by anticipations of the night's performance and nervousness about her own share in it, she must have noticed that there was still something unaccounted for in the unusual gravity, which was not sullenness, of her husband's manner. As they drove up to the stage-door she noticed that he was shaking like a girl.

"You are not well, Harry," she said, anxiously. "What is the matter with you?"

"It is only about you," said he, in a low voice.

"Oh, I shall be all right; through all my excitement I feel sure of that! Why, you are more nervous for me than I am for myself! Look here, Harry—I am sure you are not well; the shock you had this morning has been too much for you. Don't come for me to-night—indeed, there is no need; I will send for a cab and come back as safely as possible."

Rather to her surprise, he said quickly, as he helped her out of the hansom:

"Yes, yes, that will be the best; I am not very well, I think William shall bring you home."

He had paid the fare, and they had reached the stage-door together. Two of the actors were outside, and they raised their hats and began speaking to Annie. Without pausing in her talk, she gave her hand lightly to her husband, as he stood there still, anxious to be with her as long as he could. She felt again that his hand was trembling, and she turned to him to say:

"Don't watch the piece, Harry; it will make me more nervous than ever to know that you are sitting in front, in a fever lest I should make some slip."

"I'm all right; I must see you through it," said he, huskily; and he snatched away his hand, and, wishing the others, whom he knew, good-evening and success, went off very quickly, almost, it seemed to Annie, as if he were afraid of breaking down if he stayed. She went into the theater very much affected by this proof of his attachment to her, and, as she took from the box where they had been lying the flowers he had brought from Covent Garden that afternoon for her to wear that night, she raised the heavy white roses and the sweet stephanotis to her lips before she fastened them in the front of the cream-white muslin dress in which she was first to appear.

The audiences at the fashionable comedy theaters are not, as a rule, demonstrative; but, when Annie came off the stage, after her best scene that night, she knew that she had made a "hit." It was the first distinct, noteworthy success of her career, and her heart beat fast as she thought that now she had her foot firmly upon the ladder, and the future seemed to be clear before her. She did not for a moment think she had got to the top; she knew quite well that struggles and some failures lay still in her path; but that a good beginning toward a prosperous artistic career had been made was a fact which set the blood tingling in her veins and brought the fierce light of hopeful ambition into her dark eyes, when, her share in the work of the evening over, she exchanged the dress she had worn on the stage for the one in which she had come to the theater, and went down from her dressing-room to the green-room to wait for the end of the performance and the final verdict of the first-night audience upon the piece.

It was a favorable one; and Annie found her way to the stage-door, on her way out, with congratulations ringing in her ears and the knowledge that, as certainly as certainty is possible in theatrical matters, the long weeks of anxious and tedious rehearsal were to be rewarded by a calm and prosperous run of the new piece.

At the door she found William dancing about, having been with difficulty restrained by the hall doorkeeper from rushing through the door which led on to the stage. He dragged her arm through his, and in high glee helped her into the hansom, and, as he flung himself in afterward, began at once:

"Oh, Annie, you were splendid, you were immense! I didn't think you could act like that. It wasn't like acting at all, I'm sure, the way you take that toffee! Oh, well, it was just like life, just like the way you used to go on with me at the Grange! Poor, old Grange! I wonder if I shall ever see it again?"

"I used to think of you sometimes at rehearsal, when I came to that bit. Was Harry sitting with you?"

"Yes; he nearly went off his head. He kept saying, 'Isn't she perfect? Isn't she lovely?' And I had to keep him from jumping up two or three times. I think if I hadn't he would have tried to climb on to the stage to you."

"Dear old boy! How nice of him! I am so glad he was pleased with me."

"Well, I don't see much merit in that. He couldn't help being proud of you when all the people about were saying how good you were. If he had been a decent sort of husband, he would have waited himself to take you home, instead of telling me to do so and prancing off himself goodness knows where."

"Didn't he say where he was going?"

"No; he knew better than to tell me, because I should have just given him a bit of my mind about it; but I've no doubt he's gone off to supper with somebody or other," said William, with rigid disgust.

"William, how dare you talk like that? Do you know you are speaking about my husband?"

"Oh, yes, of course I know! Why, Annie, you are not really angry, are you?"

"Yes, I am—very angry. When the poor fellow has spent a miserable day, and made himself quite ill between his nervousness for me and his grief over the shock he had this morning, you take the first opportunity of abusing him to me, his wife."

"But, Annie, you haven't grown fond of Harry, have you?" said William, with pity and fear in his voice.

"Yes, I have—very fond. I couldn't help it," sobbed Annie, apologetically. "He has been so kind to me lately."

"Poor girl!" said "the child," with compassion. "Never mind; you will soon get over it when he leaves you alone again, and you are full of your success on the stage, and people will crowd round you and compliment you and tell you what a great actress you are, and——"

"When he leaves me again? What do you mean?"

"Why, he will, Annie—on some excuse or other, he will. He will never stay quietly in London without anything to ride. I know Harry."

But she was too indignant to let him go on, and for the rest of the drive she maintained a frigid attitude of offended dignity toward her indiscreet brother-in-law; and she repulsed him freezingly when he tried to kiss and be friends.

On reaching the hotel, she ran quickly up-stairs, anxious to find her husband and prove to William that she had not overestimated his devotion. But in neither room was he to be found. On her dressing-room table, however, she discovered a note directed to her in her husband's handwriting. She tore it open; but she was for some minutes too much excited and frightened to read it. It ran as follows:

"MY DARLING ANNIE,—I dont know whether you will think I am doing something very wrong and cruel or whether you wont care a straw. I am going away though I love you with all my heart just as much as ever and it hurts me awfully not to say goodby to you even but if I did I know you would ask me to stay and I cant do that and be a loafer and live on your money you would be quite right to despise me if I did and say I was nothing but an idler like I used to be. I am going to work. I dont know quite what I am going to do but I cannot try any what are called gentlemanly occupations because you know I would be so bad at them but I will make some money somehow and I wont steel it I promise you that but you must not be too particular how I make it as long as it is honestly—will you now. I have paid the bill and gone to your old lodging and paid the rent for a week and the gloves will be sent tonight and I leave you all the money I can to go on with. I am going to see you act tonight and I know you will be successfull becaus you are so clever and so pretty and all the men will try to turn your head but dont let them my darling Annie becaus all the time I am working for you and mean to get rich for you—and now you see I love you so and only go away becaus I do. I think you will try not to like *anybody* else—but to think how I can be nice to you and make you happy even though I am not clever like some of the men you know. I dont know exactly where I am going just at first—but if you write to me and give your letters to Stephen I shall get them and he will let you know how I get on. You will not see me again yet because it would knock me over just at first and I know you would not like what I am going to do and you might talk me out of it. But I shall see you very often you may be sure as long as I have a shilling to go in the gallery with

"Your ever loving husband

"HARRY."

She found a sovereign inside the letter and the hotel-bill receipted. She did not cry, but went into the sitting-room where William was waiting for her.

"Annie, you are ill! You are so white! You have overexcited yourself. Sit down and let me get you some brandy-and-water."

"No, no, I am not ill. You were quite right, William; Harry has left me already."

The young fellow stood before her, shocked, silent.

"Never mind, Annie, you have your old brother," said he, as soon as he could speak, in a soothing voice. "Perhaps, after all, it was best that he should go soon, before you had got used to him, and might have missed him. Now I have an idea, Annie, that we might be very happy if you and I were to take a cottage—now we are poor, it won't run to more than a cottage—and you might keep house for me, as lots of sisters do for their brothers; and of course I couldn't be always at home because of my military duties very soon," said he, proudly, "but I could be always running down there, even when I was away, and we should be so jolly together."

"My dear William; what are you thinking about? I am not really your sister, you know, and such an arrangement wouldn't be thought proper."

"Annie, I am afraid—I begin to think—you are really fond of Harry."

"Yes, William," said poor Annie, while the tears rolled down her cheeks, "I am afraid—I begin to think—I am."

CHAPTER XXIII.

Annie woke the next morning with a dull, uncomfortable sense of having received a great blow which quite counterbalanced the ecstasy of her first stage-success. She reasoned with herself over this feeling, but could not argue it away. She had indeed suffered two shocks yesterday—the news of George's ruin and the threatened sale of the Grange in the morning, and the letter which announced her husband's departure at night. But the first was an event which had long been impending, and George himself could scarcely be more unhappy, now the crash had come, than he had been during those long months when he had felt that ruin was hanging over him; and, as for the last, a week ago there had been no event she had so much dreaded as the possible appearance of her husband in London. It could not be that she was so weak-minded as to have changed in a week from dreading her husband's presence to desiring it. Certainly Harry had been most surprisingly nice, good-tempered, and kind, quite different from the bear he used to be at the Grange; she had caught herself turning to him for an opinion now and then, led away by the authority he had somehow assumed in his manner toward her; and his replies on such occasions had shown less imbecility than her former contempt for his ignorance had led her to expect. But then this state of things could not have gone on much longer in any case; such a very new phase as Harry's angelic patience would surely never have lasted more than another day or two, and the reaction would probably have brought on a terrible fit of savagery.

"Yet I wish he had stayed till then," she thought, regretfully. "He did not seem to have grown tired of being nice to me, and he was so very sweet while it lasted. I don't think I was ever happier than I was last week, in spite of the fatigue and anxiety of rehearsals. I wonder where he is? I dare say I should be very much disgusted if I knew. After a week of no society but mine, I should think he must be pining for some grooms or coachmen to talk to. Very likely he is enjoying himself in some stable at this minute."

But she little thought how shrewd a guess she had made.

In a wistful and restless state of mind she went back to the apartments in which her husband had found her. What few friends she had began to find her out in the course of the next few days, and to call upon her and insist upon her coming to see them and receive congratulations upon her success in "Nathalie."

This recognition of her talent was very pleasant; but it just missed being the supreme joy she had expected it to be; and, in searching for the reason of this slight disappointment, it occurred to her that there was one person who ought to have hastened forward with the rest of her acquaintance to offer her the natural matter-of-course homage of a few complimentary words upon the hit she had made in the new piece. This person was Aubrey Cooke.

She had not seen him since that unlucky meeting with her husband; and, though, in the few bright busy days she had passed with Harry, she had had little time for unpleasant reflections of any kind, she had by no means forgotten the friend whose visits and amusing talk had been the one compensation for the dullness of her home-life in London before Harry's inopportune appearance.

Why did he not come to see her again, and give her an opportunity of explaining her silence concerning her marriage? He had let fall no word, since the day of her arrival in town, when she had laughed off his sentiment, to let her think that it mattered to him whether she was under any engagement or not. Was he irretrievably offended? If he felt wounded by her want of confidence, was it not her duty to seek him out herself and offer some apology, rather than lose a friend by proud silence?

Annie felt so entirely heart-free that no further scruple about Harry's jealousy deterred her from taking such a step. Since her husband disapproved of it, she would tell Aubrey herself that she must not receive him so often; and, now that her other friends and acquaintances were flocking round her, she felt that she was not so entirely dependent upon him for companionship. So she wrote a note to him, as she had often done before, asking him to meet her at the "Stores," and help her with her shopping. She did not expect an answer, for these little civilly entreating notes he always took as commands, and she knew he would look upon it as an appointment. So, when she arrived at the "Stores" the next day, she was not at all surprised, or in any way agitated to find him there waiting for her.

But she had been but very few minutes in his society before she noticed that there was a change in his manner toward her. She had been much relieved to see that, when they first met, there was no offended dignity in his manner, no coldness in his tone; but now she began to perceive that there was even unnecessary tenderness in his voice when he spoke to her, and that he drew her hand through his arm with a gentle pressure which he had never attempted before, and when he asked her to have some strawberries, he called her "darling." The next moment he saw that he had gone too far, and turned off his unlucky speech very cleverly; but Annie felt frightened, and, while he gave her no further loophole for offense, she was constrained in her manner and dismissed him as soon as she could.

She knew what she had done, that the discovery of her deceit about her marriage had changed Aubrey Cooke's estimate of her, and that he had received this last note, written, as he must have found out, after the departure of her husband, in a very different spirit from the frank *camaraderie* with which he had responded to her former appeals to him to come and help her with her marketing. She knew that she had deserved this severe wound to her self-respect, and she went home miserable and ashamed.

But this difficulty was not yet over. At the theater a beautiful bouquet was brought to her with a note—a lover-like note—from Aubrey. She tore up the note, and gave the flowers to the dresser. But on the following night she received another bouquet, another note; and on the third night, this attention having been again repeated, she got a little teased by one of her fellow-actors, who knew Aubrey and had seen other bouquets of his and other notes.

She went home mad with shame and anger, and wrote Aubrey a curt note, asking him to call upon her; and when the next day the time she had appointed came and she heard his well-known tread upon the stairs, she felt that her whole frame was shaking violently, and that she would have hard work to receive him with calmness.

But he was experienced in flirtation as well as in love, and he had far too much tact not to know that her summons had been dictated by some feeling which was not affection. She was obliged to take the hand he held out so humbly, and his deferential attitude somewhat disarmed her.

"I got your note only just in time, Mrs. Braithwaite: I was going down to Kirby Park to see some horses a friend of mine has in training there."

"I am sorry if my note interfered with your day's arrangements. You should have sent me a line to say you were engaged."

"I am never engaged when you send for me. You must know that by this time."

Annie raised her head haughtily, while he continued:

"It is more than eight months now since you told me I was the only person in the world you could depend upon, and I have never failed you yet."

This allusion was embarrassing, and Annie could only murmur:

"You have always been very kind."

"And you have put my kindness to some hard tests, haven't you? You have snubbed me, you have confided in me—at least you appeared to do so: you have encouraged me to love you——"

"No, Mr. Cooke; I am quite innocent of any such intention."

"Then your innocence served you better than any coquetry could have done, Mrs. Braithwaite. Having innocently encouraged me to love you, you innocently allowed me to tell you so, with only such vague suggestions of 'an obstacle' as served to make me more anxious to win you. When you mysteriously left the company, you had managed to leave me not altogether without hope; when I saw you again, here in town, you managed, without compromising yourself in any way, to make that hope stronger, and it was only when I met the 'obstacle' for the first time outside your door that I was allowed to discover that it had any real existence. If you had left me alone then," continued Aubrey, in a lower voice, his agitation betraying itself, in spite of his efforts to repress it, in convulsive movements of his features and his hands, "I might at least have thought that you felt some shame at the way in which you had treated me; but you wrote me a little note just in the old way, as if the old relations between us were possible. I knew your husband was away again; it was easy for me to see by the way you met him that you hated him. I took your summons, when I at last knew the circumstances of your position, and of mine to you, as any man would have taken it. You had deceived your husband, you had deceived me; you were not the good, true woman I had thought you. Still, if you wanted me back, I cared enough about you still to come, but not on the old terms. That was impossible. You were rather reserved; I thought it a trick of coquetry, naturally enough. I sent you flowers and notes, such as I have sent to other women far less treacherous, but without any of your pretensions to immaculate conduct. To my surprise, you assume in return an attitude of the most rigid dignity and outraged propriety—you have sent for me to answer for my offenses against you. With far more reason I might summon you—if you were not a woman and therefore above laws of justice and humanity—to account for yours against me."

Aubrey Cooke stood as erect as Harry himself could have done as he spoke, with feeling and with fire, these words to the woman before him.

She had indeed been innocent of the depth of the emotions she had stirred in this man with the expressionless face and hard voice. She had expected to have some difficulty in arguing him into recognizing the fact that her conduct toward him had been dictated by the best possible motives, and that any apparent injustice she had done him was the result of circumstances; but she had not imagined for an instant that he would turn upon her with reproaches so bitter and so well founded that she would be left without a word in answer. Yet it was so; and Annie bent her head for very shame as the torrent of his passionate words passed over her, and she felt that she was without a defense.

Then, seeing her so broken and crushed before him, she who had always held herself so proudly, Aubrey relented—for he loved her still—and, as he saw the tears falling slowly from her downcast eyes on to her clasped hands, he fell upon his knees beside her, and from the stern judge became once more the humble suppliant.

"Annie, Annie, never mind what I have said! I did not want to be harsh, only to let you know—what I ought to have kept from you, I suppose."

"You said I was wicked," sobbed Annie, woman-like, seizing the advantage which his remorse at having caused her tears gave her.

"Yes, I know—I was in a passion—I didn't mean it, of course, Annie. You didn't tell me you were married—because you thought it would hurt me, and you hated him, and wanted to forget his existence. Well, you were quite right; I could see at a glance that he was an ill-tempered brute, and that you were afraid of him."

"He is not ill-tempered," flashed out Annie, with sudden fire. "And all that I am afraid of is that he won't come back to me, that some one will tell him that I am happy without him, and that he will console himself before I can let him know it is untrue."

Aubrey was silent for some minutes. He detected in this speech the ring of genuine feeling; and anger and contempt for the woman before him, who seemed to him at that moment the incarnation of fickleness and deceit, overcame his love for her and raised him to his feet again.

"I have no doubt he will wake sooner or later to a sense of what a precious thing he is neglecting in your love!" said he, in a biting voice.

"Thank you," returned Annie, brought to herself at once by this taunt. "I deserve every sneer you can cast at me; but you cannot make me regret that I have at last discovered the worth of a man who has suffered more at my hands than you have done without casting at me a single taunt."

"I congratulate you. I feel—I feel quite happy in having served as a foil to such a perfect creature. I won't take up any more of your time, Mrs. Braithwaite," said he, rushing to the door and groping blindly for the handle, having forgotten his hat in his excitement.

"Don't go away like that!" said Annie, following him and sobbing, meekly. "I have behaved very, very badly; it was all through my conceit in thinking I could not do anything wrong just because I did not mean to. Will you forgive me, Mr. Cooke?"

"No, I won't—I can't, Mrs. Braithwaite!"

"Do forgive me, Aubrey!"

He held out only one second longer, then took her little hands and kissed them again and again.

"You are the only woman who has ever treated me badly, and the only woman I shall ever care a straw about. It is always like that, I believe. Good-bye, Annie. I shall be married in a month, and dead in two, I expect. Good-bye." And he tore a little rosebud from the bouquet near her throat, and was out of the room and out of the house before she could answer.

Her faults were punishing her bitterly now. She threw herself upon the sofa in an agony of remorse and wretchedness, feeling that she had behaved badly all round, that she was abandoned by every one, and that she had deserved every pang which could torment her. She had trifled with Aubrey, despised her husband, and now they both looked down upon her and treated her as she deserved.

When the first excess of her grief and humiliation was over, her thoughts all flowed into one channel, and the question which absorbed her was, would Harry ever come back to a wife for whom he must, in spite of his patience with her through that week at the end of which he had run away, entertain at heart so great a contempt? She was herself surprised at the persistency with which her thoughts returned to the husband whom she had so disliked and despised at the time when no self-reproach at the faults in her own conduct had risen to disturb the placid superiority she felt over him.

She had begun to fret herself into a fever of anxiety at the thought that she would never hear from him again, when, on her return home from a walk one afternoon, she was told by the servant that a lady and gentleman were in her sitting-room.

"They did not come together, ma'am. The lady came first, and presently the gentleman; and, when they heard you were out, they both said they would wait for you. So I showed them both up-stairs, ma'am."

In the sitting-room Annie found Stephen, whom she had rightly guessed to be one of the visitors, and Muriel West, whom she certainly neither expected nor wished to see.

This lady, whose coarseness had in the very first days of their forced acquaintanceship on tour disgusted Annie, had nevertheless shown the latter so much good-natured kindness in many little ways, and notably when the younger actress was ill with neuralgia, that it was impossible for her not to receive the unwelcome guest with cordiality.

Miss West had dyed her hair a new color since their last meeting, but the dye was wearing off; her face was thin and ghastly, her gloves were in holes, her dress was more haphazard than ever, and her whole appearance suggestive of hard times and even of scanty fare. She greeted Annie with her old loud geniality.

"Ah, Miss Langton, you're up, and I'm down! I hardly dared to come and call upon such a howling swell as you have become. You are not sorry to see an old friend though, I see."

"I am very sorry to see you looking so ill, though," said Annie, sincerely. "You used not to look like that in the country. You want change of air."

"No, no, my dear; you're wrong there. No actress wants change of air when once she's got to London. It's an engagement I want. I've been out for six weeks, and see no prospect of being in again. I don't know whether you can help me; but I've come to ask your advice on one or two matters."

"I will come in and see you presently, Annie," said Stephen, going toward the door. "I have nothing much to say to you, and I came chiefly to see whether you had any commissions for me."

"Yes, yes, I have! I have a letter for you to take, and I want to see you most particularly. Come back and have tea with me, will you?"

He promised to do so; and Annie, who was dying to hear all he had to tell her about her husband, was obliged reluctantly to let him go, and to listen instead to the long list of grievances and complaints against London managers and things in general which Miss West proceeded to entertain her with in language much stronger than was necessary.

Annie had noticed upon her first entrance that Stephen and Miss West were in animated converse, and that the former seemed very much engrossed by his companion. He now turned with eagerness to her again, and asked whether he should have the pleasure of meeting her on his return. But Annie did not invite Miss West to stay to tea. So he left, casting at the very last moment an ardent and expressive glance at the object of his evident admiration.

The two women had not been many minutes alone together before Annie discovered that the real object of her visitor was to discover whether her more prosperous fellow-artist could oblige her with a loan. Annie had some money to spare, and could not refuse, especially as she felt that fate had been capricious in giving her a good engagement and the chance she had pined for, while Miss West, who she felt was really the greater actress of the two, was out of work and restlessly longing for an opportunity of distinction, as she herself had so long been.

Miss West had not been gone more than a few minutes when Stephen returned, and Annie asked anxiously for news of Harry, which his cousin seemed chary of imparting to her.

"Can't you tell me where he is and how he is, Stephen?" she asked impatiently.

"I can't tell you where he is, because he is traveling about, and I don't know myself where he is at this moment. But he is quite well, and I haven't seen him in such good spirits for a long time."

"Oh," said Annie, her face falling involuntarily. "I am very glad to hear that! Does he—I suppose he doesn't speak of coming to town?"

"Oh, dear, no! You know Harry hates town; he is not like the same man now he has got back into the country again, and to—"

Here Stephen pulled himself up short and Annie said quietly, with tightened lips:

"Go on, Stephen. Harry is happier now he has got back to—what?"

"Oh, I only meant the country air and the country people! You know he is a regular rustic, and Londoners don't suit him."

Annie gulped down the tears this unlucky speech brought to her eyes, and said, with forced cheerfulness:

"Yes, he is, of course, much happier in the country."

"Of course," admitted Stephen, guardedly. "He has sent you this letter."

She tore it open. It was only a short note, very affectionate, but with no definite word concerning his own movements. A sudden impulse of angry pride seized her, and shame at the long letter she had prepared in exchange for this brief, hurriedly-written note. She took up the letter she was about to send, and, excusing herself to Stephen, went into the next room, tore it into shreds, and, hastily writing a note as short and as vague as her husband's own, returned and gave that as her answer.

They were not long over tea, as Stephen seemed anxious to get away, and Annie herself was late for the theater. When he had gone, she dressed very quickly, and followed him out of the house in a few minutes. At the end of the second street she had to pass through, she saw Stephen and Miss West standing in earnest conversation. She had to pass them; but they were too much absorbed in what they were saying to notice her approach.

When she was near to them, she heard Stephen say bitterly:

"Of course you like Harry better than me, because he's such a tall, straight, handsome fellow!"

"Handsome is that handsome does. I like him because he likes me. You tell him so, give him my love, and say he'll see me before very long if he's a good boy;" and Miss West, with a laugh and a roguish glance, hurried away; and Stephen, without turning round to see Annie, followed slowly in the same direction.

Annie walked on steadily, with the hot tears burning in her eyes.

This was what Harry's desertion meant; and this coarse woman, whom she had just been assisting, was the enchantress who held his heart for the time.

"What an idiot I was to imagine for a moment that he was capable of lasting affection, and for his wife! I will never think about him again!"

But she thought about him all the way to the theater, and cried herself to sleep over her dislike of him and her contempt for him.

CHAPTER XXIV.

The nightly duty Annie had to perform at the theater was all that saved her from a serious illness, as the result of the acute misery she suffered for some time after the eventful day on which the discovery of her husband's faithlessness had succeeded to Aubrey's reproaches. How wise she now felt herself to have been in mistrusting the professions of affection which Harry had made on his recovery, in the hope of inducing her to remain at the Grange until his passing fancy for her society was quite worn out! If she had yielded to his entreaties, she would have lost the chance she had had in "Nathalie," and would have been now entirely at the mercy of her careless husband, who had taken the first pretext he could find for freeing himself from the restraint of her society, and, under the pretense of working for her, returning to more congenial companionship—perhaps to that of Susan Green, the blacksmith's daughter. And he had been so lost to all sense of decency as to use the same messenger to her and to Muriel West.

Annie was wiser now than she had been when she first came to London alone, after the few miserable months of wedded life which had ended in such a terrible fiasco at the Grange. Then she had given way to grieving in secret over the wreck of her life; but now, with the philosophy which comes of a riper knowledge of the world, she hid away her regrets as well as she could, and threw herself into the life around her, which presented many attractions to the rising young actress.

All her efforts to find out any of the members of her husband's family were unavailing. She could not leave town, or she would have returned to Beckham, to see if any of them were haunting the old place yet. She heard from William; but he was in Ireland, and had heard nothing certain about the movements of the rest. She wanted to know how George had borne the crash, and what had become of Wilfred, and whether the shock had sobered him. But she was forced to wait until Stephen, who had given her no address that she could write to, should again call and fulfill his promise of keeping her informed at least concerning her husband's health.

She had begun to wonder whether he had forgotten all about it, or whether Harry had forbidden him to hold any further communication with her, when Stephen made his appearance in her sitting-room one afternoon, looking very haggard and unhappy.

"How ill you are looking, Stephen! You have not been taking proper care of yourself. Has Lady Braithwaite seen you lately, or Lilian?"

"Lilian wouldn't care if she did," he answered, sullenly. "All she cares for is herself and her own comfort; and, when that is secured, all the rest of the world may get on as it can."

From which speech, and still more from the way in which it was delivered, Annie came to the conclusion that the lame man's infatuation for his cousin was at an end. His release did not seem to have made him any the happier, however, and it was evident from his appearance that he was in a deplorable state of ill-health.

"You have brought me news of Harry?" she asked, presently, when she had made him rest on the sofa and brought him a cup of tea.

"Yes; but there is not much to tell. He is getting on, but he has not written this time."

"Not written! Why is that? He might surely have sent me a few lines by you, if he did not choose to write by the post. I have been expecting to hear from him every day for at least a week. Stephen," she went on earnestly, drawing her chair nearer to the sofa, and speaking with all the soft persuasion she could put into her voice, "there must be some reason for this—some reason that you know and can tell me if you choose. Do let me know what it means, Stephen. You would not keep anything from me that I ought to know, would you? I am sure you could not be so cruel. He is ill, and you don't like to tell me so."

"No; he is quite well—upon my honor he is! It is only that he is not getting on so fast as he wishes to, and he is too despondent just now to write."

"But how does he live? I am sure he has no money, and he is used, poor fellow, to having it for the asking."

"No, indeed—it took a good deal of asking, and of a very pressing kind, to get money out of George lately. But it is always difficult for a man with no capital to get on."

"Look here, Stephen. I have some money that I have saved; you must take it. If Harry won't have it when he hears it is mine, you must tell him it is his share of the proceeds of the sale at the Grange. Poor old Grange! I read about the sale the other day. I can't think what has changed Harry so much; he used not to be overproud in money matters, and now he is as tiresome as possible the other way. Tell him any story you like, so that you make him take it."

"I sha'n't be able to, Annie. He is a great deal sharper than you think, and he would guess who sent it directly."

"You must say nothing about it for a few days, as he will know you have just seen me. But in about a week you can spring it upon him suddenly, and he will be off his guard by that time and believe you. Now don't raise any more objections, for you must take it; and I can spare it quite well. I know you are a man of property," said she, laughing—for Stephen had a little money of his own—"and would be offended if I offered to lend you money; but, if you ever should want 'a little check,' you must remember that I, too, am a person of property now—at least, as long as my engagement lasts; and I have just signed for another two years at a higher salary."

And, before he went away, she put into his hands a little packet containing ten pounds, which he took reluctantly, bound by a solemn promise not to let Harry know whom it came from. She sent a little note to her husband, too, begging him to write to her, telling him all about the renewal of her engagement, cheering him by all the encouraging words she could think of, entreating him not to despond if he were not immediately successful in the work, whatever it might be, which he had taken up, and saying all that a wife could think of to a better husband than Harry. She refrained from sneers or sarcasm, for she had made up her mind to take her husband as he was, to do her duty as his wife as well as he would let her; and she tried to throw all her thoughts and all her hopes into her own career, so that she might escape from the regrets which would arise in moments of depression at the thought that no home happiness would ever be possible for her.

That week, during which Harry had devoted himself to proving that happiness was possible for them together, had left deeper results than he guessed; he had paid her back in her own coin for tantalizing him during his convalescence by a kindness which was not meant to be more than a temporary effort. It was not for some time that the thought flashed into her mind that this had been a deliberately planned revenge on his part for her obstinate refusal to stay at the Grange with him. Such a refinement of vengeance did not seem in keeping with Harry's character; yet it seemed scarcely more improbable than the wild inconsistency of loving her devotedly one week and being perfectly happy without her the next.

She tried to solve the problem by acute questionings of Stephen when she saw him next; but he was more cautious and reticent than ever, seemed uneasy under the fire of her inquiries, and she soon saw that a continuance of them would only result in his having recourse to falsehood in reply. So she had to content herself with learning that Harry had taken the money; but she understood from what his cousin said that he was in want of more, and with ready generosity she sent him all the rest of her savings.

"Are you sure you can spare all this?" asked Stephen, uneasily, as he stood hesitatingly with the money in his hand.

"Quite, quite sure. You need not look so downcast about taking it," said she, laughing. "You are to tell Harry I have plenty, and whenever he wants more you have only to come to me."

"Tell Harry?"

"Oh, doesn't he know it is from me?"

"No, no; I did not dare to tell him! You told me not to. He would not have taken it."

"You are quite right. I had forgotten. Well, say that George has some more for him, and will give it to him when he wants it. Or stay! couldn't you say it comes from Lady Braithwaite?" asked Annie, brightly, more pleased than she knew to find that her husband was still too proud to accept money from her hands.

"He would not believe that. My aunt has only just enough to live upon."

"Lilian?"

"Lilian is abroad. I don't know whether she has heard anything about it yet."

"Well, say what you like, as long as you make him take it."

"And you are quite sure the want of it will not inconvenience you?"

"You are as sensitive for Harry as he is for himself. Look at the luxury I am surrounded by," and Annie pointed gayly to the bouquets and fruit on the table. "Doesn't all this speak for itself? The money, you understand, comes from somebody else; but you may take him this from me;" and with nervous, trembling fingers she pulled out from their companions a spray of jasmine and a crimson azalea, fastened them together, and put them into his hands as he left the room.

"I am afraid that poor fellow is going to die," she thought, as she listened to his slow footsteps and the thud of his crutch upon the stairs; "I never saw him look so ill as he did to-day. I wonder where he lives? He cannot be in want—I know he has money enough to keep him, and Harry even, with the money I send him, would have enough for them both. Poor fellow!"

She and Stephen had never been very good friends—indeed at the Grange he had disliked her, and she had never felt for him any warmer sentiment than pity, mingled with contempt for the slavish nature of his devotion to Lilian. His unselfish worship of the cold, proud girl had its nobler side, she knew; but she could not forgive the meanness of the actions to which he would stoop for his cousin's sake. But, now that Lilian had cast him aside like an old glove, and he appeared before Annie broken in health and forlorn, the tears came into her eyes as she thought of his wasted life, and she would have done anything in the world to smooth his rough lot for him by her sympathy or her care. But he shrunk from both, and left her each time dejected but stubborn, with the shy reserve which characterized his attitude toward most people even more marked than usual in his conversations with her.

She was feeling rather heart-sick at her inability to do anything for the members of her husband's family, from most of whom she had received great kindness, when one day she saw Sir George getting out of a hansom in Piccadilly. He was looking careworn and harassed, Annie thought; but he seemed glad to see her; and, when she begged him to come to luncheon the next day he said he should be delighted, but she must be prepared to find him more of a bore than ever.

"Well, if you bore me, I shall take the privilege of an old acquaintance and go to sleep," said she, laughing.

The next day he appeared punctually in her sitting-room, and she was even more struck than she had been on the previous day by the deep lines in his handsome face and the cloud which seemed to hang over him. She exerted herself as she had never done before to be lively and amusing; she had prepared the daintiest of luncheons, and before it was over she had the satisfaction of hearing him laugh like a man without a care. Not a particle of this delicate welcome was lost upon the keen man of the world, and, when luncheon was over, he said:

"That is the first meal I have laughed over for more than two months—since you left the Grange, in fact."

"Is it?" said Annie, carelessly, as she refilled his glass.

"Yes; and I suppose you know that as well as I do. You have the *ars celare artem*, like the accomplished actress you are off as well as on the stage; but I know you inveigled me here to-day with the base intention that your wit and your wine should get into my head, and make me forget for a little while my cares and my difficulties."

"And, if wit and wine never fulfilled a worse mission than that, they would not be so ill spoken of," said Annie, gently.

"Well said! Why did you leave us, Annie? You were the good genius of the Grange, and I am almost ready to think that, if you had never left it, we should all be there still."

"That's right. Put all the blame upon a defenseless woman."

"I am glad you were not there at the end; it was a miserable time."

He was so deeply serious that Annie grew serious too.

"Do you think I would have gone if I had known what was coming? Oh, George, you cannot think so ill of me!"

"It is better for you that you did go then; you could not have prevented the crash. I had known it must come from the time my father died. It has been nothing but wave after wave of difficulty, and getting through or over them somehow ever since. I suppose it would have been better to give up long ago; but we were so hedged in on every side that the ruin was bound to be complete when it did come, and you are just the sort of woman to understand the feeling which forces one, with or against one's will, to fight it out to the end, and stave off the fall into a broken-down swell as long as possible."

"George, George, how can you use such an absurd term? You, with your pluck, your patience!"

"I've used them all up, Annie, in the one tussle."

"Then you must let them grow again, and go in for another tussle. You are young, and have courage and energy. If I were you, I would never rest until I had bought back the Grange."

"I don't believe you would!" said George, admiringly, as he watched the proud flashing of her eyes and the varying expression of her face. "But I am not like that. I could fight on doggedly for something which was being dragged away from me; but I haven't it in me to begin a battle on my own account."

"Then what do you mean to do?"

"I shall get some appointment where I can grow gray with respectability; my people can manage that, and they will. It is a scandal for a baronet to starve, you know. Why, you silly child, you are crying! Thank Heaven, Annie! I didn't think you were so fond of me."

"I'm not fond of you—I'm disgusted with you!" said Annie, fiercely, stiffening herself rigidly as he leaned toward her. "Why, do you know that even Harry shows more spirit than that?"

"What makes you say 'even Harry?'" asked Sir George, quietly. "I could have told you long ago that Harry had pluck and spirit enough for six, in spite of his impossible manners and boorish conversation. If anybody buys back the Grange, it will be he."

Annie listened with her cheeks tingling.

"When did you first begin to think all that of him?" she asked, in a low voice.

"I knew, when we were lads together, that there was something in him; but I own I lost sight of the fact while he led his loose, lazy life at the Grange after you had left him. But, when you left the Grange this last time—more than two months ago—he let me see his best side again one night when we were talking about you."

"About me?" whispered Annie, breathlessly.

"Yes; he told me he loved you with all his soul, and he meant to win you back to him if he had to wait ten years. And I believe him."

"George," said she, in a low, uncertain voice, raising her eyes to his, after a pause, "he has done it already. But—but he won't give me a chance of telling him so. He won't let me know where he is, and—and indeed he doesn't care for me as much as you think; for, if he did, he couldn't make appointments with—with other women," sobbed she, with her head in her hands.

"Are you sure that he does, Annie?" asked her brother-in-law, earnestly.

"Quite sure. I—I overheard it," quavered she.

"Don't be so certain about it yet, my poor child! If ever a man was in solemn earnest, Harry was when he spoke to me about you, and he is far too pig-headed to change like that in a few weeks. He swore to me that you were the only woman in the world for him, and he should never look at another again. Trust me, don't make up your mind that he is faithless to you yet. His keeping away from you means something more than that, or I'm much mistaken in him."

Annie allowed herself to be somewhat comforted by these words, and she promised George, who of course managed to allow himself as many—if not more—of the small comforts of life as he had done before his ruin, to accompany him to Ascot in ten days' time, to play good angel to him and raise his spirits.

But in the meantime she had another visit from Stephen, who looked more haggard than ever; and, as he hinted to her that Harry was again in want of money, and as some dressmaking expenses had used up all she had in hand until she received her next weekly salary, she fastened up a bracelet, her best pair of ear-rings, and a diamond brooch which George had given her into a little packet, which she put into Stephen's hands, saying:

"I have been spending a lot of money upon myself this week, so I can't spare any just now. There are a few trinkets here which I never wear, and I can spare them better than money. Would you mind selling them for me and giving the money to Harry?"

"Your jewelry! No, I can't take that!" said Stephen, thrusting the packet hastily back and opening the door.

"Nonsense! You must—I insist! There is not a thing I care for among them," said Annie; and with gentle force she made him take them, pitying the poor fellow as she did so for his reluctance to let her part with her trinkets.

A few days after that was Cup-day at Ascot; and George, true to his promise, came in a hansom to take her to the station; for they were going down by train. It was a most beautiful day, Annie enjoyed herself with an unclouded delight which infected her companion, and it took all his loyalty and a little of her tact to prevent his making love to her again. She was too wise to suggest economy to him when he took her, as a matter of course, on to the grand stand and spent his money with rather more recklessness than in the old days, when he had a large establishment to keep up, and clamorous young brothers' allowances to pay. Men in difficulties always had plenty of ready money, she knew, and were much lighter-hearted companions than men who went on ploddingly paying their debts as they arose.

George left her for a few minutes, sitting, her face all smiles and sunshine, with his race-glass in her hand, examining the carriages which lined the course. He had gone into the ring, and had promised to be back in time for the next race. He returned to find her leaning back, white and shivering, with the luster gone from her eyes, and her arms hanging limply at her sides. A lady—a stranger—was supporting her head.

"Good heavens, Annie, are you ill?" he cried, in great agitation.

"She is going to faint, I am afraid," said the lady with her.

"No, no, I shall not faint; I am well already!" said Annie, rousing herself by a great effort. "Thank you very much for your kindness. I am afraid I frightened you. George, take me to have a glass of wine, please."

He led her, supported by his arm, to the refreshment-room, and in a few minutes she had controlled herself sufficiently to be able to tell him the reason of her sudden illness.

"I saw the woman I told you about, to whom Harry sends messages, on a drag on the course; and I saw Harry ride up and speak to her."

George muttered a savage imprecation between his teeth. Annie continued:

"I want you to take me down there among the carriages, to be quite sure it is she. Do take me, George! If you won't, I must go alone."

"I will take you, if you wish it; but, my child, you had better not go. If you were to see them together again, it would break your heart."

"Oh, no; my heart is not so tender as that, George!" said she, wearily. "Let us make haste."

She was afraid of her strength giving way again if there was any more delay. So he took her down, across the course, and in and out among the carriages until they came in sight of the one she was in search of. Harry was no longer beside the drag; but there sat Muriel, her complexion carefully made up, and dressed with more extravagance than good taste; and in her ears were the ear-rings and at her throat was the brooch which Annie had sent to Harry to help him out of his difficulties a week before.

She turned away quickly, and whispered to George, clinging to him like a child, and with a little tremor in her voice:

"Now let us go away—let us go away—as fast—as we can—straight back home!"

She bore up bravely all the way to the station and during the journey in the train; but when they were driving along together in a hansom, she said suddenly:

"Talk about the races, George, please."

But he could not, for there was a lump in his throat, and all he could say, as a lift to the conversation, was:

"Curse him!"

CHAPTER XXV.

"Don't go to the theater to-night, Annie! Send a note to say you are not well," suggested George, when they reached the house where his sister-in-law was living. "You are not fit to act to-night; they must get somebody else," he added, with the charming simplicity of the "outsider" in theatrical matters, who does not know how loath the rising actress is to give her "understudy" a chance of proving that she herself is not indispensable to the success of the piece.

"I must go, George; and it will be the best thing for me," said she, with a grateful look at his anxious face. "Come and see me to-morrow; I want to talk to you."

He left her unwillingly, and that night he took a stall at the theater where she was acting that he might be at hand in case she broke down. But there was no need of such a fear for the trained actress; her performance that night was, to a close observer, somewhat fitful and unequal; but she gave no other sign of the shock she had sustained that day—in fact, the excitement caused by it prevented her physical weariness from being so apparent.

The next morning, however, when George called, he found her sad and subdued, in spite of the efforts she made to seem as cheerful as usual. When she referred to the previous day, she did so quite calmly; but his self-command about the matter was not so great as hers, and he broke out in a few minutes and swore that he would find Harry out and upbraid him for his infamous conduct to the most perfect woman in the world.

"I am not that, George; and Harry knows it—that is the worst of it! If you were to tell him you and I had both recognized my jewels on another woman, he would tell you that it was only to be even with me for having preferred to his the society of another man."

George looked at her in astonishment, for she spoke with bitter self-reproach and kept her eyes away from his.

"My dear Annie, you are reproaching yourself very unnecessarily. When Harry himself behaved to you like a coal-heaver, even he could scarcely be surprised that you preferred any society to his."

"Not any society—I did not mean that."

"No, but that of men of his own rank, but not quite of his manners," said George, drawing his chair a little nearer to hers.

"I did not mean that either. As long as I preferred any society to his, it didn't matter. So I thought myself safe; it seemed quite natural to dislike and fear Harry when he neglected me and snubbed me, and bullied and at last struck me. I felt that, if I stayed with him any longer, his very presence would poison me," said she with rising excitement.

"No wonder! You were quite right to leave him, and, if you had been wise, you would never have come back to the brute."

"Do you think so? Now I think I was quite wrong. Even if I could not have loved him, it would have been safer to stay with him, safer for him and for me."

"Safer for you!"

"Yes, yes. I thought I was so strong, so hard, that I could do without affection altogether—especially as affection could, since my foolish marriage, only mean Harry's. And I was foolish and cared for him too little to ask myself whether he could do without it as well."

"He had shown that he didn't deserve yours, at all events. If you had stayed at the Grange, I think you might have been happy, Annie; but it would have been thanks to your husband's family, and not to him. You see, Lilian was just going to be married, and my mother would soon have warmed to you when her other daughter was gone; and, if Harry had not changed his tone, I would have packed him off somewhere, and then you would have been surrounded by nothing but worshipers. And, if you had liked the Grange better in those circumstances, my dear child, I don't think any one could have blamed you."

"I think they would, though. You see, my fault all through my married life has been that I looked upon my husband as a contemptible tyrant to be given way to or avoided as the case might be, never as a reasonable being whose opinions and feelings were to be considered for their own sake."

"But you see he has proved that they are not worth considering. I own to you that, when he was getting better, and he seemed never happy when you were out of his sight, and you went on laughing and talking with any of us rather than with him, and treated him like a cross, spoiled child, to be given way to and coaxed, while he seemed always longing and trying to be something more to you—it did seem to me sometimes that it was rather rough on Harry; but now I see you were quite right, and it was a good thing you did not get fond of such a weathercock. And then, when he rushed up to town red-hot to see you, and found you all dull and solitary——"

"But he didn't find me dull and solitary—that is what made him angry," said Annie, blushing. "He found an actor here whom—whom I had grown fond of when I was on tour. It was partly that I might forget him that I went to nurse Harry when he was ill," she said, hurriedly. "He used to come and see me here after I left the Grange this last time. I told him I could never marry him; but—but I did not tell him I was married already; and somehow Harry guessed that, and made me half-confess it; and then, instead of bullying me and reproaching me now that he really had something to complain of, he took me to the Bingham Hotel, and was so sweet and kind to me that I—I really think, if he had stayed with me, I should have grown very fond of him. So you see, George, I am not a martyr, and, if he has treated me badly, it is no more than I deserve."

She spoke in a very sad, quiet voice, with all the bright ring gone out of it; and George thought, as he watched her eyes fixed steadily before her, and her lips quivering a little in spite of herself, that, if her truant husband could see her now, he would realize how foolish he had been to expect that he could neglect such a pretty little wife without some more discriminating person's trying to console her.

"Well, now you must forget all about a brute who could take away your jewelry to give to another woman. And of course, it would not be right to see any more of the other man—the actor. But I will come and see you as often as you like, and take you out, and have tea with you and luncheon with you whenever you feel dull; I will come and live nearer this way—that will be the best plan—and then you can send for me whenever you want me," said George, benevolently.

"Thank you, George; I am very glad you are in town," said she, smiling; "but I won't trespass upon your kindness so much as that. I am afraid Harry isn't worth the determination; but I am not going to give him a loophole for complaint of me again."

"But he couldn't be jealous of me," said George, with eager surprise. "You can't bury yourself alive for the sake of a man who is deceiving you, who writes to say he is getting on badly"—Annie had told him that, but without saying anything about the money she had sent—"and whom you see a week after on horseback on a race-course enjoying himself as if he were rich. It isn't as if I were one of your handsome actors——"

"You are too modest, George. You are handsomer than any actor I know."

"Handsomer than——"

"Oh, yes; he is quite ugly! That was the hardest blow of all to Harry," said she, laughing. "But, handsome or ugly, Harry shall never have the least reason to be jealous again."

"Are you so sure of yourself?" asked George softly. "You know," he continued diffidently, "you thought you were quite cold and safe before."

"I have a safeguard now," said she in a low voice. "In spite of all that he has done—and you have not heard the worst—I love Harry; his forbearance to me when I was in the wrong seems to have subdued me; and nothing in this world now, not even brilliant success on the stage, has so much charm for me as the hope of some day winning him back to me."

"I hope you will, Annie—I hope you will. You deserve the greatest happiness the world can give, and Harry would be a fool not to snatch at what many a man will envy him for."

Annie did not want him to grow sentimental, and she soon turned the conversation to other matters.

She had a firm friend now in her eldest brother-in-law, whom she knew how to manage, and to whom, in this time of his ruin and consequent troubles, she did infinite service by her sympathy and encouragement. She could not, even if she had wished to do so, prevent his coming to see her constantly; for, though a man accustomed to depend upon himself in a struggle, he could find no consolation, now that the struggle was over, so great as his sister-in-law's sweet voice and kind eyes.

She had dropped much out of her circle of acquaintances since the blow she had received at Ascot; life had lost some of its zest for her, and she had grown restlessly anxious for news of her husband. She received letters from him now and then, short, affectionate, ill-spelled, but vague, requesting her to send her answers under cover to Stephen at a club he mentioned. She wrote answers in which, as he never mentioned his prospects or hers, or the money she had sent him, she never referred to them either. She also wrote to Stephen himself at the address given, begging him to come and see her; but to this she got no answer, until one afternoon she met him in the Strand and insisted on his returning home with her. He was looking as haggard as ever, and seemed more uneasy in her presence than he had been before.

"Why haven't you been here for so long, Stephen, when you knew how anxious I should be? And what have you to say to me from Harry about what I sent him? I should have thought I deserved a message of acknowledgment; but he does not even mention, in his very short notes, the help I have so often given him."

"He is ashamed to do so, Annie. But he is grateful to you all the same. He often talks to me about the sacrifices you must have made, and he thinks of them a great deal, I am sure."

"But that is not enough. He ought to speak to me about them, and, if he is too shy to do so by letter, I must hear him express his gratitude in person. Where is he living, Stephen? I must have his address," said Annie, with determination.

"I can't give it you—I can't indeed. I was afraid you would want to know it, and he has forbidden me to give it you; that is why I have kept away from you."

"And what reason have you both to give for this very singular refusal? What is Harry doing that he is ashamed to be seen by his own wife?"

"He is not ashamed exactly; but he knows how proud you are, and he thinks, if you knew how he earns his living, you would look down upon him."

"Is it something so very disgraceful then?"

"Perhaps you might call it so; at least he thinks so."

"Tell me what it is. Stephen, do tell me."

"I can't. I swore to him I wouldn't."

"Then am I never to know? Doesn't he want ever to see me again?"

"Some day, but not yet."

"But what difference can waiting make? If it is disgraceful now, it will always be disgraceful. But, if it is only that he has taken to earning his living by some employment not generally filled by gentlemen, why, I shall only respect him the more for sacrificing his pride! That is true indeed."

But all her arguments and entreaties did not move Stephen, who seemed very much agitated by her supplications, but doggedly refused to yield to them.

That night she wrote a letter to her husband, sending it as usual to Stephen to be forwarded.

"MY DEAR HARRY,—After waiting impatiently for more tidings of you than your scanty notes convey, I caught Stephen to-day, much against his will, and hoped to get him to give me your address, that I might come and see you. But nothing would induce him to tell me where you are or what you are doing, and he says you have strictly forbidden him to do so. I now appeal to you to put an end to the anxiety I am in about you, and to let me come and see you, if you will not come and see me. Stephen seems to think that you are afraid that the way you are earning your living will shock me; but indeed I think, if I were to see you with a black face after sweeping a chimney, or driving a donkey-cart full of vegetables, you would not complain of the coldness of the welcome I would give you. Please, please write to me, not one of those little hurried scrawls saying nothing, but a letter just to tell me when I am to see you again. I don't think you would be jealous of anybody I see now, except perhaps of dear old George, whom I see nearly every day, and whom I should like much better if only he would do something, like you.

I know you hate writing; but you would find time for this if only you knew how anxious I am to be sure you are well.

"Your loving wife,

"ANNIE."

She posted this letter under cover to Stephen; but she waited three weeks without getting any answer.

At the end of that time she was surprised by a visit from Lilian, who had just returned with her husband from abroad, having been traveling some months for her health, which had broken down. She was much touched by her sister-in-law's kindness to George, who had dined with Mr. Falconer and herself the night before, and had represented Annie as the guardian angel of the family.

"Wilfred has come up to town, and he was with us too," said Lilian. "And he talks of you just as well, and wants to come and see you, but he doesn't dare. You are a good little thing, Annie, to keep so staid now when every one is talking about you, and when Harry has treated you so badly."

"Who told you that?" said Annie, sharply.

"George. But never mind; you mustn't be angry with him or with me. What has become of Mr. Cooke?" she asked, in a low voice.

"Mr. Cooke! Oh, he is married, I believe; at least I am sure he is!" she answered, in an indifferent tone, but blushing.

"Married? Oh, well, I am glad of that!"

"There is no need on my account," said Annie, haughtily.

"No, no—of course not, child. Still I am glad."

"People say they get on very badly. And now he is ill, I hear."

The tears were starting to Annie's eyes; and Lilian, whom ill health had softened, began to cry too for sympathy. Annie fought down her emotion.

"Have you heard from any of the others—William or Stephen?" she asked, to turn the conversation.

"Stephen came to see me this morning. He is in wretched health, and seems to have an unaccountable dislike to talking about you. I told him to come and see me this afternoon, and I expect he is waiting for me now. I shall send Wilfred to see you to-morrow. Good-bye, you good child. I don't know what to wish for you."

And Lilian, whose movements were slow and languid, and whose beautiful face had grown thin with illness, kissed her sister-in-law affectionately and left her.

CHAPTER XXVI.

Annie did not sleep that night. Thoughts of poor Aubrey and the wreck the clever young man had made of his life, and remorse at her own share in bringing it about, occupied part of the weary, wakeful night, and brought some tears to her eyes. But her mind went back again and again to the husband who had deserted her, whose address was in the hands of Muriel West, and whom she upbraided one moment and prayed for the next. For the sentiment planted by his own forbearance and tenderness had struck deep root during these months of suspense which had followed, in spite of the shortness of his letters and the long periods of silence between, in spite of his ingratitude in not acknowledging the sacrifices she had made to help him, in spite of her doubts of his fidelity, in spite of the indifference his never once coming to see her had seemed to prove.

The fact was that Annie had at last found something to respect in her husband. During that week which dwelt so continually in her memory, he had taken his rightful place as her superior, owing to the discovery which had forced her to appear before him as a culprit. She hoped and even prayed that the reason he had given for leaving her—viz., his determination to work for himself and her, rather than live on her money—might prove to be the true one, so that he might deserve the place he had insensibly won in her heart. Yet how to reconcile the love which had prompted this determination with his acquaintance with Muriel West, his giving to this woman the jewelry she had deprived herself of to help him out of his difficulties, with the fact that it was to Muriel she had been referred for his address, and with his acceptance, without a word of acknowledgment, of her money? In spite of all, she would fain have cleared him of these charges, and, failing that, she was ready to take the greater share of the blame of his misconduct on her shoulders, and to forgive him the rest, if he would but ask for forgiveness. All the excuses which she had refused to make for the headstrong bridegroom of twenty, when she, the bride of eighteen, shut up her heart against her rough, boyish husband, now appealed to her with irresistible force. He was so young; he had been so badly brought up; his family had been "wild" for generations; he had meant to treat her kindly, and his marriage with her had been the result of a generous impulse; he had given up drinking since his illness, for her sake; while she had run away from him, treated with coldness his first protestations of love on his recovery, refused to stay with him, concealed her marriage from others. Was it surprising that he should bestow his warm affections elsewhere, when she had shown herself so indifferent to every proof of his love?

One determination she came to, as the result of a sleepless night of agitation and reflection—she would find out where Harry was, without the delay of another day, and come to some explanation with him. But how was she to do this? She could not descend to ask his address of Muriel, and the only other person she knew who could give her the information she wanted was Stephen Lawler, who had proved himself almost inaccessible to her. He had not replied to her last letter, asking for news of Harry; so that now her only plan was to hunt him out and insist upon his telling her where her husband was. Whether she would be successful in this by fair means was doubtful, as Stephen, with all his servile docility to any one to whom he was attached, was as doggedly obstinate by nature as the rest of his family, and could take refuge in stolid silence when driven into a corner. However, she must try.

The next day she drove to the club to which she addressed her letters to him and her husband, but heard that he was not there. She was not ingenuous enough to be satisfied with this answer; and, after going away and returning several times with unwearying persistency to a spot down a side street from which she could watch the entrance to the club, she at length saw the cripple descend the steps very slowly, and walk away with the aid of his crutches. She followed him. His infirmity made it easy for her to keep him in sight without going near enough for him to notice her. He left the crowded fashionable streets, and made his way at length to a narrow, quiet street in a dirty, unattractive neighborhood, where unkempt children played and screamed in the gutters in front of dingy houses where apartments were let, presumably cheap and uninviting. At the door of one of these he stopped, and taking no notice of a few howls from the ragged boys at his crutches, took out his key and went in.

Struck with wonder at such a choice of residence by the fastidious cripple, and with pity at the forlorn existence it implied, Annie hesitated about pressing her inquiries that day. But her anxiety to hear about her husband overbore all scruples, and, after allowing a short interval between his arrival and hers, she knocked at the door. A little girl opened it, and, upon being asked if Mr. Lawler lived here, nodded her head backward in the direction of the staircase, with the brief direction, "Third floor, right up top;" and, as she made no attempt at the ceremony of announcement, Annie only asked which was the door of the sitting-room, and, on being told "You go right straight into it soon as yer get up," she showed herself up without further delay. When she reached the third floor, she found the door of the little sitting-room half open, and, after knocking twice and getting no answer, she went in.

It was a meagerly furnished room, not much better than a garret, bearing evidences of Stephen's occupation of it in its extreme tidiness—for he was always neat and orderly in his surroundings. The only thing which looked out of its place was a flat hamper, which stood with the lid open on one of the chairs. Annie stood for a few minutes in the middle of the room without hearing any sound; then, attracted by the scent of flowers and by the sight of the ferns and leaves which evidently covered them, she glanced again at the hamper, crossed the room, and saw, laid on the leaves, a visiting-card with her husband's name and address upon it—"Mr. Harold Braithwaite, Kirby Park"—and penciled underneath the name, in his handwriting, were the words—"With love to my darling!"

With a throb of mad hope she seized the lid and looked outside for the direction. Then she stood looking at that, as still and almost as white as stone, for the hamper was directed in a different handwriting to "Miss Muriel West, Victoria Street." She was still standing by it when a little moan she uttered unconsciously brought Stephen from the next room. He started, and grew in an instant as white as she when he saw her.

"Stephen, I did not mean to frighten you. What I came to ask you I have found out already—here;" and she glanced at her husband's card.

But the cripple began to tremble from head to foot, and to stammer out that it was the wrong address, that Harry was no longer there, that no letter sent there would reach him.

"Tell me his right address then," said Annie, recovering her calmness. "It is of no use to try to keep it from me any longer, for I will find him out, and I will stand face to face with him before another week is over!"

"But you must not, Annie," declared the cripple, his forehead damp with agitation. "He will not see you; he will threaten you, abuse you. If you attempt to force yourself upon him against his will, I will not answer for the consequences."

"I can face the consequences," said Annie, quietly. "I can suffer anything but being cheated, and deceived, and tricked, as I have been by both of you. I shall find out where Kirby Park is, and go there without delay."

"You will not see him there. He was there; but he is gone, and they cannot tell you where."

"Very well. Then I shall find out where he is from Muriel West."

"Go to her then—go to her; ask her, if you can stoop so low, where the flowers come from that deck her rooms—that lie in her hair. And, when you are satisfied, find out your husband, if your pride does not hold you back, and enjoy the welcome he will give you."

In the midst of her own distress Annie feared for the effect of the strong excitement under which he was laboring upon the fragile frame of the cripple, and, without any further answer to his taunts, or any more reproaches for his double-dealing, she wished him good-bye very gravely, and, taking the card from among the leaves before he could stop her, she left the room as he was struggling to reach the door to prevent her exit. It seemed a horrible thing to leave him alone, cripple that he was, in a state of such utter bodily prostration as this scene had reduced him to; but she knew that he would accept no help from her hands, and she went down the narrow dark stairs sadly and slowly, listening as she went, lest she should hear him fall. But she heard no sound from the room up-stairs, and, as she left the house and walked toward home, her thoughts turned from the miserable instrument of her husband's treachery to Harry himself, with all her newly awakened love changed to a passionate wish for vengeance upon him for this cruel deceit.

Kirby Park—Kirby Park! That was where she would go—where, in spite of Stephen's worthless protestations, she believed that she should find her husband and be able to confront him, and sting him with the sharp taunts which rose to her lips now, which should make him writhe and start and feel shame, however callous he had become. Her passive hatred he had felt before, and had been able to afford to treat with indifference; she would see whether the active hatred into which his shameless neglect and ingratitude had turned her wistful affection would not make him feel some of the pangs he had caused her. Annie felt changed by that day's discovery into a wicked woman, with no feelings of pity or pardon possible, who would stop at nothing in the madness of her misery. She sacrificed even her womanly dignity, in her wish to make the husband who had despised her love feel an added pang at the sight of her. She would not simply go down, hunt him out, and confound him; she would let him think it was the worthless woman he loved who was coming to see him, so that disappointment might be added to his annoyance at meeting his wife.

It was Friday, and she could not leave town until Sunday, her only free day. As soon as she reached home, she collected some parts she had played on tour, lent her by Muriel, and copied in that lady's handwriting.

These Annie placed before her until she had mastered every detail of the slanting scrawl, and then she wrote the following note on a half sheet of paper, in an imitation of Miss West's writing:

"DEAR HARRY,—I will come down and see you on Sunday by the 2.30 train from Waterloo. Send somebody to meet me.

"YOUR DARLING."

Annie had consulted a railway time-table and found a suitable train. She posted this letter, and on the following Sunday started for Kirby Park, in a fever at the audacity of her enterprise.

She had had time, since sending off the note to her husband, to be the prey of regrets at her hasty action, to ask herself whether she was justified in giving him the shock she had prepared for him, whether it would not have been better, as it would certainly have been more dignified, to take no notice of the discovery she had made, save in a cold letter declining to hold any further communication with him, or challenging him to give some explanation of his conduct. She was beginning to fear too some outbreak of her husband's passionate temper when he discovered the trick she had played upon him. Then conjecture as to what her husband was doing at Kirby Park—he had the name on his cards as if it belonged to him—and excitement at the thought that she was about at last to solve the mystery of his occupation added to the wild confusion in her mind. She had heard of Kirby Park, but she could not remember when or how, and the most extravagant guesses occurred to her as to the position she would find her husband occupying. And through all her passionate anger, her wish for revenge, her wonder, and her sorrow there was deep down in her heart a fierce eagerness to see him again, to hear his voice, to feel the touch of his hand, even if it were not held out in welcome.

Part of her curiosity regarding her husband's occupation was satisfied before she reached Kirby. Two gentlemen had got into the same carriage with her at Waterloo, and her attention was caught by the words "Kirby Park" in their talk; and, when her thoughts had wandered off again to the subjects which were absorbing her, she was suddenly recalled to the presence of her two companions by a reference to "young Braithwaite" by one of them.

"You need not have the least apprehension on that score," said the other. "He has a sort of genius for the management of horses, and has lived more in the stable than in the house ever since he was about two. I would trust him, on any matter connected with them, before any man I know, young or old."

"He is a gentleman by birth, isn't he?" asked the younger man.

"Yes. Haven't you heard of the pranks of Sir George Braithwaite, one of the typical hare-brained scamps of a generation ago? This lad is his son; his eldest brother, the present Sir George, had to sell the estate a few months ago, and it was then young Harold came to me, reminded me I was his godfather, and said, if I didn't give him some work to do, he would hang himself on the gate-post as he went out. So I asked him what he could do, and he said he could ride. I told him I had no doubt of that; but he was a long way too heavy for a jockey. 'Well, make me coachman, groom—anything,' said he; 'and, when once you get me into a stable, you'll soon see I know more about my work than anybody there. You needn't say who I am, and they'll never find out I'm a gentleman,' he ended, rather bitterly. Well, I couldn't do that of course; but I got the lad to stay with me, for I was rather interested by his obstinacy, and thought I would find out what he could do. I soon found he could sit anything, break in anything, and could give points to most horsy men on any matter of training or going. So I made up my mind to give him a trial, and I set him up at Kirby Park and put some of my racers under his care. And of course two or three more have followed my example; and now the lad has his hands full, and has got a fair chance."

"It is a great responsibility for such a young man. He ought to be very grateful to you——"

"Well, I hope I may have reason to be grateful to him. My only fear was as to whether he would stick to it. He was very wild a year or two ago, I've heard; but he seems steady enough now, as far as I can find out. I think I've got the right man in the right place, and that he feels in his element, and will settle down all right. We shall see."

With breathless interest Annie had listened to all this. This, then, was the occupation which her husband had found, and of which, according to Stephen, he was ashamed for her to hear! He had become a trainer. But Annie felt intoxicated with pride at the thought that her husband had shown a special capacity which proved him to be much more than the lazy, incompetent idler she used to consider him, that he had shown talent and had found a field for it, that, if he had taken her money without acknowledgment, he had at least not lived upon it in idle dependence. But this discovery only made the thought of his infidelity more bitter; in the very moment when she found that he possessed all the qualities which might have earned her respect as well as her devotion, she was hastening to a meeting which would fill him with disappointment and anger, and bring down upon herself his execration instead of his welcome.

She felt afraid of him. Already she was hesitating whether she should go back without seeing him, asking herself whether she could contrive to miss him at the station, when the slackening of the train's speed and the exclamation of one of the gentlemen, "Here we are!" told her that the end of her journey was reached.

"Hallo, there's Harry himself!" said the elder gentleman, looking out of the window. "Why, how many more of us does he expect? He has brought the dog-cart as well as the phaeton. Nice turn-out, that!" he added admiringly. "Here he is! Well, how are you, Harry?" he called out, as he turned the handle of the door and stepped down on to the platform.

Annie sprung to her feet at the other end of the carriage and looked out eagerly. There stood Harry, in a light overcoat, his face rather flushed and his blue eyes sparkling, looking, she thought, handsomer than she had ever seen him. He shook hands with the two gentlemen, and then he caught sight of her. She was watching him intently; but he was better schooled than in the old days, and no one could have detected disappointment in the flash which passed over his face on seeing her. She came to the carriage door, and, as he helped her out, he said, in a matter-of-fact tone, as if he had expected her:

"So you all came down in the same carriage, Lord Lytham?"—turning to the elder gentleman. "Allow me to introduce you to my wife."

She was then introduced to the younger man, Captain King, who begged to be allowed to drive her in the dog-cart, and the other two drove in the mail-phaeton, in which Harry himself had come to the station.

Kirby Park was only three quarters of a mile off. The house was a large, heavy-looking building, which would have been ugly but for the trees about it. The park in which it stood was an extremely beautiful one, and, as the dog-cart followed the other carriage up the winding road through it, Annie's thoughts were for a few moments diverted by the loveliness of the scene around her from the doubts and fears which were agitating her.

When they reached the house her husband was standing on the steps to help her to alight. As they all went in, he said:

"You would like to rest while we go down to the stable, Annie. Mrs. Clewer will take care of you until we come back."

A very staid, elderly woman, the model of a trustworthy housekeeper, stepped forward and led Annie up-stairs to take off her mantle.

"Whose room is this?" asked Annie, as she was shown into a large front room with a beautiful view of the park and the landscape beyond.

"Mr. Braithwaite's, ma'am."

Annie trembled as she entered. She could not think yet, could not understand what this calm welcome foreboded. As his hand had touched hers in helping her from the dog-cart it had not held hers quite steadily; but Annie had not been able to see his face, had not known what emotion caused his fingers to close for an instant so convulsively on her own. What did he mean to do? What would he say when at last the time came, as come it must, for speaking to her alone?

Mrs. Clewer took her to the drawing-room—a cold, bare room which looked as if it were little lived in; and, when the gentlemen came in, and tea was presently brought, she played hostess very gracefully, doing her best to make her husband proud of her by charm of speech and manner. Whatever effect she might have upon her husband, who spoke little to her and never once looked into her face, she enchained her guests, who regretted sincerely that they could not stay to dinner, and delayed their departure until they were in danger of missing their train. When at last they left, and Harry accompanied them to the park gates, she retreated to the deserted drawing-room, threw open the window for air, and leaned against it, shaking from head to foot with excitement and fear. Then, after what seemed a long time, during which she thought with horror that he had gone away to escape her, she heard his tread in the hall.

"Oh, heavens, what will he say to me?" thought she.

CHAPTER XXVII.

Annie heard her husband open the door, but she did not turn round; then she heard his footsteps advance to the middle of the room and stop. She still stood leaning against the open French window, seeing nothing before her, and waiting for him to speak to learn what tone he was going to assume toward her. At last she heard him clear his throat, as if to attract her attention; but she took no notice. She fancied he must be working himself up to a proper pitch of indignation, and she tried to school herself to show a bold front when at last his wrath should burst out. Her case was the stronger by far, and, although that fact did not give her all the consolation it should have done at that moment, yet it would stand her in good stead when the conflict had really begun. Nevertheless, she would have given worlds for the *sang-froid* with which she had entered upon any contest with him in the old days when his opinion upon any subject was a matter of indifference to her, and when his outbursts of unreasonable anger had excited in her nothing but contempt and disgust.

He cleared his throat again, and again she took no notice. At last he spoke:

"Annie, aren't you going to speak to me?" he asked, in the gentlest, most entreating of voices.

She turned round in surprise. He stood there before her, this big, handsome young fellow who could tame the most fiery of horses with a hand and a will of iron, shy, nervous, irresolute, looking down with wistful submission on the small, slight woman at the window.

"Haven't you a word for me after all these weeks?" said he, as she was silent. "I can't help being horsy, so wasn't it better to turn my horsiness to some account? I forgave you for not answering my letters; but, now you've come to see me of your own accord, I think you might have a kiss for me."

Annie looked, listened, in utter bewilderment. Letters! Kisses! What was he talking about? Was this Harry, with the loving, pleading eyes and the gently reproachful tone, the ungrateful, faithless husband she had come to upbraid? Was this some artful plan to avert her accusations by being first with trifling charges against herself? Still in perplexity, but thawing in spite of herself under his affectionate words, she moved mechanically toward him. But the want of spontaneity in the action roused his passionate temper, and he stepped back from her, his face all flushed with wounded pride and affection.

"Don't make a martyr of yourself, pray," said he. "I don't want a little, cold duty-peck because I'm your husband. If you can't kiss me because you love me don't kiss me at all."

She was in his arms, clinging to him, her upturned face aglow with passionate love, almost before he had spoken the last words of his hasty outburst. Muriel West, money, jewelry, unanswered letters—all were forgotten, thrust aside as matters to be explained hereafter or shelved as things of no account. Whomsoever he might have loved in the past he loved her now; whatever he might have done he was holding her in his arms now; and he might condescend to prove his innocence of every charge she might bring against him, or he might treat them with contemptuous silence—he was her husband, she loved him, he loved her—what else could matter at that moment?

It was not until they were sitting side by side on the sofa in the twilight that some words of his roused in her the remembrance of the grievances with which she had come armed.

"Why didn't you come before, my darling? I have been longing for a sight of you; and the only glimpses I got of you were on the stage."

"But why was that? Why didn't you come and see me, or send for me?"

"How could I, when you were so disgusted with me?"

Annie's face fell. A cloud had come over this new happiness already. He had himself reminded her of his own delinquencies, which she had been ready enough, in the first flush of this joy in her husband's society, to believe untrue.

"I think," said she, drawing her hand out of his instinctively, "that I had reason to be."

"But I don't think you had any," said he earnestly. "I know you will be able to prove you were right, because you are so much cleverer than me that what you say always sounds right, even when I can't help thinking you're really wrong after all."

"Well, prove that I had no reason to be annoyed, and disgusted—if you can."

"Don't speak so coldly to me then, and I will tell you what I think; but I can't if you turn away your head so stiffly and speak just as if I were the old Harry that you used to hate."

"I'm not sure that I don't hate you till I have heard what you have to say for yourself."

"Yes, you are," said Harry, twining her arm about his neck with confidence. "You needn't think I'm so simple as not to know the difference between Annie who is sweet out of duty, and Annie who is sweet out of pleasure."

"Go on with your explanations."

"Well, you were disgusted with me, and thought I was degrading myself."

"Stephen told you that!"

"Yes, and that you thought it nearly as bad as being a groom, and declared I should give it up in a month and idle about again, and that it would take you a long time to get used to having a trainer for a husband."

"Stephen—told you—that?"

"Yes, of course; he was bound to tell me all you said!"

"All—I—said?"

"Yes, yes! Ah, you're sorry now, aren't you, my darling? You see you wanted me to work, and there is nothing else I'm fit for, unless I had gone for a soldier or sailor. And you see I'm not a bit horsier than I was before. You needn't even know I'm a trainer unless you like. I had all the whips taken out of the hall to-day, and I hid my spurs and top boots and things that were lying about my room, so that you shouldn't be reminded more of it than I could help. And see—I've taken out my horse-shoe pin; and I've shut up the dogs in the stable, and——Annie, Annie, what are you crying for?"

"I—I don't know in the least! Go on!"

"Well, you see it did seem rather rough on a fellow, when I was doing my best, and not drinking—and working hard, so that I might have you with me—when you hardly ever wrote, and only answered about one out of three of my letters. I know they weren't spelled properly; but, if you knew how I hate writing and what a trouble even a short note is to me—I never seem to be able to say what I mean in a letter, somehow, while your letters are just like talking—I think, if you knew how I hate it, you would answer more often than you do."

Annie raised her eyes, with a startled expression, to his face.

"I don't understand," said she, slowly. "I answered all your notes—they were very few—and I wrote you a long letter, begging you to let me come and see you; did you get that? In it I told you I should be proud of the work you were doing, whatever it was. Did you get that letter, Harry?"

He was startled in his turn, and sat looking at her for a few moments in bewilderment. Suddenly Annie sprung up, trembling.

"Harry," said she, in a low voice, "tell me quick—did you get the letter?"

"No."

"Did you—did you ever receive anything sent to you by me?"

"Oh, yes; I got three or four letters!"

"Nothing else?" she asked, breathlessly.

"Yes; once you sent me some red-and-white flowers. I've got them in my pocket-book."

"But—but, Harry—think well, dear, dear Harry, please—didn't you receive anything else from me?"

"Anything else? No, I think not; I am sure not, for I should never forget anything you had sent me, Annie."

"You never received, for instance——"

"Well, what? What is the matter, Annie? What did you think I received?"

"You never had—money or—jewelry?"

"From you, Annie? No, certainly not!"

She sunk at his feet and put her head on his knees in a passion of tears.

"Thank Heaven! Oh, Harry, I am so happy! And yet something frightens me," she sobbed; while he looked down at her, utterly puzzled and astonished.

"What do you mean, Annie? What money—what jewelry?"

"Nothing—nothing! I—I don't know what I am talking about."

"But I must know. Now, darling, tell me."

"Will you listen quietly, then, and not be angry with me—or with any one?"

"I will promise to listen quietly, and not to be angry with you. That is all."

Annie hesitated. She could not but know now on whom the blame of this miserable misunderstanding between herself and her husband lay. No explanation of Stephen's infamous conduct to both of them occurred to her yet; but, even in the midst of her indignation against him, the pity she felt for the forlorn, weakly cripple urged her to shield him from the consequences of the terrible anger she already saw gathering in Harry's blue eyes.

"I don't think I ought to tell you anything," she said, gently, "until I have found out whether there is not some explanation to be given of the matter. You are looking angry already. Don't let us spoil this beautiful, happy evening by unkind and harsh thoughts about anybody, Harry. Won't you wait——"

"No, I won't wait!" interrupted he, very sternly. "Don't shrink away, Annie; I love you for your sweet forgiveness; it is right for a woman to be ready to forgive. But there is something else for me to do. Now tell me all about it."

"Not while you are in this mood, Harry. I will tell you when you have promised to let it pass without a word of reproach, except just what you may say to me."

"You will tell me now, and without my making any promise, my darling," said he very softly, drawing her up from her knees to a seat by his side.

Annie had never before felt her will unable to carry out her purposes. She struggled with herself now as she sat in the firm but gentle clasp of her husband's arm, and saw his head bent in a listening attitude toward hers. Then, feeling at last the irresistible force of a resolution stronger than her own, she submitted—submitted in the most winning way in the world, placing her little hands on either side of his neck, and looking up at him with her sweetest, softest expression of face to coax away his anger.

"Then I must trust to your generosity, Harry. And, if you don't behave generously and forgivingly about it, I shall think you are not glad to have me again, for happiness ought always to make people's hearts softer."

He kissed her without answering in words; and she went on:

"When Stephen first came to me with a letter from you, looking very ill, very miserable—I thought he was going to die—he made me very jealous and hurt me by telling me how much happier you were now you were away from town and among country people again. He did not know how fond I had grown of you, and that I was silly enough not to like to hear how well you were getting on without me. Were you as happy as he said, Harry?"

"I was happy just then, because Lord Lytham was beginning to show confidence in me, and I saw my way to earning money and being with you again. But, if he said I didn't miss you, he told lies."

"He did not say that; and he had not the least idea how much it mattered to me. But I was angry with you for sending me such a short letter, and I thought you were enjoying yourself, and very likely didn't care; so I tore up the long, loving letter I had written, and sent you a short one saying nothing, like yours."

"Oh, you little spiteful creature! I wrote that note four times before I got one fit to send you; I was so afraid you would be offended if I told you what I was going to do. I thought I would wait until I had got on, and then come to you and show you that I could be just as fond of you as if I had never been in a stable in my life. And, at any rate, I thought, if I succeeded, you would think it was better than idling."

"Better than idling! Oh, Harry, it is better than anything for you to be successful and happy and—and fond of me!" After a pause, she continued,

"When he came the second time, he said you were not getting on as fast as you wished."

"That was true; I was in low spirits about it. Well?"

"Then he said it was very hard for a man without money to get on. He said that himself, not that you had said it. And I was afraid you were perhaps in serious difficulty for want of money, and I begged him to take some that I had put away and didn't want."

"And he took it?"

"Wait. He refused for a long time, and said you would not think of accepting my money, so at last I pushed it into his hand, and told him not to say it came from me. He was very reluctant to the last; I expect he was afraid to give it you and afraid to give it back to me."

"Was that the only time he took your money?"

"No; I gave him some two or three times—not much, of course—and it made no difference to me, for it was money I had put aside."

"And what was that you said about jewelry? Come, Annie, you mustn't keep back anything! It isn't fair to tell only half."

"It is only that once, when I was short of ready money, and anxious, in spite of poor Stephen's entreaties, to send you some, I gave him a pair of ear-rings and two other little trinkets I never wore, and asked him to sell them for me."

Harry started up restlessly from the sofa and began marching up and down; then he stopped short in front of her.

"Why didn't you write to me when you got no acknowledgment?"

"I didn't like to. I thought Stephen had kept from you the fact that the money came from me."

"And you thought I was such a booby as not to have guessed, and such a bear as not to have thanked you? Annie, that is impossible! You are hiding something from me still."

But Annie did not answer or look at him. Her eyes were fixed in front of her, as a new light broke in upon her bewildered mind.

"Harry," said she at length, raising her glittering eyes to his with an expression which was almost fear, "those flowers—you sent—by Stephen— a few days ago———"

"Oh, did you get those then? He did not condescend to—"

"Were they for me?" she asked, in a low voice.

"For you! Of course they were for you; who else should they be for?" said Harry, irritably, his excitement getting the better of him.

"Not for—not for—Muriel West!" She murmured the name so low that she had to repeat it.

"Muriel West? No. Who on earth is Muriel West?"

"You don't know!" she cried joyfully. "But, Harry, I saw you talking to her on a coach at Ascot."

"Do you mean an actress named West? Why, Annie, how jealous you are! I scarcely spoke to her, and shouldn't have done so at all if Stephen hadn't been with her. A fellow I know took me to supper once at her house a long time ago—it was the very night of my accident—and I have never seen her since, except that day at Ascot."

"Then how was it that she was wearing my ornaments?" asked Annie, quickly; and, as she spoke, the truth flashed upon them both.

"The little mean scoundrel!" growled Harry, clinching his fists. "The little crooked, lying rascal! He shall suffer for this clever trick. Then he got all he could out of both of us, and kept us apart by his lies! Of course you never said it was a disgraceful thing for me to turn trainer?"

"I never knew you were a trainer until this afternoon, when I heard those two gentlemen talking about you in the carriage as I came down. He refused to give me your address, saying you had forbidden him to do so, and I found it out only by this card." She took from her purse the card she had found in the hamper, and continued, "I went to see Stephen last Friday, determined to find out where you were. I saw a hamper of flowers with the lid open, and inside I found this card. I looked outside, and found that the direction was to 'Miss Muriel West.'"

"The direction had been changed; I directed it to you, and gave it to that wretched little hunchback for you. And, Annie, do you mean to say that, when you saw your ornaments on that woman, you thought that I had given them to her?" he asked, looking at her almost with horror.

"What else could I think, Harry?"

"And you never wrote to reproach me?"

"I could not write about such a thing—it was too dreadful! I thought I would accuse you of it face to face. But don't talk about it, Harry, please—I can't bear to think of it now; it was wicked of me ever to think it could be true."

"And you came down here to-day still believing it! And you could kiss a man you believed capable of such an infamous thing!"

"No, no, Harry; don't look at me like that! The moment you spoke to me alone in this room I felt it could not be true; because, you see, I was sure you loved me, and that cleared it all away."

And her husband drew her again into his arms, with a mist before his own eyes.

Dusk had fallen, and they were still sitting there, when they were roused from a silence of perfect happiness by the prosaic sound of the dinner-bell. Harry had great difficulty in keeping his boyish high spirits under proper control during dinner, and, when it was over, he said:

"Let us go out of doors, Annie; there isn't room enough for my happiness in a stuffy house."

So he put on her hat and mantle very carefully and very clumsily, and they went out into the park.

"Take me to see the horses, Harry. Here's your cigar-case; I saw it up-stairs, so I brought it down."

"I may smoke then?"

"Yes, of course. You are going the wrong way. Isn't that the way to the stables?"

"Yes; but I'm not going to take you there; you only ask to go to please me."

"On my word of honor, I ask to go to please myself; and, if you don't like to take me, I shall go over them with one of the stablemen, while you are sulking over your cigar by yourself. Now are you coming?"

So they went through the stables together, and Harry was quick to note the genuine ring in the interest, for what concerned him concerned her too now; and they walked all round the park together, and he said:

"Do you think you could ever live happily with me here, Annie?"

"And give up the stage?"

"Well, act only now and then. You might take an engagement for three months or more, but not give yourself up to it altogether. I know you are too clever to just settle down to keeping house for a dull, ignorant husband."

"You're not dull and ignorant, Harry."

"Well, not so ignorant as I was," said he, with, mysterious complacency. "Do you think that would be too great a sacrifice, Annie?"

"No, indeed. I couldn't throw my whole heart into my acting now if I thought I was neglecting you."

"And you will come and see me every Sunday, and stay till Monday evening now, won't you? I mustn't ask more than that yet, I suppose."

And she consented readily enough. And then came the crowning triumph of the day to Harry. He led his wife into the library, the volumes of which had luckily been collected long before his occupation of Kirby Hall, and said, turning proudly to her:

"You never thought I should get fond of books, Annie. Well, I have, and I like this room better than any in the house."

There were three photographs of her on the mantel-piece, there was a liqueur-case on a side-table, and the room was strongly perfumed with tobacco. Annie's eyes twinkled, but she only laughed contentedly.

"And now you shall hear me read aloud," said he.

So he put her into an arm-chair, and sat on a footstool at her feet, and read her a couple of pages of the *Nineteenth Century*. It was a very poor performance indeed, hesitating, badly emphasized, with the long words slurred over. He was not at his best, for he had Annie's fingers in one hand and his cigar in his mouth.

"You read beautifully now, Harry!" said she, when he looked up for approval; and the clever, well-informed woman really thought so.

"It only shows what perseverance will do," said Harry, gravely. "I've read that piece aloud to myself twenty or thirty times."

CHAPTER XXVIII.

Annie passed the night at Kirby Park; and, when she and Harry were sitting at breakfast the next morning, he told her he should come and see her act that night.

"Then will you come up to town with me?" she asked eagerly.

Her husband hesitated.

"I don't know whether I can, Annie. I have some things to see to down here before I start, and something to do in town when I get up there, so that I cannot be at your rooms till about four."

Her face clouded.

"Something to do in town!" she echoed, watching him narrowly, and noting the expression into which his face had set during the last few minutes. "Is it—to see some one, Harry?" she asked timidly.

"Yes, a business appointment."

"Oh, Harry, it is to see Stephen, I know! What are you going to do? What are you going to say? You look as if you would kill him!"

"Don't be afraid. How could I condescend to touch the little misshapen wretch, who has not as much strength in his whole body as I have in one finger? But I am going to see him, and to-day."

She saw that it was impossible to alter her husband's resolutions, so she desisted from her persuasions; but there was a terrible fear at her heart which she could not shake off. She knew the violence of her husband's temper, and feared it all the more under this new aspect of repression. She made up her mind to go to Stephen and warn him of Harry's coming, and to beg him not to exasperate her husband further by any attempt at concealment and false excuses, but to make a frank confession, such as would, she felt sure, be more likely than anything else to avert Harry's anger. Once resolved on this course, she let the conversation turn to indifferent subjects, and it was not until breakfast was nearly over that she pretended to remember an appointment with her dressmaker which would make it necessary for her to go up to town before luncheon. She did it too naturally to excite in her husband any suspicions of her good faith, and he went to the station with her, and parted with her very reluctantly, although he expected to be with her again in a few hours.

Annie herself felt something more than reluctance; she was seized with a foreboding of evil.

"Ah, Harry," she said, laying a trembling hand upon his arm, "I wish I were not married to you!"

"Why?" asked he, startled.

"Because then perhaps you might do what you did long ago, fling all considerations of business and duty to the winds and jump into the train with me."

"Do you think my love was better worth having then than now?" he asked softly.

"N-o, perhaps not. Still I wish the wife had as much influence as the girl had."

If the train had been in the station, she in it, and he at the door, these words would have carried him off. As it was, standing on the platform beside her, Harry was seized with a great trembling, and, walking away from her a few steps, he came back and said to her, low and reproachfully:

"That is the first time you have ever tempted me to what was not right, Annie. If the train had been here, your words would have made me jump in, and, for the first time since I have had work to do, I should have neglected it—and through you. I have a lot to see to at the stables this morning, and an appointment to keep with Captain King before I go up to town. But I can't resist you; so, if you love me, Annie, and if you care for what people think of me and say of me, don't ask me again, my darling, for I can't say 'No' to you."

The young wife, self-possessed and independent as she usually was, hung her head. These words of his, inspiring in her a strong feeling of respect, did much to restore her confidence in his self-command when dealing with his treacherous cousin. As she took the rebuke silently, Harry began to be alarmed at the effect he had produced.

"You are not angry with me, are you, darling? You look as if I had been scolding you, as if we had changed places."

"Changed places, Harry!" cried she, looking up in astonishment.

She had already forgotten the long period during which she had looked upon her husband as a tiresome, unreasonable child.

"Yes, when I was getting well at the Grange you didn't always treat me with proper respect, I fancy," said he, flushing, but looking down into her eyes rather mischievously.

"Oh, ah—then you were ill!" she said, blushing too.

The last words she said to her husband as the train went off were:

"Remember you are not to be with me later than four. Promise."

"All right; I promise."

And, trying to look as if her mind was at ease, Annie gave him a last smiling "Good-bye," as the train started.

On arriving in town, she drove straight to the house where Stephen lodged, and, finding that he was out, she sat down in the sitting-room to wait for him. Long ere this an explanation of the cripple's cruel and deceitful conduct had occurred to her, and it seemed more and more probable to her, as she sat in the shabby sitting-room, with its low, weather-stained ceiling and ill-papered walls. Evidently the money which he had kept back from her he had not spent upon himself; it must have gone where her jewelry had gone, and Harry's flowers—to Muriel West. Annie knew well to what depths of meanness he would descend in his devotion to a woman, for she remembered with what dogged and disinterested fidelity he had fulfilled every command, every wish of his cousin Lilian in the old days at the Grange, before her marriage with Mr. Falconer. In spite of her contempt for a man who could stoop to such acts, Annie was touched by the cripple's hapless attachment, and a great pity filled her heart as she heard the slow thud, thud of his crutch upon the staircase. Her compassion deepened when the door opened and Stephen stood before her, wild-eyed and pale with a pallor which was like that of death. She sat quite still for an instant, unable to speak, unable to express what she felt at the dreadful change in his appearance.

But when she rose very softly and held out a hand to him, she discovered, to her horror, that he still stared blankly in front of him, making no sign. He did not see her.

"Stephen," said she, in a low voice.

He started, and for the first time knew that he was not alone.

"Annie!" he said apathetically. "It is you, is it?"

With mechanical courtesy, he moved forward feebly and offered her a chair; but she took his hand and led him very gently to the hard little sofa, and made him sit down beside her there. She thought the feeling which had evidently overmastered him must be remorse for his conduct toward her and her husband, and she tried to think of the sweetest words she could to soothe his distress.

"It makes me very unhappy to see how deeply you are suffering," said she. "If I had known you would feel it so much, I would have come before."

He played idly with his crutch, not in the least moved by her words.

"It would have made no difference," said he, in a dull, cold tone.

"Oh, but I think it would! I would not have let you think so much about it!"

"How could you help that?" said he, turning upon her his lusterless eyes. "I tell you I was not rich enough, and she would have thrown me over just the same!"

Annie started. He was thinking no more of the wrong he had done her than if it had been a deed of a hundred years back. But she was not angry. Her pity rose higher than ever for this unhappy man, who had sacrificed all, even to his honesty, for the sake of a woman who did not care a straw for him now that she had got from him all he had to give.

"Stephen, I am so very, very sorry for you," said she, in a quivering voice.

"Are you?" said he, waking for an instant into something more like life. "And yet—you have no reason to be."

A feeling of shame seemed for the first time to come over him as he realized whose sympathy it was that was offered him; and he drew his hand away from hers.

"Every one has reason to be sorry for any one else who is unhappy," said she. "And when you see that even I can feel sympathy with you, you will see that you have friends who are worth living for yet."

"Not I, not I," murmured he, in a broken voice. "There is nothing left for me. She had promised to marry me—she is not a lady by birth, you know, and I could have made her one by position. I would have worked for her— I have worked for her—I have done more. But I used up all I had too fast— she saw I had no more; she said, if she married me, we should starve. And she looked at me quite coldly with her beautiful eyes, and said she was not well-educated enough to marry a gentleman—a gentleman! I, a poor cripple! It was that—it is always that! There is no happiness, no love for me; nothing but pity—wretched, miserable, scornful pity, that stings me more than taunts, more than hatred. She pitied me, I dare say, and laughed at me, and let me go;" and he broke down into incoherent words and sobbing.

Annie tried bright words of encouragement, asked him if he thought nothing of her friendship, of that of the rest of his family; but she spoke to deaf ears. When at length she rose to go, he gave her his hand and said, but still coldly:

"Thank you. I shall be glad presently that you came. It was good of you to come—generous—and I thank you. If I had a long life before me, I would try to do you some service; but I am played out now, and there is not much of my life left to run. Good-bye, Annie."

She could not stay. His last words were almost a command to go. She had not mentioned her husband's name. She thought that, in the state of mind in which she was leaving the cripple, the dread of an angry visitor might make him desperate; and she knew very well that, when Harry saw the miserable condition to which his sensitive cousin was reduced, he was no more likely to be unmerciful than she had been.

But she could not shake off a foreboding that the meeting between the cousins would be productive of evil, and she reached home anxious and thoughtful.

Her misgivings were not without foundation.

Within an hour of her departure from Stephen's lodging, Harry drove up in a hansom and was directed, as his wife had been, to the little room on the top floor. He entered with a very stern face and firm tread; but the sight of the cripple, lying half on the sofa, half on a chair, in a state of utter prostration of body and mind, made him pause. The other looked up at him without fear, without feeling of any kind.

"Do you know me?" asked Harry, abruptly.

"Yes; what do you want here?"

"I want an explanation. If you do not feel fit to give it to me now, I will come again. But I must have it, and the less delay the better."

"Ask your wife, then. She has a better head than you, and understands without so much talking. Go to her for your explanations, and leave me in peace."

"Not yet. I want some reason for your stopping my letters to her and her letters to me, for taking the presents we intrusted to your care to be given to each other, and for giving her money, my flowers, and even her jewelry to a greedy, extravagant, worthless woman whom you couldn't satisfy if you had gold mines to give her. That is what I want you to answer."

The cripple had raised himself, his eyes glittering with fury, and he sat frowning maliciously at his cousin until the latter had finished his speech.

"Then I won't answer you, except to say this; you are very good now, and look upon extravagance and waste as very wicked things. But you haven't been a saint so very long that you can have forgotten that you yourself were as greedy and worthless as any one I knew once, and that you forged your father's name to supply your own extravagance, which, it seems to me, is worse than to stoop to meanness for the sake of a woman you love and for whom you would die."

The last words he spoke in a low voice, looking straight in front of him with his glittering, feverish eyes; and his hand moved restlessly toward his coat-pocket as he finished speaking.

"Look here!" said Harry, in a softer voice. "I don't want to be hard on you. I know I've done as bad things myself, if not worse; and, if I'm a saint now, it's the first I've heard of it. But, if you're so fond of this woman as you say, I wonder how you could have the heart to play such confoundedly nasty tricks with the love of another man, and to such an angel as Annie, who had always been kind to you too?"

"Your love? Your love was nothing to mine!" Stephen burst out, contemptuously. "A woman may have a place in your heart; but your dogs and your horses fill the rest of it. You are handsome, straight; if one woman will not smile on you, another will; while I, who love sweet eyes and fair faces with a passion you cannot dream of, can only buy kindness from a woman by the ceaseless labor of ministering to all her wants, all her caprices; and then, when at last the time comes when I can give no more, I am cast aside and forgotten for—for one of your sort, with a pair of blue eyes that say nothing, and a head that can't put two ideas together."

The passionate bitterness of this speech moved Harry.

"It—it is rough on a fellow," he murmured, in a low, gruff voice.

But the pity in his tone woke the wretched man before him to frenzy.

"You can spare me your pity," said he, fiercely. "All our lives through you have got easily what I might work myself to death for, and never get, after all. You always got enjoyment, admiration, love; and, now you have sobered down, you get respect, success, money. If you had been in my place, Muriel would never have thrown you over. She had seen you only once, at a supper-party, months ago, at Beckham. Yet, when I met her in London, she remembered your stupid, red face, and sent you messages which I took care not to give you. But I will be even with you at last; the remedy I prepared for my own wrongs will do as well for yours."

And Stephen drew out from his breast, where his hand had been hidden for some minutes, a revolver, and, aiming before the other had time to realize his intention, fired it at his cousin.

Four o'clock came, and still Annie waited for her husband. He had promised so seriously, so many times, not to be later than that hour that her impatience grew quickly into anxiety as the time passed and still he did not appear. At half-past four, just as she was deciding that she could wait no longer, that she must go to Stephen's lodging and find out what had detained him, she heard a knock at the door, which, however, she recognized, to her bitter disappointment, not as Harry's but George's. He had brought William to see her, that young soldier having just arrived in town, and being mad to have a glimpse of his old play-fellow, and tell her how well he was getting on in his profession.

Poor Annie could give but a mechanical show of interest to the young fellow's eager outpourings, and at last she broke down.

"William, I cannot listen now," she said, with tears in her eyes. "You know it is not for lack of interest; but——George," she cried suddenly, turning to her elder brother-in-law, "Harry has gone to see Stephen, angrier than I ever saw him before. I can't tell you why now. But Harry and I are reconciled. It seems you knew all about his being at Kirby Park. You might have told me! And he promised to be with me at four o'clock," she went on, growing more and more excited and incoherent. "You see it is a quarter to five, and he is not here! He was very angry; and I am afraid something has happened. I must go and see!"

There was no restraining her. In ten minutes they were all three on the way to Stephen's lodging. As they approached the house, George caught sight of something from the cab-window which made him turn suddenly to his sister-in-law and advise her to return while he went in and spoke to Harry.

She saw the alarm in his eyes, and, steadying herself to speak calmly, she refused. So the cab stopped; and then Annie saw that there was a rough crowd outside the house and a policeman keeping the people away from the door. George sprung out; but she followed so closely behind him that she caught the policeman's answer to his low-voiced question:

"What is the matter?"

"Man shot, I believe, sir."

Annie kept quite still, quite calm, while George induced the policeman to let them pass in; and, as soon as the door was opened, she slipped past her brother-in-law, who had not known she was so close, and flew first up the stairs, swiftly and silently as a bird.

"He has broken his word to me," she thought in agony. "He has scattered all our happiness; and now——Oh, where is he? I dare not go in! Perhaps already they have led him away to—prison. Oh, Harry, Harry!"

She was standing outside the door of the sitting-room, which was shut. She seemed to hear a noise of low voices: but she was not sure that it was not the singing in her own ears. At last, with cold, weak fingers, she turned the handle and went in.

The only figure in the room was that of the cripple, lying motionless on the sofa.

Brought thus abruptly into what she believed to be the presence of a dead man, Annie tottered to the table for support, her face white and damp with horror; but Stephen turned, raised his head and confronted her; and she gave a low cry of relief when she saw that he was alive.

"Then Harry has not hurt you?" she whispered falteringly.

"No," said the cripple, "it was not he. You will never forgive me, Annie; you will hate me. I shot him!"

Annie did not cry this time, did not even start; she stood tapping with her fingers upon the table, struck suddenly into utter numbness. She did not feel his trembling hands clinging to her mantle as he fell at her feet and implored her to speak to him, to scold him, and not to stand before him as if his words had killed her. She did not hear the door of the bedroom open or feel the touch of a stranger's hand. But the new-comer was a doctor; and, when she woke presently from the sort of stupor which had seized her, he said, quietly:

"Now, Mrs. Braithwaite, if you will remain calm, you shall see your husband."

"I am calm," she said, simply.

She could not have cried, or moaned, or lamented her fate, if her life had depended upon her showing some emotion.

So he led her into the next room; and there, not dead, but sitting in a faded chintz arm-chair, with his left arm bound up, was Harry. It was then that her calmness gave way. She was not very demonstrative indeed over the passion of joy which lit up and transfigured her whole face; but she fell upon her knees by the side of his chair, shaking from head to feet.

"I thought—you were—killed!" whispered she.

"Why, my poor darling, who told you so?" he asked, tenderly.

"I shall never forgive Stephen!" she hissed, clinching her teeth.

"Yes, you will, Annie. He is to be pitied, not I—only we musn't tell him that. He hasn't even hurt me much—the arm is not broken; the only danger possible to me through it was loss of blood; and, if I keep quiet, I shall be all right again in no time. Is that George's voice I hear in the next room?"

"Yes; he came with me and William."

"I must get William to come down with me to Kirby Park for a day or two till I can ride again. He'll be very glad to come and I to have him. If I had to stay indoors alone, I think I should throw myself off the roof."

"Oh, Harry, won't you have me?" Annie asked, in pitiful entreaty.

"Why, how can I, my darling? I know you won't break your engagement at the theater."

"No; but I'll go down to Kirby Park every night after the performance, and come back each evening in time to dress for the theater."

"But won't that tire you too much, Annie? It is more than an hour's journey by train," he said; but his eyes flashed at the proposal.

"Why," said Annie, shyly, laughing a little, "I wanted to do so all the time. I thought of it yesterday; but then I decided to wait until you asked me; and, after all," she added, with mock petulance, "I've had to ask myself."

So that night, after the performance, Annie, escorted by George, who had made what excuses he could for not having revealed to her that he had heard of Harry's residence at Kirby Park, drove to Waterloo, where she found William and her husband. The three went down to Kirby Park together by the last train, very tired, especially Annie, but very happy.

The next day she and William had a walk together, while Harry was holding a business interview in the library; but William found that it was not quite like the old time at the Grange.

"Hasn't it improved Harry to have something to do?" said the young wife proudly.

"Oh, he's well enough!" said William, without enthusiasm. "But there's a sad falling off in you, Annie. You're quite spoiled for a sister-in-law. Why, now, when anything amuses you, you look first at Harry!"

CHAPTER XXIX.

More than six years have passed since the night when Annie returned with her husband to Kirby Park, and there are Braithwaites once more at Garstone Grange. For Harry, with a wise and loving wife at his side to comfort him in failure, encourage him in effort, and rejoice with him in success, has worked on in the career best suited to him and prospered, while she too, has striven successfully in her profession until the time has come on which the hopes of both have for years been fixed, and they have bought back the old home of Harry's boyhood, where also so many of the stormy events of their early wedded life took place.

It is Christmas-time, their first Christmas since their return to the Grange; and Annie and her husband are expecting some welcome guests to celebrate this event and Annie's final renunciation of her ambition for that entire devotion to home and husband which has now become her chief delight. For Annie has left the stage, with its struggles, its failures, and its triumphs, forever, not without some regrets at bidding farewell to old friends, old usages, and a life which had had many pleasures for her; but with new happiness in the thought that she can now devote herself more entirely than before to the husband and children in whom all her affection is centered. For in the long, dim picture-gallery where Harry saw the demure little governess playing battledoor and shuttlecock years ago two fair-haired boys are laughing and shouting at play. Their father is rather disappointed that they have his own blue eyes and curly, fair hair, and he is in great anxiety lest they should grow up like him in mind, instead of being "clever" like their mother; but Annie is troubled with no such fears, and is quite contented with her boys as they are.

Two more Braithwaites lie in the family vault in Garstone Churchyard. The first to go to his rest was Stephen, who lived but very few months after that miserable scene in which he shot his cousin in his desperate wretchedness. Those months were the most peaceful of his unhappy life, for he passed them at Kirby Park, to which Annie had herself gently persuaded him to come. She never wearied in her patient devotion to him, in her attention to his wants, in her bright endeavors to amuse and please him. Harry seconded her efforts with gentleness which was touching in the big, strong man; and the cripple's feelings were too strong and his penetration too keen for him not to appreciate rightly every kind act and tone in the people about him.

Wilfred lies in the vault too; he was killed by a fall from his horse in the hunting-field in the winter following the sale of the Grange, and they buried him beside his father and cousin.

A better fate is in store for the youngest brother, William. "The child" is now Captain Braithwaite, and his letters to Garstone are full of references to the loveliest girl that ever was seen and mysterious hints that he has a surprise in store for them—from which and a certain incoherency of style in his letters Annie does not need much penetration to decide that he is going to be married.

Sir George passes most of the year in chambers in town, and has never found the courage to begin a new battle with fate; he is still unmarried, and there seems every probability that the title will pass in course of time to Harry and his eldest son.

He and William are now at the Grange to spend Christmas with Harry and his wife; they are all expecting two other guests, for whom the warmest welcome of all has been prepared. Lady Braithwaite, growing old now, and reconciled to her daughter-in-law at last, is about to return to the home where her wedded life was passed, never to leave it again until the time comes for her too to sleep peacefully by her husband's side in Garstone Churchyard; and Lilian is coming with her to spend a week at the old home.

The winter sun is setting when Annie, on the alert for the sound of wheels, starts up from her seat in the morning-room and goes out on to the doorstep with William and George to receive Lady Braithwaite and her daughter, whom Harry had gone to meet at Beckham Station. Harry, who jumps out of the carriage first, gives way to his elder brother, and it is on Sir George's arm that the stately old lady leans as she steps down from the carriage and meets her daughter-in-law. Lilian follows. She is thin and pale, and looks much older than Annie, who has recovered almost all the beauty of the shy little governess of eighteen who first attracted the attention of the wild Grange boys more than ten years ago. Lilian's love of excitement and pleasure has told upon her health; she is not exactly an unhappy woman or an unloving wife; but her passionate nature has found something wanting in life, and in the eagerness of a vain search for it she has grown old before her time.

When they are all together in the drawing-room after dinner, and the little boys, having begun to make themselves obnoxious by playing at ball over their grandmother's head, have been kissed and sent to bed, the talk turns to town and what is going on there.

"Oh, Annie, have you heard of the success of your old friend Aubrey Cooke?" asks Lilian. "I went to see him in this new piece in which they say he is so good, and I never felt myself so entirely carried away by any acting before. Everybody says he will be the greatest actor of the day."

"Ah, I thought I was going to be the greatest actress once!" Annie says, rather slowly.

"Then he has fulfilled his ambition, and you have given up yours unfulfilled. Don't you regret it just a little? Come—be candid!"

Lilian speaks in a low voice, meant only for her sister-in-law's ear. Annie hesitates, looking down at the fire with an expression which it is not easy to read.

She is startled by finding her husband's hand laid quietly on her shoulder. He has overheard these last words of Lilian's, notices his wife's reluctance to answer, and leaves his seat to speak to her.

"Are you sorry you are not the wife of a great actor instead of a plain country gentleman, Annie?"

"No, not in the least; I never thought of such a thing."

"Then why are you looking so thoughtful?"

"Any news of people one has known well and lost sight of sets one thinking."

"I could give you some more news of him but that I am afraid it would make you sad."

"Never mind; I should like to hear it. Go on."

"His home-life is a very unhappy one. They say he ill-treats his wife; I know they are never seen together. George told me all about it yesterday; but I did not tell you, because I knew it would pain you. However, it is something for him to have satisfied his ambition, and you see he has done that."

"While I have let mine go———"

"Just to settle down into a mere quiet wife and mother. Is that what you are thinking? Do you regret it, Annie?"

She turns her soft, dark eyes, bright in the glow of the firelight, toward him, with her head raised proudly.

"No, no: I have never regretted it—I never shall. My ambition was very strong, but I did not throw it away; I kept it and clung to it until it was swallowed up in something stronger still; and I think you can guess what that is."

Talk and laughter are going on brightly round them among the members of the reunited family gathered round the glowing fire. Harry does not answer his wife in words; but the firm pressure of his hand as it clasps hers unseen by the rest tells her that he understands that the passion which had absorbed all others in the brilliant actress and the true-hearted woman is her love for him.

[THE END.]

9 789362 094490